STANDING IN THE GAP

✶ ✶ ✶ ✶ ✶ ✶ ✶ ✶ ✶ ✶ ✶ ✶ ✶

ARMY OUTPOSTS, PICKET STATIONS,
AND THE PACIFICATION
OF THE TEXAS FRONTIER
1866-1886

STANDING IN THE GAP

✖ ✖ ✖ ✖ ✖ ✖ ✖ ✖ ✖ ✖ ✖ ✖ ✖

ARMY OUTPOSTS, PICKET STATIONS, AND THE PACIFICATION OF THE TEXAS FRONTIER 1866-1886

LOYD M. UGLOW

FORT WORTH

TEXAS CHRISTIAN UNIVERSITY PRESS

Library of Congress Cataloging-in-Publication Data

Uglow, Loyd, 1952-
Standing in the gap: picket stations, minor posts, and the pacification of
the Texas frontier, 1866-1886 / Loyd M. Uglow.   p.cm.
        Includes bibliographical references (p.) and index.
        ISBN 0-87565-246-8 (alk. paper)
        1. Texas—History, Military—19th century. 2. Fortification—
Texas—History—19th century. 3. Frontier and pioneer life—Texas. 4.
Indians of North America—Wars—Texas. 5. Indians of North America—
Wars—1866-1895. 6. United States. Army—History—19th century. I.
Title.

F391 .U39 2001
355.7'09764'09034—dc21

                                                    2001037601

Cover and text design by Bill Maize; Duo Design Group

To
my wonderful wife,
Carol, the love of my life.
This book is yours
as much as it is mine,
because you are a part
of everything I do.

CONTENTS

✗ ✗ ✗ ✗ ✗ ✗ MAPS ✗ ✗ ✗ ✗ ✗ ✗

In the years immediately following the Civil War, the United States Army faced a tremendous challenge on the Texas frontier. Military authorities had to do more than simply defeat an enemy in battle. They had to overcome major obstacles in mobility and communications, including both logistical support and channels of communication, in order to bring the enemy to battle, and they had to learn a far different kind of warfare from what they had practiced during the Civil War.

Those considerations had a great bearing on the army's decisions concerning placement of its military posts, their size, and their number, with the overriding goal of using them to aid in the pacification of the frontier. An analysis of the significance of outposts during this period depends upon an understanding of those other vital elements of the military picture; outposts did not exist in a vacuum.

In analyzing the role and importance of military outposts in Texas between 1866 and 1886, two questions stand out: Did those outposts accomplish the objectives for which they were established? If they did, what conditions proved necessary to their success?

In answer, the use of outposts proved successful in certain instances and unsuccessful in others. Little evidence exists that subposts in the zone along the Red River succeeded in preventing Indian depredations in North and Northwest Texas. The tribes responsible for raids in that region did not stop their hostile activities until the army crushed their power in offensive campaigns against strongholds on the Staked Plains. The story is similar along the lower Rio Grande, though the army took no major offensive action against outlaws and cattle thieves there. Almost certainly if such outposts had not existed there, depredations would have been greater, but the presence of those posts did not stop depredations or reduce them to an insignificant level. The presence of troops did reduce the likelihood of such attacks on stage stations and mail lines and contributed to the defeat of the attackers. Picket stations, however, played only a minor role in the overall struggle.

Although outposts failed to accomplish their objectives in some areas of the frontier, their establishment and use proved quite effective in the region west of Fort Concho and throughout the trans-Pecos area in the late 1870s and early 1880s. The army's system of subposts played a key role in bringing Victorio and other Apaches to bay and in depriving them of their earlier advantages in mobility and initiative. Without the series of subposts controlling critical points, various bands might have continued to elude military forces for years longer.

Several conditions proved necessary to the success of subposts in the campaigns. Colonel Benjamin Grierson and other officers formed a comprehensive plan for a system of outposts rather than establishing individual posts in response to isolated needs. Grierson coupled his plan with extensive reconnaissance and mapping of the region, giving him as thorough a knowledge of its resources and terrain as the Indians had. With that intelligence, he placed his outposts in key locations that enabled him to control the region. A second condition that proved important to the success of the outposts concerned the availability of water. Indians required water just as troops did, and only a few sources existed in that arid country. When Grierson established his outposts at every water hole and spring, he robbed the Apaches of their mobility. They had no choice but to remain in areas where they could obtain water.

A third condition aided the success of the army's use of outposts against the Apaches—the absence of a sanctuary in Mexico.

With Mexican troops cooperating against a common enemy, American units no longer faced the frustration of a safe zone for the Apache. That, combined with the natural scarcity of water, in effect reduced the vast area of the campaign to a finite series of points that the army could effectively control and deny to the enemy.

Space and mobility — the allies of Victorio and his brethren— were lost because of the judicious use of subposts by the army under favorable conditions. In other circumstances such outposts proved much less effective. Regardless of their success or failure, however, the subposts, minor forts, and picket stations held a significant, if not often prominent, position in the pacification of the Texas frontier.

⁂

I first became interested in United States Army outposts on the Texas frontier after a camping trip to Grierson's Spring in the desolate country west of Fort Concho during the winter of 1991. My companions and I found the post in ruins, as one would expect after more than a century of abandonment, but the absence of the restoration and improvements typically found at a historic site gave the old post a certain timeless quality that fascinated me. The only artifact we ran across was a single cavalry uniform button. That button, the crumbling stone walls of barracks and stables, and the old cisterns that used to hold the only water for many miles, stirred my curiosity about the post and the men who had served there.

A large number of secondary works on the military history of the Texas frontier covered major forts in great detail but contained only passing references to outposts such as Grierson's Spring. Nothing remotely approaching a comprehensive study of the smaller military posts of the region existed.

To investigate those outposts in relation to the major forts that controlled them and to determine their place in the context of the military situation on the Texas frontier became a mission. The sheer numbers of outposts that existed during the period, approximately seventy, indicated their importance to army strategy. The fact that the military continued to use them over a twenty-year span served as additional evidence of their significance to defense and pacification of the frontier.

This volume details the periods in which each outpost existed, their major functions and accomplishments, and something about the troops who manned them, as well as the reasons for establishing and, ultimately, deactivating them. I also explore the role of outposts in relation to other elements of concern to the army on the Texas frontier, such as mobility and communications. From the study, I draw conclusions about the utility and effectiveness of those outposts as they fit into overall strategy and thus shed light on the larger military picture.

Several kinds of primary sources for material on Texas outposts were consulted. A few memoirs and reminiscences of army officers and enlisted men of the time, such as Mason Maxon, provided valuable references to some of those small posts. In like manner, a handful of accounts left by army wives of the period furnished bits and pieces of information. Dependents usually stayed at major forts, however, and had little contact with the small outposts at which their men often served.

Official reports of scouts and expeditions contained in the archival records of major forts offer more precise and significant details of many of the outposts along with original maps, which put directions and distances into perspective. Letters and orders prove extremely fruitful sources on both the outposts and the major forts with which they were associated. Post and regimental returns, held by the National Archives and available in microfilm, provide a great deal of hard information.

Annual reports of the secretary of war contain tabular listings of major forts and the outposts under their control, along with details on their garrisons. In addition, those reports present summaries of operations involving troops at various outposts and indicate the establishment or closing of certain outposts and the reasons for doing so. In some cases, military commanders evaluated the effectiveness of the outposts on the Texas frontier and explained tactics that troops employed.

Newspapers of the period would seem to be a logical source for more primary material on frontier outposts. Unfortunately, the great majority make little mention of outposts or the troops that manned them. That absence may have resulted from the remoteness of many of the posts from towns that had newspapers, or possibly from the fact that troops at those bases very seldom saw or fought Indians. When newspapers did describe military actions, official reports of those operations supplied more accurate, if often less thrilling, accounts.

Secondary sources prove particularly valuable in two areas, the background and history of major forts and the course of significant campaigns.

This author faced several choices in organizing this work. Arranging the material chronologically seemed to have advantages, chiefly the ability to take the reader through the period in a beginning-to-end narrative without the inconvenience of going back and forth in time. That benefit, however, could not counteract the equally great disadvantage of having to jump spatially from post to post. The loss of continuity in the coverage of individual posts would have been too great a burden on the reader.

Discussing outposts by size or some other category would have provided some interesting comparisons and allowed the reader to see those posts from certain aspects not present in other approaches. I have dealt with them according to function and type.

I settled on a geographical organization based on a discussion of each major fort and its accompanying outposts, as the most logical and easiest to follow. Granted, some difficulties exist, primarily the continual movement back and forth in time. But any study encompassing an area as large as the Texas frontier over a period of twenty years would likely have that problem. This approach allows a logical and manageable examination of the state's outposts in relation to the area and the other posts most closely related to them.

As the ancient Israelite prophet Ezekiel wrote, "And I sought for a man among them, that should make up the hedge, and stand in the gap before me for the land, that I should not destroy it: but I found none" (Ezekiel 22:30). Almost 2500 years later a different group of men took up the challenge to stand in the gap, to protect the land and people from destruction.

INTRODUCTION

Pacification of the Texas frontier during the late nineteenth century posed great difficulties for its guardian, the United States Army. The size of the region, the nature of its land, and the characteristics of adjacent regions provided some of the problems. The army's human opponents in this contest—primarily several nomadic Indian tribes and, secondarily, Mexican raiders from across the Rio Grande— proved to be elusive and deadly foes. Problems associated with mobility, supply, and communications placed constraints on military operations and affected the final outcome of the struggle as much as the actual combat effectiveness of the units involved. These and other variables influenced the nation's military leaders to establish a network of forts, often several days' travel apart, supplemented by subposts, minor posts, and picket stations at particularly critical points. This network, both offensive and defensive, played a leading role in the eventual pacification of the Texas frontier between 1866 and 1886.

In 1866 Texas' size alone presented military protectors with a tremendous challenge. The region consisted of three separate, but interrelated, zones. Starting in Grayson County on the Red River, the first zone stretched 400 miles in a long curve toward the south-west, coming to an indistinct end on the western edge of the Hill

Country. This zone had a depth of a hundred miles or more in many places, with widely scattered ranches and mail stations on the western fringes and increasing settlement as one moved east. The second zone ran close to 400 miles northwestward up the Rio Grande from the Gulf of Mexico to Del Rio. The third zone consisted of isolated ranches and occasional stage stations running westward from the junction of the first two zones to El Paso. Between 1866 and 1886 the number of ranches and small settlements in this last zone multiplied and spread into areas increasingly remote from the main roads. During the same period the first zone edged westward as daring settlers drove cattle onto ground that had belonged to the buffalo just a short time before.

The most significant natural characteristic of this vast frontier from a military point of view was its lack of water. Although this aridity posed no problems to commands operating close to the Rio Grande or the more northerly rivers as they curved down toward the Gulf, men traveling cross-country had to choose their routes carefully to take advantage of scarce springs and water holes. Lack of water often caused troops to break off pursuit of raiding Indians and in summer even endangered their lives. One of the key features in the army's eventual success in defeating their Indian opponents was ongoing reconnaissance of the land until every possible water source had been located, charted, and in some cases garrisoned.

In addition to vast size and lack of water, a third feature of the frontier that affected the military situation was the presence of adjacent regions that offered protection to raiders. Two such areas, Mexico on the south and Indian Territory on the north, served as political sanctuaries from which attackers could operate and to which they could safely return. To the west rugged mountains and the intimidating Staked Plains provided havens made safe by nature rather than politics. Eventually a combination of diplomacy and military necessity opened the Rio Grande and Red River barriers, and determined marches by officers such as Colonel Ranald S. Mackenzie, Fourth Cavalry, and Lieutenant Colonel William R. Shafter, Twenty-fourth Infantry, proved that troops could operate on the Staked Plains.

Texas offered enticing booty to Native Americans who had swept through the region on annual raids for decades or even centuries. Parties of Comanches and Kiowas, large and small, penetrated far into the settlements from the north and west, taking horses, scalps, and captives back with them to villages in Indian Territory or on the Staked Plains. Small groups of Lipan and Mescalero Apaches wreaked havoc from the west. Kickapoos, exiled far from their native hunting grounds in the north, practiced hit-and-run attacks on the Rio Grande frontier from the safety of Mexico. These tribes moved fast, knew the country intimately, and usually vanished before troops sent after them could close in.

Especially on the lower reaches of the Rio Grande, Mexican cattle thieves made frontier ranches dangerous places to live. Unlike Indians, who might ride hundreds of miles on a raid, these bandits merely had to slip a few miles across the river, capture an unguarded herd, and dash back into Mexico. Ranchers who resisted often paid with their lives. During some periods of Mexican political unrest, warring factions might cross or be driven over the river, adding yet another problem with which the army had to contend.

Whether raiders were Indian or Mexican, the army faced a tremendous challenge in attempting to find and catch them. The ability to move troops rapidly, to supply them in the field, to communicate with scattered units, and to position soldiers at a network of strategically placed military posts would prove to be important in making the frontier safe for settlement. From the beginning, it became obvious to military commanders that success in stopping well-mounted raiding parties required mobility. A static defense was of little value except in warding off attacks on remote mail and stage stations. Mounted patrols, coupled later with large-scale offensive operations against enemy sanctuaries, became the primary tactic of the Texas frontier army. These patrols usually consisted of cavalry units, but infantry riding horses or mules saw considerable action.

Maintaining an adequate number of serviceable horses proved difficult for some units. During late 1866 and early 1867, for example, the garrison of Buffalo Springs, A and E companies of the Sixth Cavalry, lacked mounts for some of the men.[1] A shortage of horses continued to plague units as the decade drew to a close. Garrisons at Forts Richardson and Griffin found it extremely difficult to keep even small parties properly mounted for escort duty and impossible to provide enough horses for a large detachment on a twenty-four-hour forced march. In some cases, cavalry units had twice as many men as horses, and less than one-third of those animals were fit.[2] Occasional epidemics reduced the number of serviceable animals even further.[3]

In addition to epidemics and limited numbers, the performance of cavalry horses often failed to measure up to required campaigning standards. When forced to subsist primarily on grass during lengthy pursuits, government horses often gave out while the tough little ponies of their adversaries pulled away and carried their riders to safety.[4] Even infantry units tended to outdistance cavalry on long campaigns, once the mounts had begun to tire and grain ran short.[5]

Railroads provided another means of mobility. The Texas & Pacific Railroad reached Fort Worth by July 1876 then pushed rapidly westward toward El Paso. The Southern Pacific, building eastward from California over a route that sometimes trespassed on Texas & Pacific surveys, got to El Paso before the T&P. The two lines joined at Sierra Blanca in mid-December 1881, linking the state from east to west.[6]

Railroads promised rapid movement for troops and supplies over long distances, a provision seemingly tailor-made for conditions on the Texas frontier. President Ulysses S. Grant and General William T. Sherman both supported the construction of railroads for their military utility. Railroads also encouraged settlement. As an area filled up with farmers and ranchers, the numbers of buffalo decreased, and safe havens for Native American war parties became fewer and fewer.[7]

Those advantages had less significance in the pacification of the Texas frontier, however, than they might have had. The railroads did not cross the state and begin to bring the tactical military benefits mentioned until 1881, a year after Victorio's rampage had ended. After that last major threat, only sporadic raids by small groups of renegades troubled the frontier. Essentially, the railroads came too late to Texas to provide the army a significant advantage in mobility or logistics in its struggle to pacify the frontier.

Supply had a close connection with mobility in other ways. Large columns of troops in the field required considerable quantities of food, ammunition, and forage if they were to operate effectively over periods longer than a few days. Supplying those columns became one of the major obstacles to successful pursuit and engagement of Indian raiders by the army.

Mule-drawn wagons carried large quantities of supplies but had very definite disadvantages in frontier fighting. Such wagons moved slowly and required fairly level ground. Soft sand or mud could slow a supply train to a painful crawl. In the rugged terrain characteristic of the Texas frontier and frequented by hostile Indians, supply wagons simply could not keep up with the troops they were supposed to support.[8]

Rather than wagons, army columns learned to depend upon pack mules to provide supplies. Packtrains could keep up with columns of cavalry or infantry over almost any kind of ground. Their disadvantage lay in the fact that they carried much less than a similar number of mules hitched to wagons. For a period in the mid-1870s the army even experimented with a cross between the wagon and the pack mule, a two-wheel cart pulled by a pair of mules. Such a vehicle could carry 1200 pounds, as compared with 500 pounds that could be packed on the backs of two mules. Carts never attained widespread use, however, and troops continued to rely on packtrains.[9] Probably the best combination of pack mules and wagons occurred in campaigns such as the Red River War, in which wagons hauled large quantities of food and forage to advanced supply camps where packtrains loaded and carried them to columns in the field.

That essential commodity, water, sometimes proved to be decisive in an action or an entire campaign. Its importance varied with the area. In regions along the Red River and the edge of the Staked Plains, and the lower Rio Grande, water played a much less crucial role because of its greater availability than it did in the arid region of the trans-Pecos. Water often determined the location of military posts and even the sites of some military actions. Probably no fight would have occurred with Victorio at Tinaja de las Palmas in July 1880 in far West Texas if that spot had not held the only water available for many miles. As the army learned the location of most water sources in the trans-Pecos, it gained the ability to use that information to force Indian bands to retire from the region or to fight on the army's terms.

Mobility and supply had a close association with methods of communication for the military on the Texas frontier. Good communications between posts allowed more rapid concentration against the enemy. In addition, certain channels of communication such as roads doubled as avenues of supply.

Long before the Civil War the military had realized the importance of roads connecting the posts on the Texas frontier with one another and with towns and settlements. During the 1850s troops completed the skeleton of a basic road network in Central Texas and the trans-Pecos region.[10]

Federal troops renewed their road-building efforts after the Civil War. Two black regiments in Texas, the Twenty-fourth and Twenty-fifth Infantry, did the lion's share of construction. Often companies from those regiments remained in the field for months at a time linking one post with another or shortening an existing route.[11] Probably more than any other officer, Colonel Benjamin Grierson, Tenth Cavalry, contributed to the building of military roads in West Texas during the post-war years. His comprehensive program of scouting, mapping, occupation of water sources, and road construction provided a true defensive framework for the region that ultimately allowed the army to wrest control from the Indians.[12]

The telegraph, another channel of military communications, allowed even greater coordination between various commands and a much faster response to developments in the campaign area than the system of roads. Those advantages were not lost on Colonel J. J. Reynolds, commanding the Department of Texas. He made repeated requests beginning in 1868 for the materials and manpower to build a network linking the posts in the department.[13]

After several attempts at passing a bill for construction, Congress finally approved the measure in June 1874. The army's Office of the Chief Signal Officer placed Lieutenant Adolphus W. Greely, Fifth Cavalry, in charge of the project in April 1875, relieving Lieutenant Allyn Capron, First Artillery, who had already completed preliminary surveys for the grid. Greely coordinated the work of parties of soldiers on various portions of the line throughout the state. Under his direction the line reached virtual completion by the following spring.[14] It linked Denison, Texas, with Fort Richardson, Fort Griffin, Camp Colorado, Fort Concho, and Fort Stockton on one line. A branch from Fort Richardson made connections with Fort Sill, Indian Territory. A second major line connected Fort Concho with Fort McKavett, San Antonio, Fort Clark, Fort Duncan, and the posts on the lower Rio Grande.[15] Troops extended the telegraph in the trans-Pecos region beyond Fort Stockton to Fort Davis and El Paso by early 1879, and units throughout the state kept the network in good repair.[16] The telegraph proved its military worth during the Victorio campaign of 1880, when Colonel Grierson and other officers used it extensively to transmit and receive orders and information between the many commands involved in the operation.

Solving mobility, supply, and communications problems would have meant little to the army, however, without a network of posts from which troops could operate. The posts were the framework, the skeleton, around which the entire military defense structure was built.

The first United States military posts in Texas were constructed during or shortly after the Mexican War. The Indian Frontier Line, built in 1849, consisted of Forts Worth, Graham, Gates, Croghan, Martin Scott, Lincoln, and Inge. As the name of the line implied, these forts served to protect the frontier and advanced settlements from Indian incursions from the north and west.[17] Fort Graham stood on the Brazos River, between Fort Worth and Waco. Fort Gates was placed fifty miles southwest of Fort Graham. Next came Fort Croghan, sixty miles northwest of Austin. Fort Martin Scott occupied a key strategic position outside Fredericksburg and within a hundred miles east of several major Indian trails. Fort Lincoln was located next to the German settlement of D'Hanis. Fort Inge, eighty miles southwest of San Antonio protected the road from that city to El Paso. Even at this early date the army made efforts to tie these posts together by a series of direct, all-weather roads.[18]

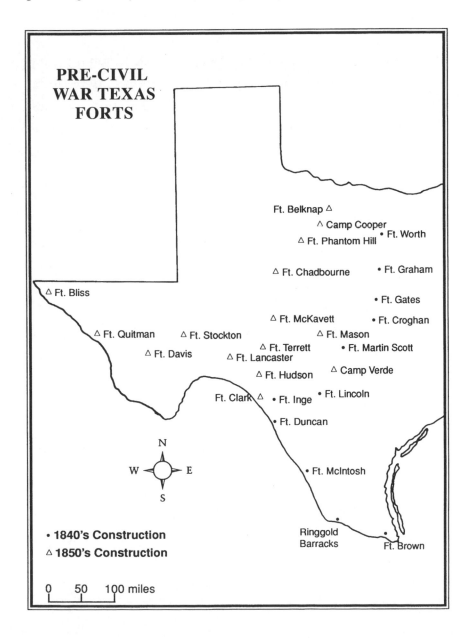

PRE-CIVIL WAR TEXAS FORTS

Ft. Belknap △

∧ Camp Cooper

△ Ft. Phantom Hill   • Ft. Worth

△ Ft. Chadbourne   • Ft. Graham

△ Ft. Bliss

• Ft. Gates

△ Ft. McKavett   • Ft. Croghan

△ Ft. Quitman   △ Ft. Stockton   △ Ft. Mason

△ Ft. Terrett   • Ft. Martin Scott

△ Ft. Davis   △ Ft. Lancaster

△ Ft. Hudson   △ Camp Verde

Ft. Clark △   • Ft. Inge   • Ft. Lincoln

• Ft. Duncan

N

W E

S

• Ft. McIntosh

• 1840's Construction

△ 1850's Construction

Ringgold Barracks   Ft. Brown

0   50   100 miles

A second line covered the Rio Grande frontier. Fort Brown, built during the Mexican War, already anchored the southernmost end of the zone. The army extended its protection upriver by building Ringgold Barracks near Rio Grande City, Fort McIntosh at Laredo, and Fort Duncan at Eagle Pass as part of the program begun in 1849.[19]

These two lines of forts failed to provide adequate protection to the frontier for two main reasons. First, settlements advanced westward at such a rate that they soon passed beyond the protection of the forts. Second, the government stationed too few troops in the state to patrol adequately the many avenues through which raiding Indians might slip to attack settlers.[20]

As a result of pressure for better protection and the government's desire to guard the mail route to the Pacific, the United States started a new series of forts in 1851. The line roughly followed the stage route that entered Texas at Preston on the Red River and continued southwest to El Paso.[21] On the northeast end of this line, Fort Belknap stood next to the Brazos River, 150 miles southwest of Preston. Next came Fort Phantom Hill in Jones County and Fort Chadbourne in Coke County. In 1854 the government erected Camp Cooper between Belknap and Phantom Hill.[22]

From Fort Chadbourne a branch swung south toward the Rio Grande, with Fort McKavett, Fort Terrett, and Fort Clark placed to provide a defensive barrier for settlers in the Hill Country. McKavett, northernmost of the trio, overlooked the San Saba River. Thirty miles southwest lay Terrett on the North Llano River. Fort Clark stood at the end of the line, eighty miles south of Terrett and just twenty-five miles from Mexico.[23]

Continuing west from Fort Chadbourne along the mail route, the main line of posts included Forts Stockton, Davis, and Bliss.

Fort Bliss, built in 1849 then deactivated for a time, was brought back into service in 1854. Although an important link on the mail route and in protection of the international border, it was too remote from Texas settlements and most of the enemies that menaced them to play a vital role. Fort Davis, constructed in 1854, assumed a much more active part in the pacification of the frontier, primarily because of its central location in lands frequented by parties of Indians and often crossed by settlers and immigrants. The government did not establish Fort Stockton until 1859, but it, like Fort Davis, held a key position. It sat at the junction of the mail route and a major Comanche war trail and covered the best living spring for many miles around.[24]

Additional posts built in the 1850s met specific local needs or protected areas not defended by the major lines of forts. The United States established several of these in the years just prior to the Civil War. They included Forts Lancaster, Hudson, and Quitman at vital points along the roads from San Antonio to El Paso.[25] Camp Verde, near Kerrville, and Fort Mason, farther north in the Hill Country, also fit into that category.[26]

At the beginning of the Civil War the United States Army evacuated all of its posts in Texas and did not return to them until the war ended. Initially, troops reoccupied posts on the lower Rio Grande during the summer and fall of 1865. These included Fort Brown, Fort McIntosh, and Ringgold Barracks. Fort Bliss at El Paso also received a garrison. Troops at these points could offer protection against cross-border forays by bandits and Indians from Mexico and against threats from the forces of Emperor Maximilian, but they offered no defense for the rest of the frontier.[27]

During the late summer of 1866, when Indian raids caused severe loss of life and property in many Texas settlements, James W. Throckmorton, the state's new governor, began to request federal

troops. Although inclined to dismiss Texans' claims of Indian depredations as either exaggerated or completely false, military authorities led by General Philip Sheridan began sending troops back to
resume defense of the ungarrisoned majority of the frontier. By the
end of the year, soldiers had reoccupied Forts Inge, Clark, and
Mason, and Camp Verde; elements of the Sixth Cavalry Regiment
moved into Jacksboro in North Texas.[28]

Over the next two years troops reactivated most of the forts on
the outer edge of the frontier and up the Rio Grande, including
Stockton, Davis, Hudson, Chadbourne, Belknap, Quitman,
Duncan, McKavett, and Lancaster. The army abandoned several of
these, plus Fort Inge, Fort Mason, and Camp Verde, as permanent
posts shortly afterward but still used them when the need arose as
temporary outposts.[29] In addition, troops built three large new
posts to cover the northern and central portion of the frontier. Fort
Richardson stood just outside Jacksboro. Sixty-five miles west, Fort
Griffin commanded high ground along the Clear Fork of the
Brazos. Fort Concho guarded the confluence of the three branches
of the Concho River.[30]

The government added three more independent posts before
1886. Fort Elliott, established in 1875, guarded the Texas
Panhandle and points in western Indian Territory and southern
Kansas. Fort Hancock, initially known as Camp Rice, began as a
subpost of Fort Davis in 1882 then became an independent post
in 1884. Hancock stood on the Rio Grande west of Big Bend
along the road to El Paso.[31] Camp Peña Colorado, south of Fort
Davis, also served as a subpost of Davis originally, but later
achieved independent status.

Although strategy dictated the general placement of the forts,
it was not the only factor involved. In determining the precise location for a new post, officers charged with making the decision had

to consider several practical requirements. First among these was adequate water. A garrison of 150 men with an equal number of horses needed an abundant, permanent source of fresh water. In some instances officers choosing a site for a new post were deceived

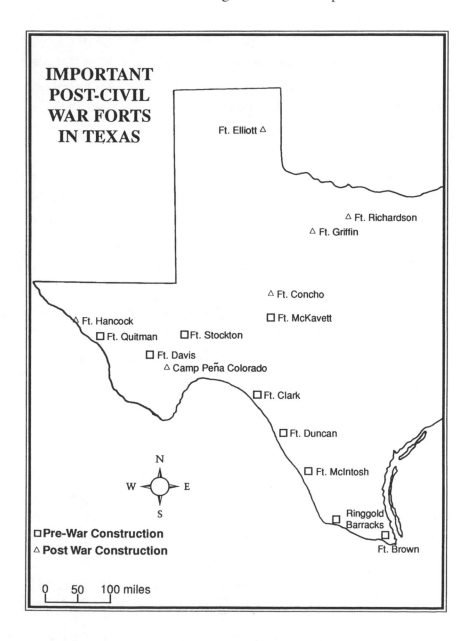

IMPORTANT
POST-CIVIL
WAR FORTS
IN TEXAS

Ft. Elliott △

△ Ft. Richardson
△ Ft. Griffin

△ Ft. Concho
□ Ft. McKavett

△ Ft. Hancock
□ Ft. Quitman   □ Ft. Stockton
□ Ft. Davis
△ Camp Peña Colorado

□ Ft. Clark

□ Ft. Duncan

N
W — E
S

□ Ft. McIntosh

Ringgold
Barracks
□
Ft. Brown

□ Pre-War Construction
△ Post War Construction

0   50   100 miles

about the adequacy of the water supply. Creeks and springs often quit running in exceptionally dry years. Streams and rivers sometimes contained water too salty or alkaline for animals to drink. Such a shortage caused more than one post to be abandoned.[32]

Other necessities for a suitable post location included sources of fuel, building materials, and forage. Wood served as the universal fuel for both cooking and heating at military posts on the Texas frontier. In drier areas, wood could be scarce, forcing some commands to send detachments many miles to cut timber or to dig roots. If wood were plentiful near the site chosen for a post, buildings and corrals might be constructed of it. Several forts operated small sawmills in remote stands of timber to furnish their lumber needs. In the absence of suitable timber, commands employed stone or adobe for construction. In the early stages of construction, soldiers often lived in tents or crude temporary shelters made of wooden pickets.[33]

Finally, military stations required ample quantities of grass and hay, either available at hand or in close proximity to allow detachments or civilian contractors to bring in supplies regularly.

When choosing the site for a post, military authorities considered comfort of the troops to be desirable but not a necessity. If tactical factors favored a certain location, a post would be established, regardless of unfavorable climate or absence of a spot suitable for growing vegetables.[34]

Major frontier posts followed a design pattern that seldom varied significantly. An open rectangular parade ground formed the center of the post. Along one of the long sides of the rectangle stood quarters for officers. Enlisted barracks stretched the length of the opposite side. At some distance behind the barracks, troops constructed stables and a corral. Headquarters, hospital, and quartermaster's buildings occupied the short sides of the parade ground. Kitchens, a powder magazine, a guardhouse, a post trader's store, and various additional structures stood away from the parade ground.[35]

Just as the army used a common pattern for arrangement of buildings, it provided blueprints and specifications for certain types of structures usually found at a post. Within the scope of building materials available at the site, troops had to follow design specifications. For this reason, hospitals and officers' quarters at widely separated forts often looked identical. Structures considered less important, such as enlisted barracks or laundresses' quarters, were not as standardized.[36]

The army intended its Texas forts to serve as bases for mobile operations rather than fortresses, so very few had defensive works such as palisade walls. On the very rare occasion when Indians did strike, they seemed more interested in capturing government animals than in destroying the garrison.

In close connection with the elements of mobility, supply, and communications, the army had to incorporate a plan involving the use of its military posts. Military leaders faced several questions in addressing that issue, including the most effective size for posts, best utilization of the garrison at each post, and the fundamental role that those posts were to fulfill in the overall strategy for protecting and pacifying the frontier. Officers had to consider the nature of the threat as well as the limitations on their own resources in making their decisions.

Military authorities differed in their opinions about the best size for posts on the frontier, some advocating many small garrisons and others preferring a few large ones. Those favoring a few large posts argued that a greater percentage of a given force could be put in the field from one large base than from several smaller ones, which would require a larger total force to be left behind. They also spoke in favor of benefits to good order and discipline that came from having an entire regiment at a single fort.[37]

The argument for many small posts had support and political backing from frontier settlers. With Indian raiding parties able to strike any of virtually thousands of locations in the state, troops had to be spread out to cover the largest amount of territory to protect the citizens beyond the edge of civilization. The capability for rapid movement of troops by rail did not alter that situation until significant Indian danger in Texas had already passed. Because Native Americans usually traveled in small numbers, garrisons did not have to be large to engage those bands successfully. In addition to purely military reasons, portions of the local economy in the vicinity of every post relied upon the military market for sale of their produce, and local citizens opposed every attempt to close even the smallest army posts.[38]

For twenty years following the Civil War, neither side in the controversy over size could claim total victory. Regardless of the size of the major forts, the army continually dispatched troops to remote outposts to cover far-removed strategic points. These outposts took on a variety of designations depending on their function and the number of men assigned to them.

The generic designation, *minor fort*, described a post smaller or less significant than a major fort, but independently reporting to department or district headquarters and the adjutant general's office. Camp Peña Colorado, Fort Elliott, Fort Hancock, and Fort Quitman—during part of its existence—fit the category of minor forts. *Subposts* were usually manned by one or two companies on detached service from larger bases. Commanding officers reported to senior officers at the larger forts rather than directly to department headquarters or the adjutant general's office. Commands frequently sent detachments to establish *scouting camps* in country often traversed by raiding bands. Patrols fanned out to cover trails, fords, and water holes likely to be used by passing hostile Indians.

Scouting camps tended to be more temporary than subposts, although the functions of the two were quite similar.

When a particular site, such as a mail station, ranch, or water hole needed ongoing protection, the nearest post detached a detail of a dozen men or fewer to establish a *picket station*. The parent post usually relieved the detail monthly. If the picket station was on the mail and stage line, its detail supplied a man to ride guard to the next station on each coach or wagon that passed through. Picket stations came under Indian attack far more frequently than other posts on the Texas frontier.

On the major offensive expeditions undertaken against hostile Native Americans in Texas after the Civil War, the army used supply camps as logistical bases of support. Columns piercing unknown regions of the Llano Estacado relied on such advance camps to provide the food, forage, and ammunition that never could have reached them directly from headquarters. Supply camps gave troops the extra reach necessary to run the mobile warriors to ground and attack them in their wilderness homes.

Various other types of camps existed for special purposes, primarily logistical. Several of the major forts on the frontier line set up semi-permanent sawmills in distant areas if the timber near the fort were inadequate. When grass played out around posts, some commands located choice grazing land up to a day's ride away. Troops would establish a grazing camp at the location and rotate cavalry companies through it, allowing a month or more for each company to fatten its horses before returning to the main post. Forts where forage was in short supply and could not be bought from contractors occasionally stationed a detachment in a grassy area to cut hay and haul it to the fort on a continual basis. Such a hay camp usually provided much harder work for its men than the troops at the main post experienced.

Unfortunately for the military and the settlers, the size of the army remained too small to establish or man a completely effective network of smaller posts.[39] Major forts in Texas from 1868 to 1886 usually had garrisons ranging from two to five companies— approximately 100 to 300 men. One company normally manned a regular subpost, and a detachment of two to fifteen men held a picket station in most cases.

As time passed, military authorities refined and improved tactics and doctrine for their units on patrol. In 1871, Colonel J. J. Reynolds, commanding the Department of Texas, kept half the strength of each major fort on patrols and scouts in the field. In his opinion such a policy extended "the greatest protection possible to the frontier counties with the force at hand."[40] The following year, the new department commander, Brigadier General C. C. Augur, decided to issue revised standing orders for scouts and subposts in the state. Fearing that the routine pursuit of hostile bands offered little hope of success, he instituted a more vigorous policy demanding relentless action to follow, engage, and punish Indians marauding in the state. He also gave fort commanders authority to establish subposts and picket stations where they thought best.[41]

That same year the commanding officer of Fort Richardson proposed a comprehensive network of subposts and signal stations running from Fort Sill to San Antonio. The line would consist of a series of subposts approximately twenty-five miles apart, each holding a half company of infantry for garrison purposes and a half company of cavalry for scouting and pursuit. Signal stations would stand at intervals of ten to twelve miles between subposts. From three to ten men would garrison each station. The stations and subposts would occupy high ground to keep all the land between posts and stations under observation. If a war party attempted to pass the line and enter the settlements, troops would spot it, flash the word to the other posts up and down the line, and launch a coordinated pursuit. Because of the tendency of Indians to raid in small parties, the cavalry unit at each subpost could almost certainly outmatch any raiders they found.[42]

The plan offered concrete benefits to the settlements in the northern and central parts of the state but addressed nothing of problems in the extreme west or along the Rio Grande frontier. Military authorities never accepted the proposal, possibly because it involved too much construction and expense, or possibly because such an effort had never been undertaken before.

A series of military offensives culminating in the Red River War of 1874-1875 broke the power of the Comanches and Kiowas who had menaced the northern and western frontiers of the state for so long. Similar but more limited cross-border excursions by the army neutralized the threat from Kickapoos and related tribes in Mexico during the mid-1870s. By the latter part of the decade, army victories left only the Apaches in far West Texas to pose appreciable danger to frontier settlements.

Against the Apaches in 1879 and 1880, the army's system of subposts and picket stations proved most effective. Kept from water by garrisons at virtually every spring, and deprived of sanctuary south of the Rio Grande by the cooperation of the Mexican and United States governments, Victorio's band and others found themselves without the mobility and room to maneuver. Able to force battle on their own terms, the United States and Mexican armies brought superior force to bear and destroyed any Apaches who chose to continue the fight.

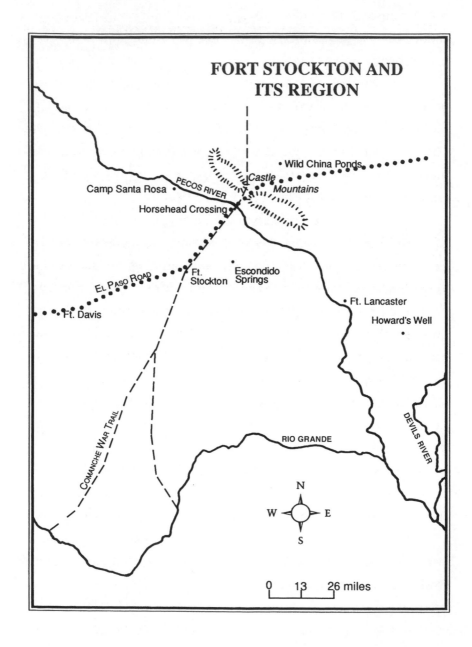

FORT STOCKTON AND
ITS REGION

Wild China Ponds

Castle
Mountains

Camp Santa Rosa

PECOS RIVER

Horsehead Crossing

El Paso Road

Ft.
Stockton

Escondido
Springs

Ft. Lancaster

Howard's Well

Ft. Davis

COMANCHE WAR TRAIL

RIO GRANDE

DEVILS RIVER

N

W   E

S

0   13   26 miles

FORT STOCKTON
AND ITS OUTPOSTS

Fort Stockton, in the center of present-day Pecos County, occupied one of the most strategic locations on the Texas frontier. Established near the abundant artesian flow of Comanche Spring, the fort controlled a major source of water in that region. Stockton's men also guarded the junction of the San Antonio-El Paso road, the Overland Mail route to the Pacific, and the Comanche War Trail.

The Comanche War Trail served as the principal route along which raiding parties traveled to Mexico from their hunting grounds above the Red River. These raids occurred virtually every year from the late eighteenth century until the mid-1870s. Large bands of Comanches usually chose late summer or early autumn, when Mexican horses and mules reached prime physical condition, to hit the northern settlements and ranches of Chihuahua.[1]

Parties, sometimes of several hundred Comanches, rode south along the trail into northern Mexico. Occasionally raiders would penetrate farther south, even approaching the forests of Central America,[2] where they set up advance camps. From these they struck targets in the region over a period of weeks or months, gathering large herds of captured horses and mules, as well as numbers of captive Mexican women and children. In winter or early spring the bands turned north, joined the trail, and followed it until they reached the southern fringe of their territory.[3]

The track consisted of a number of individual branches in the north converging into a single broad route. That route ran south until it broke up into a series of smaller trails in the Big Bend country, each leading to a particular section of northern Mexico.[4] The trail varied in appearance at different points on its length, but always presented a striking image to those who passed it. Near Fort Stockton it resembled a wide road made up of twenty-five smaller parallel tracks worn deep into the ground and running close together. Huge Comanche horse herds packed the earth hard and eliminated grass along much of its length. At certain points the trail widened to two miles or more, and in many places observers on high ground could see it from miles away. About sixty miles south of Fort Stockton, the trail branched into two main arteries, one passing east of the Chisos Mountains and the other west, before crossing the Rio Grande.[5]

A raiding party using the trail forded the Pecos River at Horsehead Crossing. The war chief rode in the rear while his second-in-command led the column. Small detachments—separated a mile or two from the main body—served as advance guards and rear guards. On occasion, similar detachments rode on either flank for additional security. The war chief might send out single scouts far from the band in particularly dangerous areas.[6]

Running west from San Antonio, the El Paso road carried military supply wagon trains to a number of frontier posts and served as a major route for immigrants heading for California. The United States mail also used that road, as well as the more northerly Overland Mail route angling southwestward from Preston on the Red River to El Paso and beyond. These roads and the Comanche War Trail intersected at the site of Fort Stockton for one reason: Comanche Spring. An average of 60 million gallons of water per day flowed from the spring, providing more than enough for the largest Comanche raiding party, the longest

Not all Comanche raids on Texas were successful. This man was the sole survivor of a war party of twelve (The Center for American History, University of Texas at Austin).

immigrant train, or the thirstiest military column. Water rose from a number of locations and formed a stream twenty feet wide and two feet deep that ran for ten miles onto the arid plains before returning to the ground.[7]

Companies A, B, E, and K of the Ninth Cavalry Regiment under Colonel Edward Hatch reestablished Fort Stockton on July 7, 1867, the first United States troops at the fort since before the Civil War.[8] Typical of many senior officers on the frontier, Hatch had served through the Civil War, rising from captain to colonel in an Iowa volunteer cavalry regiment. Later brevets for gallantry made him a major general. After the war, he became commanding officer of the Ninth with a colonel's commission in the regular army.[9] Hatch had to quarter his troops in tents because the buildings had deteriorated during the war years. He pressed his superiors in the District of Texas to allow rebuilding of permanent structures as soon as possible because the steady high winds at the site would ruin tents within sixty days.[10]

Hatch also worried about rumors in San Antonio that Stockton was last on the list of Texas posts in order of priority for rebuilding. In his opinion it was one of the most important forts on the frontier and rated top priority. He suggested using adobe for most of the buildings, as no building timber stood within twenty miles of the fort and local stone was inferior.[11] To provide lumber for construction, Hatch ordered Captain George Gamble, Ninth Cavalry, and a detachment to scout the Guadalupe Mountains for a suitable location for a sawmill. A steam-powered saw had already arrived at Fort Stockton, and a sawyer and engineer accompanied Gamble's command into the mountains.[12]

Duties of Hatch's command at Fort Stockton included pursuing raiding bands of Indians, scouting the region to prevent incursions, and escorting mail carriers and travelers on the roads that intersected at the fort. Fort Davis stood seventy-five miles to the west and Fort Clark 260 miles to the southeast, leaving the troops at Stockton with a huge area to protect.

Hatch favored reoccupation of a number of the abandoned posts and garrisoning several additional points to provide protection where it was most needed. He suggested stationing one company of the Ninth Cavalry at old Fort Hudson, another at Fort Lancaster, and four at Fort Davis. One of the companies at Fort Davis should be detached to hold Fort Quitman on the Rio Grande. Of the four companies remaining at Fort Stockton, he proposed sending one to guard Horsehead Crossing on the Pecos.[13]

Heavy Indian activity east of the fort, including a bloody skirmish in which a large band killed two soldiers and captured the first mail sent west from San Antonio in October 1867, prompted Hatch to make further recommendations.[14] He suggested reopening Howard Springs, which had been silted in by floodwaters earlier. It provided the only water on the eighty-six-mile stretch between the head of Devils River and Fort Lancaster on the Pecos. Presumably, Hatch wanted to place a garrison there to deny that water to Indians.[15] His proposal prefigured a strategy used with great effectiveness by Colonel Benjamin Grierson more than ten years later in far West Texas.

In addition, Hatch proposed turning Fort Davis into an infantry post because he thought its mountainous location favored the use of foot soldiers over mounted troops. Lancaster, Stockton, and Quitman, he believed, were the most important posts on the line. Quitman stood in an area that Hatch considered one of the most dangerous, and thus one of the most crucial, on the frontier. Lancaster's importance lay in its location at a point where engineers were bridging the Pecos and in its ability to provide escorts for sojourners.[16]

Fort Stockton's location continued to prove extremely valuable in succeeding years. Lieutenant Colonel Wesley Merritt, Ninth Cavalry, commanding the post after Hatch's departure, emphasized its success in intercepting Indian war parties attempting to pass through the region and in providing protection for cattlemen driving herds to New Mexico and for other immigrants.[17]

Much of the fort's effectiveness, however, lay in the work of its outposts. Without them, Fort Stockton would have faced an impossible task in attempting to cover the massive area under its jurisdiction. Subposts at Fort Lancaster and Camp Santa Rosa, along with smaller stations at Escondido Springs, Howard's Well, and other locations, extended control and protection to many vulnerable, outlying points.

The first attempt at extending Stockton's power began on July 30, 1867, when Lieutenant Fred Smith, Ninth Cavalry, received orders to proceed from the post to what remained of Fort Lancaster. Like George Gamble, Smith had started the Civil War as a private, then had won a commission in a black cavalry regiment, so his transition to the Ninth, after the war, was natural.[18] Smith and his men cleaned up and repaired the old Lancaster buildings and put them in defensible condition. They remained for several days until a force from Camp Hudson to the east relieved them.[19]

A steep bluff towered over Fort Lancaster. An old road from the plateau above led down to the fort around huge boulders littering the face of the bluff. Horses could scarcely descend the rugged trail.[20] The fort stood on the east bank of Live Oak Creek, four miles from where the main road crossed the Pecos.[21]

Detachments scouting out of Fort Stockton crisscrossed the country around Lancaster during the following months. One of those scouts was led by Captain W. F. Frohock, Ninth Cavalry.[22] In late December, Frohock bivouacked within the ruins of the old

fort. After the command had unsaddled and several troops designated as wranglers had taken charge of the horses and mules, a
force of several hundred men staged a surprise attack upon the
camp. Most of the attackers appeared to be Indians, but a number
of white renegades rode with them.[23] The Indians made a determined assault on the camp from the north and reached the ruins of
the old post trader's store before being driven back. Many of the
government animals stampeded as the firing increased. The frightened horses helped break up the attack, but they scattered into the
countryside outside the camp, where Indians captured most of
them. Frohock formed a skirmish line and drove the enemy back,
but the troops could not get close enough to recapture the horses,
thirty-two of which were lost.[24]

The attackers tried a coordinated assault from several directions at once in an effort to overrun the camp, but the troops held
their ground and repulsed the attacks, killing several Indians.[25]
Frohock lost three men who had been taken by surprise in the
initial assault, lassoed, and dragged away to their deaths.[26]

The road from San Antonio to El Paso, which became a major
route for the United States mail in 1867, crossed the Pecos near
Fort Lancaster. Indians frequently attacked coaches carrying mail,
even if they had military guards. A war party killed Corporal Samuel
Wright and Private Eldridge Jones of D Company, Ninth Cavalry, as
they rode escort to a mail coach in October 1867.[27] The need to
protect travelers and the mail led to establishment of a temporary
outpost at Lancaster in March 1868.[28]

Troops used the site intermittently as a base for scouting and
escort operations over the next two years. To supply large bodies of
cavalry on extended patrols, quartermasters sometimes hauled
rations and forage to the old fort and stored them under guard
there.[29] Detachments out of Fort Stockton made camp in the ruins

and sent out patrols that scoured regions around Howard's Well and along Live Oak Creek. Such an arrangement allowed a company to remain in one vicinity longer and cover it more thoroughly than if the company operated directly from Stockton or another major fort.[30]

By the end of 1870 several officers believed that Fort Lancaster should become a permanent subpost. Lieutenant Colonel James H. Carleton, Fourth Cavalry, urged headquarters, Department of Texas, to station twenty infantry and fifteen cavalry at the site, to be relieved monthly. The mounted troops could patrol the main road out to a distance of twenty miles east and west of the post every ten days. Supplies would pose no problem, as wood and grass were abundant in the area, and grain for animals could come from Fort Stockton.[31]

A few months after Carleton's report, headquarters, Department of Texas, decided to establish a permanent subpost at Fort Lancaster to replace the small picket detail stationed there. Government transportation would furnish supplies from Fort Stockton for the men garrisoning the subpost, and a fresh company from Stockton would relieve troops at Lancaster every thirty days. Tents would house the troops until they could build huts for themselves. Duties of the company included patrolling the main road west toward Fort Stockton and east as far as Howard's Spring, which was to be visited at least once per month, and repairing the roadway and all stream crossings over the same stretch.[32]

Life at the new subpost had fewer comforts and amenities than a post such as Stockton. William E. Friedlander received appointment from the secretary of war as official post trader in August of 1871. He supplied canned goods, tobacco, and other small luxuries to troops for a hefty price.[33] Sardines, canned meat, and canned oysters proved to be some of the most popular items for soldiers accustomed to a monotonous diet of government dried beef, hard bread, and coffee.[34] The commanding officer at Fort Stockton also made arrangements to assign an acting assistant surgeon to Fort Lancaster.[35] Soldiers at the subpost faced health risks typical of the frontier—risks often stemming from a poor diet. Scurvy posed a particular threat, especially in the winter months when fresh vegetables and fruits were nonexistent. One soldier had died of the ailment at Lancaster when it had been a temporary camp.[36] On November 30, 1871, Private William Lewis, Ninth Cavalry, died in the post hospital of an intestinal disorder.[37]

Troops at Lancaster found indications of increased Indian activity in the area as winter approached. Soldiers discovered a trail left by two Indians on December 8. The next day a two-man patrol bound for Camp Melvin with mail exchanged gunfire with four Indians on the road, and the following day a party of mounted Indians appeared on the Stockton road. Patrols went out regularly toward Howard's Well, Camp Hudson, and other points to counter these threats, but the garrison had too few men to scout as vigorously as Captain Louis Johnson, Twenty-fourth Infantry, in command of the subpost, desired.[38] For scouting Johnson requested four additional cavalrymen or at least four saddle horses on which to mount his infantrymen. He preferred cavalry because they were armed with revolvers, weapons not furnished to foot soldiers but valuable for fighting from horseback.[39]

Rather than receiving more men, however, Fort Lancaster faced an imminent decrease in its troop strength. Wanting to free more men for scouting and garrison duty at Fort Stockton, Lieutenant Colonel Merritt recommended that the force at Lancaster be permanently reduced to twelve infantrymen and six or eight cavalry—numbers he believed adequate for the patrol and escort duty required of the post.[40] On January 2, 1872, the commanding officer of Fort Stockton ordered G Company, Twenty-fourth Infantry Regiment, to return from Lancaster, leaving one noncommissioned officer and three privates at the subpost along with a small detachment of cavalry. Supplies and forage remained at Lancaster to be used later by commands operating in the area and by the garrison left behind. The commanding officer of G Company had the option of leaving two or more saddle horses with his detail for use at the camp.[41]

The steady decrease in Lancaster's garrison illustrated a trend toward small detachments for outposts all over the Texas frontier. Given the limited troop strength available for duty at virtually every major fort, commanders had to choose between abandoning most of their outposts in order to garrison one or two with a large number of men, or manning a number of points with a handful of men at each. They invariably chose the latter course, desiring to retain control over the maximum number of locations, even though that choice meant spreading their strength thinly. Actually, small garrisons usually proved sufficient to discourage raids. Indians in Texas almost always traveled in parties of no more than forty or fifty, often fewer. A handful of troops, seasoned and well led, sufficed in almost every instance to deter or even pursue any war party they encountered.

Small details continued to use Fort Lancaster for routine scouting and escort duty and as a supply station at various times over the remainder of the decade. The last major period of activity at the post occurred in 1879. By that time Comanche, Kiowa, and Kickapoo raiders no longer troubled the frontier, but small bands of Apaches still posed a significant threat.

In the spring of 1879, Colonel W. R. Shafter used Fort Lancaster as a base for scouting columns that crisscrossed the area in search of Apache bands. Lancaster served as supply depot for the large amounts of forage required by 125 horses and mules operating out of that post.[42] A company of cavalry from Fort Duncan at Eagle Pass reinforced the troops already using Lancaster in April. The commander of the District of the Nueces planned to replace that company with a detachment of Seminole Negro Indian scouts under Lieutenant John L. Bullis, Twenty-fourth Infantry.[43]

The scouts descended from original Seminole Indians and runaway black slaves living with the tribe. They were removed from Florida to Indian Territory in the 1830s. A portion of the tribe split off and settled in Mexico but later crossed the border and made their home in southern Texas in and around Forts Duncan and

Ka-ya-ten-nae, Apache war leader and close follower of Victorio (National Park Service, Fort Davis National Historic Site, Texas).

Clark. The army used these men extensively in its campaigns, and they proved to be expert scouts and courageous fighters. Lieutenant Bullis led them for a number of years and showed himself to be a brave and intelligent officer.[44]

Instead of Bullis and his scouts, however, Lieutenant Mason Maxon and a detachment under his command relieved the company from Fort Duncan. Maxon had entered West Point during the Civil War and received his commission upon graduation in 1869. Posted immediately to the Tenth Cavalry, he served virtually

Kiowa warrior Tow-an-Kee—his death on a raid into Texas sparked a savage retaliatory campaign by his father Lone Wolf (The Center for American History, University of Texas at Austin).

his entire career in that regiment.[45] He and his detachment used Fort Lancaster as a base for scouting in the direction of Camp Peña Blanca.[46]

Frequent patrols in the area yielded no further sign of Indians during the spring. The center of Apache activity eventually shifted to the country farther west and never returned to Fort Lancaster's vicinity. Its importance as a base for scouting operations and as supply point declined sharply, and the army used it thereafter only on rare occasions.

Troops from Fort Stockton established another outpost in July 1868 at Escondido Springs, sometimes referred to as Tunas Springs. Stockton relieved the unit at Escondido Springs with a fresh detachment every thirty days.[47] Military authorities chose to garrison the site because the mail route from the east shifted its crossing point on the Pecos southward, from Horsehead Crossing to Camp Melvin, also known as Pecos Station. The route then continued west through Escondido Springs to Fort Stockton.[48] The springs lay along the old mail road between San Antonio and San Diego, about twenty-five miles east of Fort Stockton.[49]

In a medical inspection during September, Acting Assistant Surgeon Rudolfo Gausetsky found the men at Escondido Springs comfortably quartered in tents pitched around the inner side of a stone wall enclosure. Their field kitchen turned out adequate meals, rations occasionally being supplemented by fresh beef. The springs furnished plenty of good, clear water. Abundant mesquite trees provided firewood. Gausetsky noted problems only in a shortage of adequate clothing for the coming winter, and low morale because of boredom and the absence of a commissioned officer to maintain discipline.[50]

Transfer of two companies of the Ninth Cavalry from Fort Stockton to Fort Concho in early 1869 caused reduction of the garrison at Escondido Springs. Only five men guarded the mail station and springs after that change. A detail now served two months at the post before being relieved.[51]

Troops at a picket station such as Escondido Springs guarded the mail station buildings and livestock and provided a one-man escort to ride most stagecoaches to the next point on the route. The small number of soldiers usually proved effective in deterring major attacks on their station, if not quick raids to run off horses and mules. The tiny garrisons did not discourage every attack, of course, and the presence of a single soldier on a stagecoach could not prevent a determined war party from taking a stage. The troops did, however, discourage most war parties from attacking the guarded station or stagecoach in favor of easier prey. Native Americans in Texas could exhibit extreme courage, but they seldom cared to press home an assault in the face of vigorous return fire.

Eventually infantrymen replaced cavalry troopers at Escondido Springs. Wagons from Fort Stockton regularly carried the men sent to relieve garrisons at the springs and other stations on the mail road.[52] The road remained in good condition in the vicinity of the post, and the springs supplied good water. The once abundant wood, however, grew scarce by 1874, apparently from constant use for the fires of men stationed there.[53]

When Apache troubles increased in the area in 1878, troops at Escondido Springs faced more frequent action. A band of Indians killed one civilian mail rider near the post and captured the mail before chasing a second civilian to the station. The small detachment could not pursue the attackers, but troops from Fort Stockton did.[54]

Increased depredations prompted reinforcement of the detachment at Escondido Springs. Twelve infantrymen and five cavalrymen garrisoned the post by the summer of 1879. The men came prepared for a long, dangerous campaign, as indicated by

Camp Santa Rosa (Fort Concho National Historic Landmark).

their larger than normal ammunition issue of one hundred rounds per man and rations for four months.[55]

By the end of the following year, army units west of Fort Stockton had put an end to organized Apache raiding. The military used Escondido Springs as a patrol base only sporadically afterward. In early 1883 Captain George Armes, Tenth Cavalry, led a column of forty-two men out of Fort Stockton to pursue a war party reported in the vicinity of Escondido Springs but found no Indians during the ten-day scout.[56] Following Armes' patrol the army had little need for Escondido Springs, and the post fell into disuse.

Camp Santa Rosa, also identified at times by military authorities as Frazier's Ranch, stood three miles west of Frazier's Crossing on the Pecos, just downstream from Pecos Falls and served as another of Fort Stockton's outposts. The surrounding country contained little except mesquite and sparse grass, but a good road ran from Fort Stockton past the camp to Frazier's Crossing. The ford could prove treacherous at times because the banks on each side rose steeply from the riverbed.[57]

Troops from Fort Stockton used Camp Santa Rosa, twenty-six miles away, as a camping spot for patrols as early as 1874.[58] The heaviest activity at the camp, however, occurred in 1879. During that year of increased Apache raiding, Camp Santa Rosa became one of the primary bases for patrols scouring the region in search of small bands of Indians. In June, an entire company of troops occupied the camp and scouted the area in all directions.[59] By order of the commanding officer, District of the Pecos, Camp Santa Rosa became an official subpost of Fort Stockton during this period. Troops at the camp had responsibility for forcing hostile Indians from that part of the district and keeping them out, thus protecting the mail route and settlements. In carrying out these responsibilities, cavalry units at the camp logged more than 1000 miles per month on patrols.[60]

Captain George Armes commanded Camp Santa Rosa and his cavalry company stationed there in the early summer of 1879. He often had two or three patrols out at one time looking for hostile Indians. Noncommissioned officers commanded the smaller patrols, while Armes or one of his lieutenants, such as Calvin Esterly, Tenth Cavalry, led sorties of a dozen men or more. Some patrols traveled hundreds of miles in their search.[61]

More often than not, army patrols out of Camp Santa Rosa saw no Indians. Occasionally, however, they did make contact. Lieutenant John McMartin, Twenty-fifth Infantry Regiment, commanded one such scout. He and Esterly were both 1877 graduates of West Point and, thus, lacked the wartime experience of many of the other officers in their regiments.[62] McMartin led twenty-one enlisted men of B Company, Tenth Cavalry, and a civilian guide along the Pecos out of the subpost in late July. Coming across fresh signs of Indian raiders, McMartin began pursuit, aided by three local cowboys who agreed to serve as scouts. On August 16, the troops caught sight of a mounted party of Indians in the distance and gave chase. After twenty miles of rapid pursuit, McMartin reined in his horses and stopped the chase, knowing he could not catch the band. He did not return to camp, however. Instead he headed west for the Fort Stanton reservation in New Mexico on the assumption that the Indians were bound for that point. On reaching Fort Stanton, he did not find the raiders, so McMartin rested his command for three days then marched back to Camp Santa Rosa. His patrol had lasted over a month.[63]

Patrols virtually anywhere on the Texas frontier between 1866 and 1886 followed a pattern very similar to those originating from Camp Santa Rosa. Although there were occasional exceptions, such as McMartin's scout, very few columns ever caught sight of Indians, and not many even found fresh sign. Men and horses seldom had enough water. Fatigue, poor rations, and bad weather wore down troopers as well as their mounts. Despite difficulties, some men liked patrols because they provided a break from the monotony of garrison routine. More important than their effect on soldiers, however, patrols did serve an essential purpose. They placed a military force in the field where it had at least a chance of finding and engaging hostile raiders. Although the odds of doing so were poor, they remained better than if the unit stayed at its post. In addition, scouting hardened soldiers and their mounts and provided training for those rare occasions when the troops actually came to grips with their enemy.

Morale at Camp Santa Rosa suffered during those hot summer months of 1879, not only because of the difficulties of frequent patrols but also because of the strictness of Captain Armes. In one instance, the captain returned an ambulance from Fort Stockton empty after it had journeyed to his subpost to pick up sick men.

Armes believed that the men who were supposed to return to Stockton for medical care were shirkers, and he kept them on duty. He even requested ten additional infantrymen to guard the camp, freeing more cavalrymen for patrol.[64]

Some of Armes' men went to extremes in their dislike of their commander. Sergeant Frank Lewis, leading a detachment and wagon from Fort Stockton back to Camp Santa Rosa on the night of June 12, left his men and returned to Stockton. He told them he had forgotten his pistol and wanted to retrieve it. According to Armes' report, when Lewis reached Fort Stockton, he attempted to break into the Armes family house and tried to kill one of their servants. He fled the post and rejoined his detachment at dawn. No record exists of any disciplinary action against Lewis for the alleged assault.[65]

A number of other officers, including some of his superiors, thought Armes was a poor officer and unreasonably hard on his men. Orders came from the Department of Texas to inform him that a medical officer, rather than Armes, was to make decisions as to the physical health of men in the command.[66] Armes tried to regain the initiative in this situation by cancelling the contract of a civilian physician, Dr. M. F. Price, serving temporarily at Camp Santa Rosa, but the Department of Texas ordered Armes to reinstate Price.[67] With a shift of Indian activity to the west, Camp Santa Rosa became unimportant as a base for patrols. Its use declined dramatically after the fall of 1879.

Several other points held small garrisons for limited periods in the region around Fort Stockton, including Howard's Well, Castle Mountain, Wild China Ponds, and several camps along the Pecos. Howard's Well, located a few miles southwest of Fort Lancaster, served on occasion as a depot for forage and supplies or as base for a small detail. In March 1872, quartermaster wagons with a detachment commanded by Captain Louis Johnson left 9000 pounds of forage to be used for cavalry units conducting extensive scouts in the area.[68] Johnson detailed a sergeant and four privates to remain and guard the supplies. Indians stampeded four horses from Johnson's command while it rested at Howard's Well before continuing to Fort Clark, costing him valuable time in trying to recover the animals.[69]

A month later two companies of the Ninth Cavalry passing Howard's Well came upon a burning government freight wagon train. Nine civilian drivers and passengers lay dead at the site. Troops set out after the Indians, who had just ridden away. After a stiff fight eight miles from the scene of the massacre, the soldiers broke off the engagement. Lieutenant F. R. Vincent died later that day from wounds received in the fighting.[70]

A small detachment of Ninth Cavalry troopers under Captain Johnson encamped at Castle Mountain in June 1868. At this location a gap in a range of rugged hills funneled traffic west toward Horsehead Crossing on the Pecos River. Johnson's troops changed their camp to Wild China Ponds, east of Castle Gap, a short time later.[71] A few days after the move, twenty-five Indians tried to sneak up to the water; Johnson's men drove them off. The water supply proved insufficient for a permanent camp, forcing the detachment to abandon the area.[72]

Camps along the Pecos occupied intermittently included Horsehead Crossing and Pecos Bridge. Horsehead Crossing lay just west of Castle Gap. Pecos Bridge stood in the vicinity of Fort Lancaster.[73]

With such a large array of outposts, Fort Stockton extended its control over a wide area and helped in pacification of a particularly vulnerable portion of the Texas frontier. Still, the army at Stockton labored under circumstances that made their outposts no more than partially effective in protecting settlers and travelers in their region. The combination of a huge land area, a multitude of potential targets, a limited number of troops, communications no faster than a galloping horse (at least until the construction of a military telegraph network), and small groups of fast-moving opponents made the military's task almost impossible.

FORT CLARK
AND ITS OUTPOSTS

Fort Clark, near the town of Brackettville, served as the pivot point between the line of forts protecting the lower Rio Grande; the arc running north and east through Fort McKavett and the post-Civil War posts of Concho, Griffin, and Richardson; and the series of trans-Pecos forts from Stockton westward. As such, it faced danger from three directions.

Scattered settlements, which lay to the north, often attracted long-range Comanche and Kiowa raiding parties from beyond the Red River. Troops at Fort Clark also kept their eyes trained westward on Apache bands that preyed on mail stages and solitary travelers. Finally, two enemies threatened from south of the Rio Grande, Mexican marauders and Kickapoo warriors. Fort Clark's garrison battled each of these enemies at various times from the end of the Civil War to the mid-1880s.

Realizing Fort Clark's important location, the army reoccupied it at the end of 1866.[1] Fourth Cavalry troopers garrisoned the post during the early months, but companies from the Ninth Cavalry soon replaced them.[2] In addition to the cavalry, by 1868 Fort Clark was occupied by men of the Forty-first Infantry Regiment.[3] Fort Clark also served as home for the army's Seminole

Negro scouts. In 1870 the government enlisted many as guides and allowed the men to settle their families on government land adjoining the fort. They served for the next eleven years, primarily under the command of Lieutenant John L. Bullis.[4] During the years under Bullis, the scouts fought in twenty-six engagements without the loss of a man. Several of them won Congressional Medals of Honor, and Bullis owed his life to them after one particularly hard fight with Comanches.[5]

Fort Clark earned a reputation in army circles as an unpleasant post for a tour of duty. The majority of enlisted men lived in poorly constructed huts and had few opportunities for relaxation except across Las Moras Creek in the village of Brackettville. Officers lived in better housing but found the post lacking in anything beyond the essentials.[6]

Some considered the climate at Fort Clark healthy, but significant risk of dangerous disease—particularly malaria—existed in the area. The high malarial fever had to run its course, and doctors could do little more than bathe their patients in the coolest water available. Patients who survived the weeks of fever usually emerged pale and emaciated after the struggle.[7]

Fort Clark briefly came into prominence in 1873 because it served as the base of operations for Colonel Ranald S. Mackenzie in a strike south of the border.[8] Mackenzie had a long and distinguished military career. His performance as a cavalry officer in the Civil War made him a favorite of General U.S. Grant and gave Mackenzie a reputation as one of the brightest young officers in the army. Following the war he served in the frontier army and, over a period of years, usually seemed to be where the action was hottest. In addition to hard service in Texas, he campaigned with his regiment against Sioux and Cheyenne in Wyoming and Montana, Utes in Colorado, and Apaches in the Southwest. His skill and judgment made such an impression on subordinates that some of them, even many years later, would find themselves modeling their tactics after his.[9]

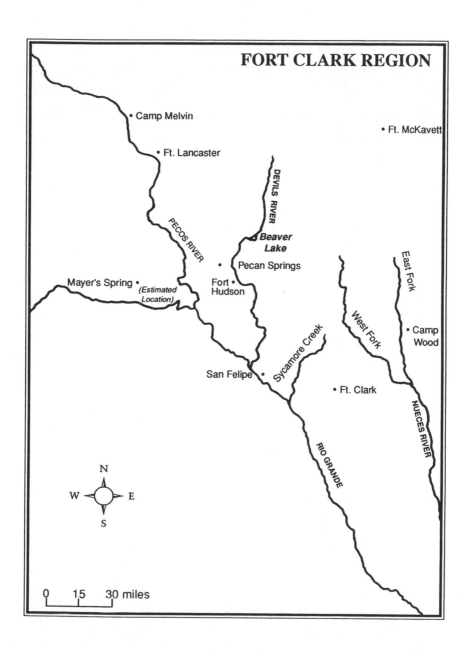

Kickapoo warriors had raided Texas settlements in the border counties for several years, killing people and stealing hundreds of head of livestock. Mexico provided not only a home but a sanctuary for the raiders, one that United States troops could not violate until 1873. In that year General Philip Sheridan and Secretary of War W. W. Belknap met with Mackenzie and gave him the dubious honor of striking Kickapoo villages a day's ride inside Mexico. He was then to return before Mexican troops or angry Indians could retaliate. When Mackenzie questioned the order and his own responsibility for such a violation of another nation's border, Sheridan assured him that President Grant assumed responsibility for the move.[10]

The Kickapoo villages that Mackenzie planned to hit stood just across the Rio Sabinas, more than sixty miles into the state of Coahuila. Slipping out of Fort Clark, elements of the Fourth Cavalry Regiment traveled a full day and night, and a few hours of the following day before reaching their objective. Immediately officers put their troops into formation and led them at a dead run through the villages. Most of the warriors were raiding elsewhere at the time of the attack, although a few offered resistance. Troops killed nineteen Indians and captured more than twice that many women and children. The soldiers destroyed the villages, including their stocks of food, then pulled out for the Rio Grande. The Fourth Cavalry returned to Fort Clark safely. After the attack, Kickapoo raids seldom seriously bothered Texas settlers again.[11]

Fort Clark continued as an active post between 1866 and 1886 and well beyond. During the years when Indians remained a very real threat to the safety of that segment of the Texas frontier, the fort operated a number of outposts that extended its protection and its offensive capabilities a great distance in several directions. Fort Hudson, Camp Melvin, Beaver Lake, and Mayer's Spring functioned as subposts of Fort Clark at various times. Additional outposts or picket stations existed at San Felipe; along Devils River, the Pecos, and the Nueces; and at a number of other sites in Fort Clark's geographical area.

Fort Hudson (also referred to as Camp Hudson) stood at the second crossing on the west bank of Devils River.[12] Sixty miles south lay Fort Clark.[13] Late in the spring of 1867 advance elements of the Ninth Cavalry occupied Hudson, which had been deserted since the beginning of the Civil War.[14] After these units had moved on to other posts, D and G Companies of the same regiment took station at Fort Hudson. Captain John M. Bacon, commanding officer of G Company, assumed command of the post with eighty-four enlisted men under him and Lieutenant Francis Dodge of D Company. Dodge served as acting post commissary and quartermaster.[15]

Bacon had already proven his competence and courage through three years of commissioned service in a Union cavalry regiment from his native Kentucky during the war. His regular commission as captain in the Ninth came in July 1866. During the remainder of a long career, he would twice be cited for gallantry against hostile Indians in Texas, including once in an action along the Pecos River shortly after his arrival at Fort Hudson. A thirteen-year stint—1871 to 1884—as aide-de-camp to General Sherman undoubtedly paved the way for promotions into the upper ranks of the Seventh Cavalry and command of the Eighth Cavalry.[16]

Dodge proved an able subordinate to Bacon during the officers' time together at the little post. Following service in a Massachusetts infantry regiment early in the Civil War, he had gained a commission in a black cavalry unit and ended the war a captain. A year later he joined the Ninth, taking a reduction in rank to first lieutenant. In the summer following the transfer of his company to Fort Hudson, he would win his captaincy.[17] A month after its arrival at Fort Hudson, the garrison suffered its first casualty when a man from D Company died after an illness. Troop strength increased to ninety-four at the post, however, because a number of men previously on detached service at other locations returned to their companies.[18] In October, during an Indian attack, D Company lost two enlisted men escorting mail near Fort Lancaster. As a result, the company shifted upriver to Beaver Lake to protect the region better, while G Company remained at Hudson.[19]

For a brief period that fall the quartermaster department at the post hired two civilian employees to handle supplies, indicating a certain degree of independence for the post, as did the assignment of Dr. J. C. Whitehead to Fort Hudson as acting assistant surgeon.[20] The following February a civilian wheelwright hired on at the post. The same month several new recruits for G Company arrived from Fort Stockton under charge of Lieutenant Francis S. Davidson, Ninth Cavalry.[21] Events took an unexpected turn in April, however, when orders came in from headquarters, District of Texas, to transfer the garrison at Fort Hudson to Fort Clark. A handful of men stayed behind to guard government property at Hudson, but only until it could be removed to Fort Clark.[22]

The army reactivated Fort Hudson as a subpost three years later. Three officers and fifty-nine enlisted men of the Ninth Cavalry and the Twenty-fifth Infantry reoccupied the post on May 23, 1871. Captain Lemuel Pettie, Twenty-fifth Infantry, assumed command.[23]

Reactivation of Fort Hudson occurred in the same month that army attention focused on the Texas frontier as a result of the Warren wagon train raid by Kiowa warriors. Indians killed seven teamsters in the attack near old Fort Belknap in the northern part of the state. The war party narrowly missed catching General William T. Sherman—on an inspection trip to look into reports of depredations that he felt were exaggerated—at the same location a few hours earlier. Sherman changed his mind about the seriousness of the Indian menace when he heard firsthand reports of the massacre from survivors who stumbled into Fort Richardson immediately after it occurred.[24]

Fresh troops relieved the garrison of Fort Hudson every two months. They saw no sign of Indians in the vicinity through the summer and fall. In the absence of combat, soldiers at the subpost kept busy repairing quarters and working on the road between Fort Clark and Fort McKavett. Infantry constituted the great majority of the garrison at Fort Hudson, but a few Ninth Cavalry troopers remained for mounted scouting duty. By the end of the year, two cavalrymen still served there as messengers, along with the infantry detachment.[25] On February 21, 1872, the army abandoned Fort Hudson once again. Although troops there had had no contact with hostile Indians during the preceding months, they had completed work on a long stretch of the road from Fort Clark.[26]

Such road building occupied soldiers on the Texas frontier almost as much as pure military duties. Military road construction consisted of finding the most favorable natural route from one location to another and then making it more passable at certain difficult points such as hills and stream crossings. Troops used blasting powder but often paths were cut over rocky hills with picks and shovels. Troops rooted out persistent scrub cedar, mesquite, and prickly pear. Where a route led across a river or creek, men often had to cut down the banks to make an easier grade. Along hillsides they sometimes built stone retaining walls to prevent slides or washouts. Soldiers at outposts in the southwestern part of the state did more than their share of construction.

Fort Hudson saw occasional use after its abandonment, at times serving as a convenient supply depot for forage used by government animals in units operating nearby.[27] In other instances, troops used it as a staging area for further operations. Colonel W. R. Shafter, operating against Mexican Indians in the spring and summer of 1876, camped with his command at Fort Hudson for a short period before moving to the Pecos and eventually into Mexico after the hostiles. During the campaign his men opened a wagon road between Hudson and the Rio Grande.[28]

Although far beyond Fort Hudson from Fort Clark, Camp Melvin (beginning in the late 1860s) also served as a subpost in Clark's area of responsibility and a picket station on the stage route west. Melvin stood on the Pecos River fifty-five miles east of Fort Stockton.[29] The site bore a great number of names over many years, but Pecos Station and Camp Melvin were the most frequently used. Stagecoaches used the Pecos River crossing at Camp Melvin from 1868 to 1881, and much of the post's importance stems from that use.[30]

On July 1, 1868, Colonel Edward Hatch, commanding the Ninth Cavalry, ordered Captain George Gamble to change the mail route between Fort Stockton and San Antonio. The route had forded the Pecos at Horsehead Crossing opposite Castle Gap, but Hatch wanted the ford shifted south to Pecos Station. He ordered a company of his regiment to that point with instructions to make a suitable crossing. The work involved cutting down steep banks so that a wagon could safely descend to the river and make it up the other side.[31] Gamble entrusted the assignment to Lieutenant Robert Neely and troops of the Forty-first Infantry.[32]

Neely's A Company at Camp Melvin enjoyed a healthy climate and location. They slept in common tents. A hospital steward cared for their minor medical needs, which included nothing more serious than applying bandages and dispensing a few medicines. Dr. Rudolfo Gausetsky, an acting assistant surgeon, found slight symptoms of scurvy in one man during a medical inspection of the camp in the fall, but nothing that warranted major treatment. He recommended that no doctor be assigned to Camp Melvin because no medical facilities or equipment existed there yet and because the garrison showed no indication of need for a physician. For cases too serious for the hospital steward to treat, a wagon could transport patients to Fort Stockton.[33]

In addition to guarding the crossing and cutting down the banks for wagons, the company established a ten-man outpost on the mail route ten miles east of camp. Heavy work on the banks at the crossing fatigued animals as well as men, and Fort Stockton had to send additional forage for the company's mules.[34] By the following summer most of the troops had transferred to other locations, a detail of just eight men remaining at Camp Melvin, primarily as guards for the mail route and stage station. Fresh troops relieved the detail every sixty days. No Indians had attacked that section of the mail line since its establishment.[35]

Although a ferry crossed the river at Camp Melvin, the army made efforts to bridge the Pecos there in late 1869. Major C. M. Terrill, a military paymaster, recommended such a bridge and provided measurements of possible crossing points. The Pecos averaged approximately forty-six feet in width from the top of one bank to the top of the other. Terrill estimated that a fifty-foot bridge would be sufficient.[36] A span already stood near Fort Lancaster, but when troops dismantled it and transported it to Camp Melvin, they found it too short, so they returned it to its original location.[37] Engineers eventually erected a pontoon bridge. Colonel Benjamin Grierson's command and the post of Fort Davis depended on that bridge as part of their supply line. At one point, it broke loose from the west bank, causing considerable worry on the part of Grierson's staff.[38]

Small details of troops guarded the stage station at Camp Melvin throughout the 1870s.[39] Occasionally, soldiers used it for other purposes. Early in 1873, for example, a small infantry detachment escorted a survey party on the Texas & Pacific rail line from Camp Melvin to New Mexico.[40]

During its existence as an active post, Camp Melvin usually functioned under the control of Fort Clark. Part of that time, however, it came under Fort Stockton's authority.[41] With the passing of the Apache threat in West Texas in the early 1880s, Pecos Station, or Camp Melvin, no longer required the protection of the small military detail.

A few months before the first troops arrived at Camp Melvin, the army began using a small post at Beaver Lake, twenty-three miles north of Fort Hudson where Devils River and Johnson's Run converge. Lieutenant Francis Dodge and forty-two enlisted men of D Company, Ninth Cavalry, occupied the site late in 1867.[42] In December, Dr. J. C. Whitehead arrived at the camp to serve as acting assistant surgeon.[43] Dodge, newly promoted to captain, evacuated the camp the following April and marched his troops to Fort Stockton on orders from headquarters, District of Texas.[44] By the end of the year, however, soldiers again garrisoned the camp at Beaver Lake.[45]

In addition to the regular detachment assigned to Beaver Lake, other troops sometimes used the camp for a rendezvous point or staging area. In January 1870, twenty mounted troops with a noncommissioned officer in command met an army major at or near Beaver Lake for a period of intensive patrol.[46] Three years later Colonel Ranald Mackenzie and a large contingent of cavalry operated in the area near Beaver Lake against hostile Indians. A trader named August Santleben camped with Mackenzie's command at the lake. Santleben's wagon train, carrying freight for

Mexico, left the troops and proceeded less than three miles when approximately forty Indians ambushed the train's advance party. Indians killed two of the men before the train could make it back to the safety of Mackenzie's camp.[47]

Troops occasionally provided escort to travelers passing Beaver Lake. Captain John Craig and twenty-three men of his G Company, Tenth Infantry, escorted a wagon train from Fort Clark to Beaver Lake in March 1876 during a particularly dangerous period.[48] Like many other outposts, Beaver Lake frequently served as a depot for forage or supplies. Fort Clark provided the supplies, and teamsters hauled them to the camp.[49] Although its use by the army declined after the mid-1870s, Beaver Lake continued to serve on occasion as a camping site for other forces such as Texas Rangers. In the summer of 1876, a large Ranger force under Major John B. Jones used Beaver Lake as a staging area to operate against Kickapoos and Lipan Apaches along the Pecos.[50]

For a brief span in the early 1880s the army maintained a camp at Mayer's Spring near the Rio Grande on a road between San Felipe and Peña Colorado. During the summer of 1880, several companies of the Twenty-fourth Infantry marched from Fort Clark to Fort Stockton along this route. They investigated the area near Mayer's Spring for water but found no permanent sources except for the spring itself.[51] Troops occupied Mayer's Spring at the beginning of 1881, along with several other key points near the Rio Grande. Elements of the First Infantry Regiment garrisoned some of those locations, with A Company holding Mayer's Spring.[52] These units operated against small Apache bands that slipped back and forth across the Rio Grande to hit undefended ranches and to steal livestock.

At the end of April, the infantry left Mayer's Spring, replaced by H Company, Eighth Cavalry. By July two additional companies of that regiment occupied Mayer's Spring and patrolled the region along the border.[53] A month later another company of the Eighth Cavalry left Fort Clark for duty at the spring, along with a detachment of Seminole Negro scouts. Troops operated out of Mayer's Spring for the remainder of the year.[54]

Indian activity in the area diminished by the beginning of 1882 to the point that troops no longer needed to garrison Mayer's Spring, although they still passed through or made camp there on occasion. Captain George Armes and a patrol looking for a party of Indians rode into the area in April 1883. By that time many ranchers lived there, and Armes picked up guides from among them as his patrol scouted the mountains. He saw two mounted men, believed to be Indians, at one spot, but could not catch them. Otherwise, his patrol found no recent sign of raiders.[55]

In addition to Mayer's Spring and the other subposts of Fort Clark, several minor camps and stations existed during the period. The fort established one such outpost at Camp Wood during the early 1870s. The camp stood beside the east fork of the Nueces River, ten miles north of the town of Montell. Camp Wood occupied the site of an old Spanish mission, San Lorenzo de la Santa Cruz. At various times the Texas Rangers maintained a camp there.[56]

On June 1, 1871, forty-six men of the Twenty-fourth Infantry and fifteen men of the Ninth Cavalry, under Captain Henry C. Corbin, Twenty-fourth Infantry, occupied Camp Wood. A fresh infantry company relieved the troops there every month, and command of the post passed to the commanding officer of the new company. Men at Camp Wood saw no serious action but spent most of their time building corrals and stables for the post's animals and constructing a road from Fort Clark, forty-four miles south, to Fort McKavett, approximately eighty miles north. Camp Wood retained a four-man cavalry detachment for escort and courier duty after most of the cavalry withdrew. On Christmas Day, 1871, the army abandoned Camp Wood and removed its government property and records to Fort Clark.[57]

Troops from Fort Clark used an outpost at San Felipe on the Rio Grande for several years in the 1870s and 1880s. The post stood near a series of springs less than two miles from the river along the road from Fort Clark to Peña Colorado.[58] Between March 1873 and February 1876, units of the Ninth Cavalry operated out of San Felipe on patrol for Mexican cattle thieves and Indians.[59] When Indian activity increased in the area again in the spring of 1878, troopers from the Fourth Cavalry and Eighth Cavalry used San Felipe as a base for scouting. Being only twenty-eight miles from Fort Clark, the camp received supplies from the main post easily. Even a section of light artillery helped protect San Felipe briefly, before it returned to Fort Clark. Troops continued to occupy the outpost through the early months of 1881.[60]

Several outposts under Fort Clark's jurisdiction existed along Devils River. D Company, Ninth Cavalry, took station twenty-eight miles west of Fort Hudson at the head of Devils River in November 1867 to protect the mail and locate additional sources of water.[61] The following January a seven-man detachment under a corporal garrisoned the first crossing of Devils River.[62] Like many other small outposts, this one also served as a supply and forage depot for troops scouting in the area. In March 1872, for example, troops deposited 3000 pounds of forage at the crossing and maintained a guard there to protect it.[63] Another camp on the river held cavalry troopers during the hectic spring of 1878.[64]

On a more temporary basis, troops from Fort Clark made use of a number of scouting camps over the years. Such outposts existed on the Nueces River (1872), at the head of the Sabinal

River (1873-1877), in Frio Canyon and Sabinal Canyon (1877), on Pinto Creek (1877-1879), at the mouth of Sycamore Creek (1878-1879), on Texaquila Creek (1878), at Strickland Springs (1878-1881), on Las Moras Creek (1878), near Twin Mountain (1879), at the mouth of the Pecos (1881), and at Del Rio (1881). In addition, troops under Lieutenant John Bullis built a small hut and stockade at Pecan Springs for detachments operating in the area.[65] The site lay close to Devils River in extremely desolate country.[66]

Such an intricate network of outposts greatly aided Fort Clark in providing protection to the area for which it had responsibility. If that protection often proved inadequate, one could blame a shortage of troops and the skill of Indian opponents rather than arrangement of the defensive posts.

FORT MCKAVETT
AND ITS OUTPOSTS

On the south bank of the San Saba River, 110 miles north of Fort Clark and 160 miles east of Fort Stockton, sat Fort McKavett, another pre-Civil War post. Like Fort Clark, McKavett defended a region threatened by raiding Indians from north, south, and west. In addition, soldiers at the fort had to deal with recalcitrant citizens who resented changes wrought by the Civil War.

Responding to urgent requests from settlers on the frontier and from officials in the Texas government, United States troops reoccupied Fort McKavett early in 1868. On April 1, A Company, Fourth Cavalry, under Captain Eugene B. Beaumont, rode into the fort and established camp. The post stood in virtual ruins, the buildings so dilapidated that the unit had to live in tents.[1]

Another company of the Fourth Cavalry and three companies from the Thirty-eighth Infantry arrived later that month, giving the garrison plenty of men for construction work.[2] This side of soldiering must have been irksome for most of the officers and men, especially one like Lieutenant Peter Boehm, Fourth Cavalry, who had seen combat and had been cited three times for gallantry in action against hostile Indians.[3]

At Fort McKavett using stone for the buildings proved impractical, so the troops began cutting cedar pickets. A detail under
Lieutenant Boehm established camp near old Fort Terrett for that
purpose, and by late summer was cutting 200 pickets per day.
Captain Beaumont estimated that three weeks at such a rate would
provide all the pickets necessary to rebuild the fort.[4] The reconstruction effort continued into 1869.[5]

Military operations out of Fort McKavett consisted primarily
of scouting for hostile Indians. On many occasions troops would
respond to a report of Indians raiding in a certain vicinity and
launch a pursuit. Very few of these efforts met with success. At other
times patrols rode out of the fort on random searches in areas where
Indian activity had been heavy in the past. Again, success eluded
most of the patrols.

Fort McKavett also provided support and additional troops for
expeditions from posts closer to the home ground of raiding Indians.
Sometimes during this post-Civil War period, officers at McKavett
found the post stripped of so many troops in support of remote
campaigns that they had too few men to protect their own region
adequately. Colonel Henry B. Clitz, Tenth Infantry Regiment,
found himself in this situation in late 1875. Command of two companies would have allowed him to maintain continual patrols along
both the San Antonio road and the road between Forts Terrett and
Mason, effectively guarding the main routes that Indians might
take in trying to slip into the settlements from either north, south,
or west. Because Clitz had only one company for local operations,
however, he had to keep it at the post in case of danger.[6]

By the mid-1870s Fort McKavett no longer faced a significant threat from Native Americans in its own vicinity. Troops had
forced Comanche and Kiowa warriors onto reservations north of
the Red River. To the south, soldiers had blunted the hazard from

Indians across the Rio Grande to such an extent that raids no longer penetrated as far as the McKavett area. Apaches to the west and southwest still raided settlements and attacked travelers, and McKavett provided troops for the continuing struggle against the

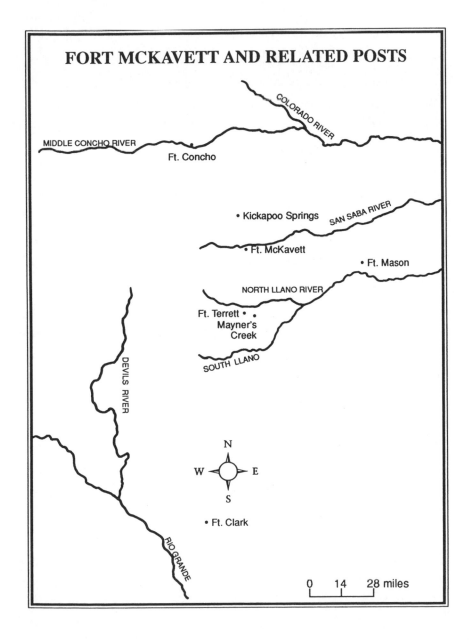

FORT MCKAVETT AND RELATED POSTS

Apaches through 1881. The last scout for hostile Indians left the fort in March 1880.[7]

Fort McKavett operated a number of subposts and picket stations in its region between 1868 and 1878. Its troops garrisoned old Fort Terrett and Fort Mason at times or maintained camps nearby. In addition they established stations or camps at Kickapoo Springs, Mayner's Creek, Splitgarber's Ranch, and various other sites.

Two locations called Kickapoo Springs existed in the vicinity of Fort McKavett. One lay well to the south on the way to Fort Clark. Troops from Clark bivouacked there for brief periods while working on a road between the two forts in 1872.[8] The other site of the same name was a place of much greater significance to military operations around Fort McKavett. That Kickapoo Springs bisected the route from Fort McKavett to Fort Concho. It occupied a spot about twenty miles north of McKavett near the San Antonio-El Paso road.[9] Troops from the fort garrisoned Kickapoo Springs periodically from the reoccupation of Fort McKavett in 1868 until 1877.[10] The first detail to occupy Kickapoo Springs consisted of Corporal William Somerz and two privates of the Fourth Cavalry, sent to protect the mail station at the springs. Apparently the men remained at the station for just a few days.[11]

Colonel Ranald Mackenzie took command at Fort McKavett in early 1869 and reestablished the picket station at Kickapoo Springs on March 27. He did so on request of Ben Ficklin, operator of an extensive stage line that passed through the location. A long-running argument began at that point between Ficklin and Mackenzie over maintaining a permanent detail at the station.[12] Mackenzie withdrew the detachment on May 20 because of a shortage of troops at Fort McKavett caused by the absence of two major scouting parties. Ficklin complained that the United States mail, which passed through Kickapoo Springs, needed military protection.[13] While

Kickapoo Springs, 1887 (Fort Concho National Historic Landmark).

Mackenzie was temporarily absent from Fort McKavett, the Fifth Military District headquarters ordered the station reoccupied. Captain Henry Carroll, Ninth Cavalry, acting post commander at McKavett, complied.[14]

The situation angered Mackenzie, and he stated his disagreement in writing to district headquarters. He did not believe a permanent station at Kickapoo Springs was warranted because troops could occupy the site whenever it was threatened. He also resented Ficklin's actions in principle. As military commander in the immediate area, Mackenzie believed he was best qualified to decide when and how to protect the mail, citizens, and government interests.[15]

Mackenzie kept a detachment at Kickapoo Springs for the time being, but replaced the infantrymen with cavalrymen, who could patrol nearby areas whenever reports of Indian activity reached them and more actively protect the region than foot soldiers. Mackenzie gave strict orders about the care and protection of horses and ensured an adequate guard would be left for the station if the majority of the command left on a pursuit.[16]

Ficklin continued to pester Mackenzie with requests for more troops. He went so far as to ask for an entire company of cavalry to cover the stretch between Fort Concho and the head of the Concho River. Mackenzie considered small permanent detachments at points like Kickapoo Springs detrimental to the army's ability to protect an area. They drained resources of men and horses, hampering a post commander's ability to conduct real offensive operations. Mackenzie thought placement of troops at temporary picket stations could be effective, but he believed offensive patrols and long scouts that penetrated Indians' home ground to be the best tactics.[17] In late August, Mackenzie withdrew the remaining troops from Kickapoo Springs for use in just such an extended scout.[18]

The entire Ficklin-Mackenzie controversy over garrisoning Kickapoo Springs illustrated a common problem faced by the army on the frontier in Texas and elsewhere. Many military officers believed, correctly or incorrectly, that civilians demanded the presence of troops at various locations out of financial motives rather than for protection of life. In most cases those financial motives focused on the army garrison as a potential market for local agricultural produce, which often sold at inflated prices to vegetable-starved troops. In the case of Kickapoo Springs, no such sales motive existed, but Mackenzie still suspected, no doubt correctly, that Ficklin was trying to use the army to protect his business from personal enemies rather than to protect lives and property from marauding Indians. The November after Mackenzie pulled out the rest of his troops, five men under command of a non-commissioned officer reoccupied Kickapoo Springs. The soldiers, carrying rations for thirty days, pitched tents at the station.[19]

At times no troops occupied Kickapoo Springs, but units from Fort McKavett still made frequent patrols in the vicinity. One such patrol under Sergeant Emanuel Stance, Ninth Cavalry, spotted a band of Indians with a horse herd near the springs on May 20, 1870. Stance and his patrol rode for the Indians at a dead run, scattering them and capturing several horses. After camping for the night at Kickapoo Springs, Stance's patrol started back for Fort McKavett with their captured animals. A short distance along the way they saw a party of Indians preparing to attack a small group of wagons, and Stance again ordered a mounted attack, catching the war party by surprise and taking a few more horses. When the Indians worked around his flank and tried to hit his unit from the rear, Stance and his men used their carbines to good effect and drove off the enemy. For his actions in the fighting at Kickapoo Springs, Sergeant Stance won a Congressional Medal of Honor.[20]

Stance's action illustrated the fact that the small detachments of troops typical of outpost and patrol duty in Texas almost always outfought the similarly small bands of Indians they encountered, if the Indians made any fight at all. Most of the time, however, war parties fled at the first sign of military pursuit. Because Native Americans routinely traveled with two or more horses per man, Indian bands usually had little trouble outdistancing cavalry units, with their one-horse-to-one-man ratio. The great majority of military patrols, of course, resulted in no sign of Indians whatsoever.

Mixed cavalry and infantry detachments usually served at Kickapoo Springs. Troops built necessary structures such as corrals but lived in tents themselves. In addition to guarding the mail by providing escorts to ride stagecoaches between the springs and the next station at Coghlan's Ranch, soldiers also protected cattle herders in the vicinity. Cavalry at the station mounted small patrols when reports of Indians came in.[21]

On occasion soldiers lent a hand in enforcing the law. In October 1876, the sheriff of Tom Green County and a posse chased two killers into a thicket near Kickapoo Springs. When the posse attempted to go in after them, the outlaws opened fire and killed one of the group. At that point the sheriff asked the military detachment for help. A lengthy gun battle took place, ending finally with the killers shot dead.[22]

In the summer of 1877, Colonel H. B. Clitz, in command of Fort McKavett, decided that no further need existed to garrison Kickapoo Springs and ordered the detachment there to abandon the station.[23]

Whereas Kickapoo Springs occupied a strategic location north of Fort McKavett, old Fort Terrett stood to the south. Before the Civil War, Fort Terrett served as one of the major posts guarding the Texas Hill Country settlements, but after the war it never regained the status of an important post. At various times during the 1870s, however, it was garrisoned by detachments from Fort McKavett.

A few months after troops reactivated McKavett, a detail from the post camped near Fort Terrett to procure cedar pickets for building purposes.[24] To protect the working party, five enlisted men served as a guard. Wagons hauled the rough pickets back to Fort McKavett.[25] Fort McKavett continued to take advantage of the cedar brake at the old post for at least another year, sometimes stationing work details there for two weeks at a time.[26]

Fort Terrett also served as a scouting camp. Ninth Cavalry troopers under Captain E. M. Heyl used it as a base for supplies and forage when conducting a reconnaissance of the area in the fall of 1869. Wagons from Fort McKavett hauled supplies to the old post, where pack mules waited to carry those supplies on with the patrols.[27] For a brief period in 1871, Fort Terrett served as a regular subpost of Fort McKavett. During this time the post received a permanent medical officer.[28] Soon, however, the army disestablished the post, and Fort Terrett reverted to use as an occasional camp.

Late in 1876 in response to a number of raids in the region, troops again occupied Fort Terrett and used it as a base for scouting. In addition to such patrols, the command there also cut more cedar poles, provided escort to cattle herders, and hunted for outlaws who had fired on an army paymaster's detail shortly before.[29]

Probably the most bizarre assignment of any detachment at Terrett fell to Captain Henry Carroll and twenty men of the Ninth Cavalry.[30] In addition to scouting, Carroll's command had the extraordinary duty of disinterring the bodies of all soldiers buried in the old post cemetery so the quartermaster could haul the remains back to Fort McKavett for reburial.[31]

Like Fort Terrett, Fort Mason had functioned as a major post before the Civil War but only housed scattered detachments after the war. Two companies of the Fourth Cavalry reoccupied the fort at the end of 1866 as part of the initial post-war force sent to defend the frontier.[32] Located approximately fifty miles east of Fort McKavett, however, Mason stood too far inside the settlement line to serve as a permanent post. The troops there transferred to Fort McKavett when that post returned to active status in early 1868.[33]

Although Indians raided in the region for several years, some of the most significant action around Fort Mason concerned white cattle thieves. After the reestablishment of Fort McKavett, that command sent a detachment under Captain G. W. Budd, Ninth Cavalry, to Mason. Budd reported trouble in the vicinity, where unknown outlaws were killing cattle. Eight cavalrymen left Fort McKavett to help Budd and to relieve the infantry detachment with him. With the mounted troops to aid him, the captain spent the next three weeks investigating the cases and taking affidavits before returning to Fort McKavett.[34]

Two months later in July 1869, military commanders at Fort McKavett and at Fifth Military District headquarters discussed permanently stationing one company at Fort Mason to deal with continuing problems of murder and cattle theft. Troops from Fort McKavett always arrived too late to do any good when local citizens around Mason called on them for help. Estimates for repairing the old fort to house a company ran between $3000 and $5000, however, and nothing came of the idea.[35]

At election time the following November, the commanding officer of Fort McKavett detailed Lieutenant W. W. Tyler, Ninth Cavalry, to Fort Mason as a member of the Board of Registrars for Mason County. Ten enlisted men went with Tyler to enforce rules laid down by the Fifth Military District, and the detail remained until after the election.[36] Afterward Mason served only as a temporary campsite for patrols.

Captain John Clous, Twenty-fourth Infantry, was responsible for another outpost of Fort McKavett.[37] In May 1871, Clous led two other officers, citizen physician Thomas Davis, and sixty-two enlisted men from Fort McKavett to a point where Copperas Creek flowed into the North Llano River, a few miles east of old Fort Terrett. He established a camp there known as the subpost on the North Llano, or Mayner's Creek. For the next year fresh troops from Fort McKavett relieved detachments at the subpost monthly. The garrison contained both foot soldiers and mounted troops and varied between thirty and sixty men during most of that period.[38]

The detachment at Mayner's Creek decreased to six men in June 1872, probably as a result of a manpower shortage caused when Colonel W. R. Shafter led an expedition of almost 200 men from Fort McKavett toward the Brazos and Colorado Rivers. Troops abandoned the post altogether the next month.[39]

Fort McKavett maintained several other small posts or picket stations in its area at various times. On May 16, 1871, four enlisted men of the Ninth Cavalry established a picket station at Splitgarber's Ranch, seventeen miles from the fort, to guard the mail station. Fresh troops relieved the detail monthly. The picket station remained active through November.[40] Although too small to mount patrols, the four-man garrison fulfilled the general objective of a picket station—to discourage raids by small bands of Indians on the station and its livestock. The next January, a detachment under Captain H. C. Corbin, a former brigadier general of volunteers during the Civil War and a future major general who would become adjutant general of the army, occupied a camp at Bear Creek. Troops remained at the camp through April. They spent most of their time working the road between camp and Fort McKavett.[41]

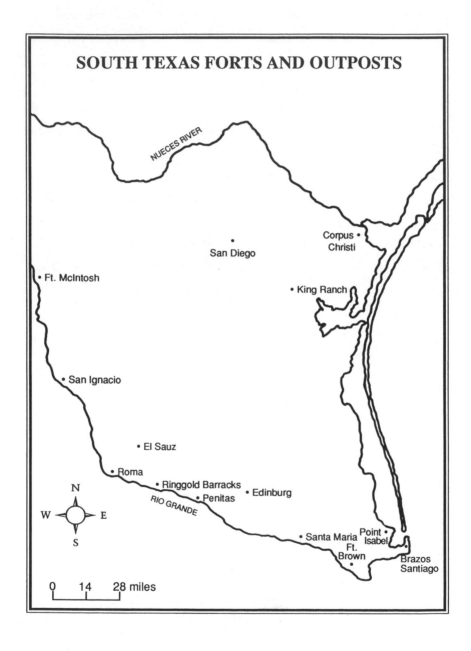

SOUTH TEXAS FORTS AND OUTPOSTS

NUECES RIVER

• San Diego

Corpus • Christi

• Ft. McIntosh

• King Ranch

• San Ignacio

• El Sauz

• Roma

• Ringgold Barracks
• Penitas   • Edinburg

RIO GRANDE

N
W ⬥ E
S

• Santa Maria   Point •
Isabel
Ft. •
Brown
Brazos
Santiago

0   14   28 miles

FORTS AND OUTPOSTS OF THE LOWER RIO GRANDE

Southeast of the region covered by Forts McKavett, Clark, and Stockton, a line of posts stretched down the lower Rio Grande, from Fort Duncan at Eagle Pass through Fort McIntosh near Laredo and Ringgold Barracks at Rio Grande City, to the mouth of the river. Fort Brown anchored the line at that point. Mexican cattle thieves and other lawless elements across the border constituted the primary danger to this zone all the way up to Fort Duncan, where Indians began to replace Mexican outlaws as the main threat.

United States troops returned to Fort Brown immediately after the Civil War to protect the border, not only from outlaws, but also from incursions by forces of French-supported Emperor Maximilian of Mexico.[1] A succession of units rotated through the post. On occasion they came into conflict with Mexican irregulars or civilians. Late in 1866, two companies of the Fourth Cavalry actually crossed the border into the town of Matamoros during a civil disturbance. The soldiers kept watch over Americans and their property for several days before returning to Fort Brown.[2] On their own side of the border, detachments protected various points in the town of

Brownsville, such as the United States customs house.[3] In addition, troops out of Fort Brown conducted regular patrols to combat cattle thieves northwestward along the border.[4]

Commanders at Fort Brown oversaw a number of outposts along the river and at points farther into the interior from 1866 to 1886. The post of Brazos Santiago, northeast of Brownsville and directly on the coast, received a small garrison in 1865, and army quartermasters improved the site early in 1867.[5] In 1871, when a military hospital moved to Brazos Santiago, it became an official subpost of Fort Brown. The hospital came from another small post just abandoned at Point Isabel, a few miles west.[6]

The detachment then at Brazos Santiago consisted of thirteen enlisted men under the command of Lieutenant James Cranston,[7] Tenth Infantry, a reliable but rather undistinguished officer.[8] By the following March, Cranston's command had decreased to just five men.[9] The post continued in operation for another year, when the army closed it and sent its garrison back to Fort Brown.[10]

In the summer of 1874, a company of the Twenty-fourth Infantry reoccupied Brazos Santiago. In September, however, the army again withdrew, this time permanently.[11]

Unsettled conditions in Mexico and a resulting increase in raids along the border led military authorities to order a major increase in cavalry patrols of the region in early 1872.[12] As part of this effort, on April 18, 1872, troops established an outpost at Santa Maria Ranch, thirty miles upriver from Fort Brown. Captain Francis E. Lacey, Tenth Infantry, an Irish immigrant with an up-and-down military record that included citations for gallantry at Gettysburg and a brief dismissal from the service in 1864,[13] and thirty men of the Tenth Infantry under his command had orders to prevent armed groups from crossing into United States territory from Mexico and to arrest individuals north of the river who attempted to enter

Mexico in violation of neutrality laws. Lacey's troops remained at Santa Maria only a few days before returning to Fort Brown.[14]

The following October, an unusual amount of activity by cattle thieves near the ranch brought troops back to Santa Maria. Detachments from two other outposts plus a patrol out of Fort Brown converged on the area.[15] M Company, Fourth Cavalry, operated out of Santa Maria during that winter but returned to Fort Brown in February. The company rode out again almost immediately as escort for a group of United States commissioners conducting an investigation of troubles on the border for the United States Congress.[16]

Troops of the Ninth Cavalry continued to scout out of Santa Maria in the following months. In October, the Department of Texas officially charged Fort Brown with responsibility for protection of the entire stretch of border between the fort and Santa Maria.[17] The next month, C Company, Ninth Cavalry, changed station from Santa Maria to Roma, a post far upriver and under command of Ringgold Barracks.[18]

In July 1874, a company of the Ninth Cavalry again used Santa Maria as a base for patrols.[19] For a brief period the next summer a detachment of the same regiment operated out of Santa Maria. Beginning in February 1876, companies of the Eighth Cavalry occupied the site continuously for three and a half years.[20] During a three-month span near the end of that period, Santa Maria functioned as an independent post but reverted to the control of Fort Brown afterward. Finally, in October 1879, the Eighth Cavalry transferred to Fort Clark, leaving Santa Maria ungarrisoned.[21]

When the army remanned Santa Maria the following January, it sent only one officer and twelve enlisted men rather than a full company. The troops came upriver on the steamboat *Andrew Ackley*. From that time until the end of 1886, small detachments of as few as five men used the post as a base for patrols along the river.[22]

Troops from Fort Brown also operated from an outpost at Penitas Ranch, eighty-five miles up the Rio Grande. In late June 1872, Captain Robert P. Wilson, Tenth Infantry, and forty-seven men of that regiment, mounted for scouting purposes, took station there, with orders to patrol the country between Ringgold Barracks and Edinburg and to stop cattle thieves and armed bands from crossing the border. Citizen physician O. J. Eddy rode with the party.[23] The following October, Wilson moved the command to Santa Maria to join other detachments traveling to the site.[24]

Troops returned to Penitas in May 1873. A detachment of nineteen enlisted men of the Ninth Cavalry under the command of a sergeant used the ranch as a base while guarding one of the crossings of the Rio Grande. Other detachments followed at the outpost. Troops from the same regiment returned the next summer for the last time.[25]

Increased Indian activity including the murders of nine settlers in April 1878, in the vicinity of San Diego, Texas, led the army to place a garrison at that location.[26] San Diego lay 150 miles north northwest of Fort Brown and only eighty miles east of Fort McIntosh, but the post came under the jurisdiction of Fort Brown. Captain Albert B. Kauffman, commanding E Company, Eighth Cavalry, occupied San Diego in late summer of 1878. His command logged more than 1000 miles in scouts between that time and June 1879. Patrols ranged in all directions after Indians and other marauders were reported in the area but never made contact. They also explored possible routes for new wagon roads connecting San Diego with the major posts in the region.[27]

Kauffman's command continued scouting out of San Diego for two more years. During that period Indians made no more trouble in the vicinity, and the troops concentrated their efforts on stopping Mexican raiders and horse thieves but apprehended few, if any, offenders. Nevertheless, the presence of active troops helped bring a greater measure of security and order to the vicinity.[28] Finally, in September 1881, E Company evacuated and transferred to Fort McIntosh.[29]

Troops from Fort Brown temporarily garrisoned several additional posts, primarily for use as scouting camps and bases for guarding river crossings. Those sites included a camp on the Nueces River (1871), Santa Rosaria (1872), Garcia's Ranch (1873-1874), Mezquito Ranch (1873), and El Sauz (1875). In addition, Fort Brown and Ringgold Barracks shared control over a subpost at Edinburg that remained active for several years.[30] After the Civil War, troops reoccupied Ringgold Barracks.[31] The command engaged in much the same activity as that at Fort Brown, concentrating their efforts on scouting close to the Rio Grande to prevent incursions from across the border and pursuing outlaws or Indians who invaded the region.

In early 1872 this policy became especially difficult to carry out because of increased revolutionary activity across the river. Parties of Mexican government troops as well as revolutionaries crossed the Rio Grande repeatedly in January. The next month, Mexicans living in Texas made two raids on the town of Mier in Mexico, harming residents and stealing property both times. At first the army left investigation of the attacks on Mier to civil authorities, but troops eventually went into action to apprehend some of those responsible for the raids.[32]

As a result of the increased potential for trouble in the area, military authorities transferred additional cavalry units to Ringgold Barracks and Fort Brown for a time to allow those posts to cover their stretches of the border more effectively.[33] Border troubles grew worse in 1874 and 1875. Reports from reputable sources attributed much of the theft and murder committed by Mexican bands on the American side of the river to wealthy Mexican merchants and officials who encouraged such activity by providing a ready market for stolen goods and livestock brought across from the north.[34] As late as 1880, General E. O. C. Ord, commanding the Department of Texas, believed a strong force was essential at Ringgold Barracks even though the border had become relatively quiet and safe in the preceding years.[35]

Ringgold Barracks maintained several subposts and camps between 1866 and 1886. The most important ones included Edinburg, Roma, and San Ignacio. Edinburg became a subpost of Ringgold Barracks in October 1868, at the same time as San Ignacio. Both had functioned as independent posts before that time. Edinburg's garrison consisted of forty-six men of I Company, Twenty-sixth Infantry, under Captain Welcome Crafts. A detachment of the company occupied Las Cuevas nearby.[36]

The following February, I Company abandoned Edinburg and returned to Ringgold Barracks on orders from the Fifth Military District. Troops did not return permanently until May 1873 when G Company, Ninth Cavalry, transferred to the camp. Daniel McLean, a civilian physician, joined the garrison as medical officer.[37] Various companies of the regiment served at Edinburg through August 1875 when the regiment transferred to New Mexico Territory.[38]

Troops at Edinburg engaged in regular small patrols. On one of the few that actually fought a party of raiders, Sergeant James Randolph and three privates of L Company, Ninth Cavalry, attacked Mexican cattle rustlers near Havana Rancho on the night of November 24, 1874. The patrol captured one man and scattered the remainder of the thieves.[39]

Units of the Eighth Cavalry occupied Edinburg regularly through October 1879, when they abandoned the subpost on orders from the District of the Rio Grande.[40] The following January, a detachment of thirteen men from the regiment regarrisoned Edinburg. From that time through September 1884, troops operated out of the camp, sometimes in small detachments and sometimes in company strength.[41]

The first significant army activity in Roma, a village fifteen miles upriver from Ringgold, occurred in September 1870 when a fourteen-man detachment out of Ringgold Barracks spent five days protecting the United States customs house there.[42] Three years later Roma received a more permanent garrison. At that time, C Company, Ninth Cavalry, rode to Roma from their old station at Santa Maria.[43] The company pulled the normal border duty of scouting and guarding river crossings. A medical officer was originally assigned to the unit, but he left in December 1873 for the post at Edinburg.[44]

The company at Roma performed extensive scouting in small detachments during the winter. In February alone, patrols rode almost 450 miles.[45] The following year in April, C Company saved the town and the customs house from an attack by forty armed Mexicans returning from a raid on ranches farther into the Texas border counties.[46] Even larger bands crossed the border near Roma at times, threatening to pillage entire towns. In an open letter to the president of the United States, Texas Governor Richard Coke appealed for more protection along the lower Rio Grande. Secretary of War William Belknap assured the president and Texans in general that he would take immediate steps to protect the area.[47] Shortly after Belknap made his statement, however, the troops at Roma pulled back to Ringgold Barracks.[48]

Although soldiers patrolled the area around Roma on occasion, troops did not return for any length of time.[49] Not until May

1884 did the army again garrison the town. Even then only a detail of nine men occupied the post, and they stayed just through the summer before evacuating permanently.[50]

Periodically over a decade, units from Ringgold Barracks used the village of Carrizo, often referred to as San Ignacio or Rancho Ignacio, as an outpost. The village stood fifty-eight miles upriver from Rio Grande City. H Company, Twenty-sixth Infantry, first occupied Carrizo in May 1868. The company returned briefly to Ringgold in September, but moved back to Carrizo the next month. At that time, Lieutenant Daniel F. Stiles commanded the twenty-eight man detachment. E. A. Spohn, a civilian physician, served with the troops as medical officer. In February 1869, Stiles and his command evacuated the subpost on orders from the Fifth Military District.[51]

Troops under John M. Thompson of I Company, Twenty-fourth Infantry, plus a medical officer returned to Carrizo in the fall of 1877. A detail of the Eighth Cavalry joined the foot soldiers there in April 1878, but Carrizo's days as a permanent outpost were drawing to a close.[52] In November, the last garrison of Carrizo, G Company, Twenty-fourth Infantry, under Captain Louis Johnson, withdrew. Although patrols out of Ringgold scouted near the village when reports of Indians came in, no soldiers occupied the site again.[53]

In June 1873, Lieutenant Daniel Floyd and troops of his B Company, Ninth Cavalry, established an outpost of Ringgold Barracks at the King Ranch. Floyd's twenty men left the King Ranch for El Tule Ranch, ninety miles from Ringgold, in October. The next month, B Company of the same regiment established a scouting camp at Los Conchos near the King Ranch and patrolled the area for cattle thieves until April. The troops crisscrossed the vicinity thoroughly, riding 550 miles on scouts in one month alone.

Other companies of the Ninth Cavalry continued to occupy the outpost until September, scouting and, on one occasion, providing aid to the sheriff at Corpus Christi.[54]

Other small posts and picket stations operated under direction of Ringgold Barracks during the mid-1870s. Those included La Pena Ranch, also identified as Salineno (1872-1873), El Tule Ranch (1873), Penitas (1873), Las Puneas (1874), and Las Ruscas (1875). Farther to the northwest up the Rio Grande, in mid-1865 Fort McIntosh at Laredo was reactivated at approximately the same time as Fort Brown and Ringgold Barracks. Troops from the Fourth Cavalry engaged in long scouts out of McIntosh, each covering well over 200 miles.[55]

By 1872, military authorities in Texas had begun to consider closing Fort McIntosh. Brigadier General C. C. Augur, commanding the department, thought McIntosh too remote from settlements on the Nueces River that needed protection and believed a subpost at Carrizo would suffice for protecting the immediate Rio Grande area.[56] Fort McIntosh remained open, however, and by 1878 troops operating from it engaged in a large amount of scouting. The following two years saw similar patrol activity by the several companies of troops stationed at the fort.[57]

Located on a stretch of river having few villages and towns, Fort McIntosh had less need and opportunity for establishing outposts than the forts farther downriver. Troops from McIntosh did use a subpost at Souz's Ranch during 1878 and 1879. Soldiers based at the ranch conducted normal patrols along the border looking for Indian or Mexican raiders. They also provided escort to United States customs officials. In April 1879, troops from Souz's Ranch captured a party of smugglers along the river.[58]

The next major post on the river, Fort Duncan, served as a junction between Fort McIntosh and those posts farther down the Rio Grande on one side, and Fort Clark on the other. In many

ways Duncan had a closer connection to Clark than to those other
forts, because troops from Duncan and Clark often operated
against the same enemies, and those enemies were Indians rather
than Mexican cattle thieves. Unlike the other three forts of the
lower Rio Grande, Fort Duncan did not become an active post
again until 1868. On March 23 of that year, I Company, First
Infantry, occupied the site. The command consisted of three commissioned officers and forty-eight enlisted men. The troops found
the post in bad condition, buildings stripped of doors and windows and no portable property of any value remaining.[59]

In April, Lieutenant Colonel W. R. Shafter assumed command
of Fort Duncan. The garrison increased to more than 180 officers
and men with the addition of companies from the Forty-first
Infantry, which was Shafter's regiment, and the Ninth Cavalry. The
post's effectiveness for scouting and escort duty declined over the
summer, however, because a majority of the cavalry horses were
unserviceable and were not replaced.[60]

Shafter earned a reputation as a tough and energetic cam-
paigner both before and after his tenure at Duncan. He rose to the
rank of brevet brigadier general of volunteers in the Civil War,
winning a Medal of Honor along the way for heroism at Fair Oaks,
Virginia, in May 1862.[61] With the massive reduction in the army
at the war's end, he went home to Michigan and cut wood for a
living while he waited for Congress to consider his application for
a major's commission in the regular army. By a curious twist,
Congress had no place for another major but offered him instead
a commission as lieutenant colonel, an offer he quickly accepted.
His career from that point included long, hard service on the
frontier where subordinate officers learned to fear the short,
overweight Shafter and his high professional standards and sharp
tongue. As the crowning achievement of his military service, he

would command the successful Santiago expedition in Cuba during the war with Spain in 1898.[62]

Fort Duncan received a boost to its combat strength in the summer of 1870 when the first Seminole Negro scouts crossed the

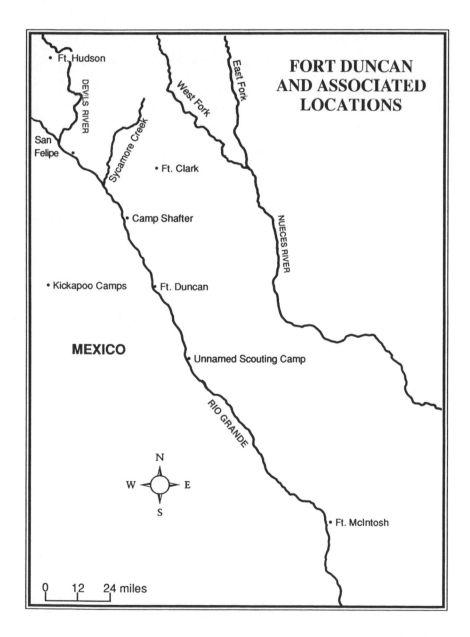

FORT DUNCAN AND ASSOCIATED LOCATIONS

border from Mexico and enlisted. More came in over the next three years, and some remained at Duncan, although most went to Clark.[63] Fort Duncan served as one of the staging areas for Colonel Ranald Mackenzie's attack on the Kickapoo villages in Mexico in May 1873, the Seminole Negroes guiding the cavalry columns to their targets below the border.[64]

The primary duty of units at Fort Duncan at most times consisted of scouting. Patrols covered vast distances of the arid countryside along the border. Occasionally, troops from the fort participated in larger expeditions that kept them away for months at a time. One such undertaking took two companies of the Twenty-fourth Infantry and a detachment of black Seminole scouts away for six months on a 2000-mile scout to the northwest.[65]

Despite such expeditions and constant smaller patrols, Indian danger in the region near Fort Duncan remained strong in the late 1870s. Certain villages and towns well south of the border carried on a profitable trade in stolen American livestock with Indians living there. Those towns feared punitive raids by Mackenzie or other commanders, and some Texas citizens called for just such attacks to end the danger in the border region.[66]

Other thrusts into Mexico did occur, but troops from Fort Duncan engaged in road building much more than they did in combat, especially after 1879.[67] Duncan's importance declined rapidly after that, and the army abandoned the fort in August 1883. In April 1886, Fort Clark established a subpost on the site of Fort Duncan for maintaining order along the Rio Grande and protecting citizens from Mexican raiders and extremists.[68]

After the Civil War, Fort Duncan operated a handful of outposts, the most significant of which was Camp Shafter, also known as Camp San Pedro Springs. Troops from the fort had scouted frequently in the vicinity of the Cariza and Pendencia

Ranches in early 1872, but in May of the following year, over 120 men from two companies of the Fourth Cavalry established an outpost there. The camp stood about twenty-five miles up the Rio Grande from Fort Duncan. Seminole Negro scouts acted as couriers between the camp and Forts Duncan and Clark.[69]

Lieutenant Colonel Shafter established the camp to protect the border from an expected raid by Kickapoos and Lipan Apaches in retaliation for Mackenzie's recent attack on their villages. Shafter sent another detachment to set up a similar scouting camp thirty miles downstream from Duncan. Although Indians did not avenge Mackenzie's attack, Camp Shafter remained in use for several months. Cavalry from the camp patrolled the Rio Grande during this period in efforts to stop cattle thieves and Mexican political extremists reported in the area.[70] The following summer, cavalry from Fort Duncan used Camp Shafter as a grazing camp to fatten their horses when the grass became too poor near the fort.[71] Other outposts of Fort Duncan included another grazing camp twelve miles from the fort, used in the early spring of 1876, and Fort Hudson, used as a scouting camp by Lieutenant Colonel Shafter's command from April through October of that year.[72]

Together, the forts on the lower Rio Grande and their outposts provided a network of points from which patrols operated. Those patrols tried, primarily, to reduce cross-border depredations in the border counties of Texas. Troops at those outposts operated under disadvantages even worse in some ways than those faced by the army in other areas of the state. Sanctuary for Indian and, especially, Mexican marauders existed just across the border. Ranches lay all along the north side of the Rio Grande. Raiders had merely to ford the river, ride a few miles, strike an isolated herd or ranch house, and return to safety in Mexico with their stolen cattle. Chances were extremely slim that a military patrol would happen along during the few hours that a raiding party was in Texas. Additionally, many ostensibly law-abiding Mexican inhabitants of the Texas border counties, as well as ranchers and businessmen south of the river, helped and protected Mexican outlaws in their forays into the state. In the part of Mexico opposite Eagle Pass and Fort Duncan, some towns did a thriving business with Kickapoo and Lipan warriors who often struck targets in Texas. Only with better cooperation from Mexico, realized late in the 1870s, did the army on the lower Rio Grande achieve a significant measure of success in pacifying the region.

FORT RICHARDSON
AND ASSOCIATED POSTS

Just as the Rio Grande marked the southern border of Texas, the Red River formed most of the state's northern boundary. Above the Red lived enemies every bit as dangerous and resourceful as those in Mexico. The allied Comanche and Kiowa tribes, assigned to vast reservations in Indian Territory near the site of Fort Sill, considered the northwestern half of Texas their rightful domain and the Texan inhabitants of that region their perpetual enemies.

Ever since the first settlers had moved into North Texas in the 1830s, the two tribes had raided their settlements and ranches incessantly. After settlers forced Comanches off a reservation in North Texas in the late 1850s, the attacks increased, and they increased again in the wake of the withdrawal of federal troops from the frontier at the beginning of the Civil War. Soldiers did not return to the northern frontier zone immediately after the war, although many occupied the interior of the state and attempted to reestablish federal authority over the growing Anglo population.

A demand from settlers and Texas government officials for frontier protection finally brought the army back to North Texas. One company of the Sixth Cavalry Regiment rode into the town of Jacksboro in the summer of 1866 to take up the defense of that area. Six more companies of that regiment joined the vanguard at Jacksboro over the next five months. The troops lived in tents at first, but early in the new year work began on a permanent post of log pickets.[1] In April 1867, the army transferred the companies at Jacksboro to two other locations that seemed to offer better protection to the frontier line. Four companies went west forty miles to old Fort Belknap, and the rest of the troops moved north to Buffalo Springs, twenty miles closer to the Red River. Although the army had intended those new stations to be permanent, most troops left them within a few months and returned to Jacksboro, where they began work on Fort Richardson.[2]

The fort formed one link in a chain of four new posts planned to cover the northwestern frontier of the state. Beginning with Fort Concho near the confluence of the three branches of the Concho River in Tom Green County, the proposed chain stretched north and east to Fort Griffin on the Clear Fork of the Brazos, to Richardson, and on to Fort Burnham. Military authorities wanted to locate Fort Burnham, to be named in honor of Brigadier General Hiram Burnham, who was killed near Richmond in 1864, on the Red River near the mouth of the Little Wichita. The post would house four companies of cavalry and two of infantry. General J. J. Reynolds, commanding the District of Texas, would determine the exact location for the post.[3] To help make that determination, Lieutenant Thomas Tolman, Sixth Cavalry, a young officer who had spent the entire Civil War as a cadet at West Point, made a tour of northern Montague County in the late winter of 1868, looking for the best site. Officers designated A and C Companies, Sixth Cavalry, to garrison the new post. In June, however, the army cancelled plans for Burnham, primarily because no good site existed near the mouth of the Little Wichita. That stream flooded frequently, making a major cavalry post there impractical.[4]

With plans for Fort Burnham scrapped, Fort Richardson served as the northernmost link in the defense chain. As such, it had responsibility for patrols through the Red River counties and those just to the south. In addition, large-scale offensive expeditions striking at

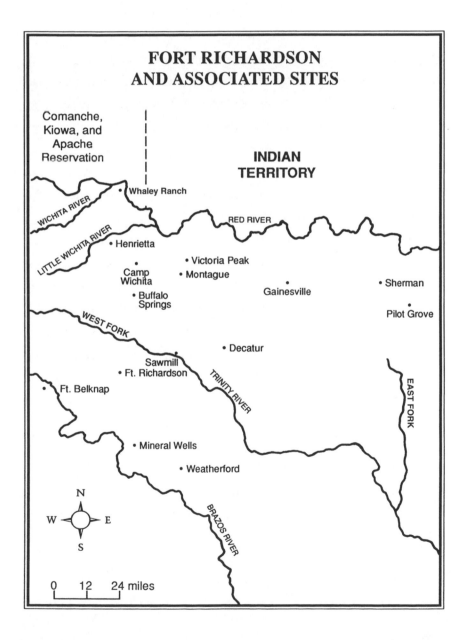

FORT RICHARDSON AND ASSOCIATED SITES

the home ground of certain Indian bands originated at the fort. For a time, however, the garrison remained too weak and the horses too poor to perform even escort and patrol duty adequately.[5] A shift in troops eventually remedied that situation, but civilians in the area clamored for permission to organize local defense companies to provide protection the army seemed unable to give. As early as 1866, the Texas legislature had provided for state forces to help defend counties in North Texas, but General Philip Sheridan had vetoed the plan.[6] By late fall of 1868, however, raids in the area reached such proportions that the commanding officer of Fort Richardson authorized temporary enrollment of citizens in Wise, Denton, and Montague Counties to pursue hostile bands marauding in the area. The fort could spare only four or five soldiers to join with citizens on any such pursuit.[7]

Commanders at Richardson refined their instructions a few days later, allowing permanent organization of civilian companies, to permit a quicker call to arms in the event of attack. The orders limited each county to 100 men and required that names and addresses of each be filed with the fort. A citizen captain commanded each unit, and either he or the county judge could call the men to action. Citizens had to furnish their own horses and weapons, although the fort could lend surplus arms and supply food when available. Volunteers served without pay.[8]

Despite the expressed desires of settlers to organize defense companies, the effort met with indifferent success. Only twenty-three men enlisted in the vicinity of Jacksboro. They elected Edward Wolffarth as their captain. Following a raid on May 23, 1869, only Wolffarth and ten men responded to the call to arms. They, along with a small military detail, launched a pursuit lasting several days but failed to destroy the war party. Even fewer men volunteered for service in Cooke and Montague Counties.[9] Further

Kiowa warrior White Horse (The Center for American History, University of Texas at Austin).

The Kiowa chief Kicking Bird, who was generally an advocate of peace but did challange the military around Buffalo Springs (The Center for American History, University of Texas at Austin).

efforts at cooperation between civilian and military forces in the vicinity accomplished little. Large-scale military offensives against the raiders on their home ground seemed to promise better results.

The army undertook its first major offensive from Fort Richardson in response to the massacre of several teamsters west of the fort by a large party of Kiowa and Comanche warriors. On May 18, 1871, over a hundred Indians from the reservations in Indian Territory hit the Warren wagon train transporting corn from Weatherford to Fort Griffin along the stage road. The war party swept down on the procession from a low hill and overran it before the twelve teamsters could prepare a defense. Five of the white men fled on foot to the concealment of a stand of small oaks and escaped, but the other seven died at the hands of the warriors.[10]

As a result of this attack and the grave impression it made on military leaders in the region and in Washington, a large force under Colonel Ranald S. Mackenzie left Fort Richardson in July to operate against the Kiowas. The column accomplished little in its attempt to locate and punish certain bands of that tribe. A second Mackenzie expedition onto the Staked Plains in the fall skirmished with Kwahadi Comanches, but later the troops lost many horses in a night raid by the Comanches. Again, the troopers enjoyed no decisive result.[11]

In the summer of 1872, Mackenzie launched a new offensive from Fort Richardson against the Comanches of the Staked Plains. He moved farther north into the Texas Panhandle and destroyed a major Comanche village on the North Fork of the Red River on September 29. His command took more than a hundred Comanche women and children prisoners along with a horse herd numbering in the hundreds. Although warriors repeatedly hit Mackenzie's men that night, the prisoners did not escape. The army would keep them in custody as an effective means of forcing warriors to go to the reservation.[12] The captured horse herd and its guards, under Lieutenant Peter Boehm, did not fare so well. Boehm had put the horses into a natural depression a mile from the rest of the command. He knew the Comanches might make a try for the herd that night and thought the draw would offer some protection. It did not. When the Indians came upon Boehm's little command, they started a stampede that carried away all of the captured ponies plus a number of cavalry horses. Boehm and his men did not suffer any losses but took the brunt of a good laugh from the main body of troops when the horse guards straggled to camp the next morning with a few burros carrying the men's saddles.[13]

Fort Richardson did not serve as a base for any further major offensives because it stood too far east of the Staked Plains.[14] Richardson did provide continuing protection for settlers near the Red River, however, and in that way aided pacification of that portion of the frontier. The number of settlers in the region increased rapidly in the late 1870s to the point that existing mail and transportation facilities felt the strain.[15] Finally, on May 23, 1878, the army abandoned Fort Richardson because Indian danger from north of the Red River had largely ceased.[16]

Fort Richardson had a connection with several smaller posts. Those posts existed primarily to protect settlements or stretches of the mail route westward. In some cases they served as independent posts, and in others as subposts, picket stations, or special-purpose camps.

Buffalo Springs, some twenty miles north of Jacksboro, functioned as an independent post for a significant period of time and later as a subpost of Fort Richardson. In fact, the army at one time intended for Buffalo Springs, rather than Richardson, to be the major fort in the region. When the military evacuated Jacksboro in April 1867, two companies, along with their supplies, went to Buffalo Springs to establish a permanent post.[17] Twenty miles northeast lay the little village of Victoria, the next place beyond Buffalo Springs with any settlers. At Buffalo Springs, the two companies of Sixth Cavalry troopers camped in a grove of trees near the springs.[18]

Captain Benjamin T. Hutchins, commanding A Company, assumed command of Buffalo Springs when the troops arrived.[19] At Buffalo Springs, Hutchins faced problems from the beginning. The command lacked enough horses and saddles to mount all of its men. Nevertheless, when Indians appeared in Clay and Montague Counties in June, Hutchins and thirty-five men rode after them. The troopers scouted to the Little Wichita at Van Dorn's Crossing, followed the river for a while, then explored a section of the road between Belknap and Camp Radsminski before returning to Buffalo Springs. They found tracks believed to be made by Indians but the sign was too old to follow.[20]

The following month, Hutchins again led a scout out of Buffalo Springs. He took seventy men after a party of Indians who had stolen several government mules from a detachment of troops and civilian teamsters cutting timber eighteen miles from the post. The Indians killed one civilian in the action, and the detachment returned to Buffalo Springs to make their report.[21] Forty-five men remained behind at the post, unable to join the scout because of the lack of saddles. The day after Hutchins left, a group of citizens from Decatur passed through, telling Lieutenant Theodore Majtheny, Sixth Cavalry, the officer in charge of the post, that they were trailing a party of 250 Indians, probably the same band, and that the Indians were at that moment only five miles from Buffalo Springs.[22] The lieutenant apparently thought they were lying, for he had them disarmed and thrown into the guard house. Majtheny and a sergeant issued ammunition to the troops and placed pickets at some distance from the post to give advance warning in case of attack. Approximately 100 civilian workers building the post had camped a half mile north of the military bivouac. They had no weapons.[23]

At about 7 P.M. just as the bugler was blowing "Retreat," sentries shouted a warning, and a very large party of Indians rode into view. Thirty soldiers deployed in a skirmish line and advanced, firing as the Indians charged. The Indians halted their attack, and the troops pulled back and took up defensive positions in and around the corral, which was in the middle of the camp, where the command's horses and mules had been herded for protection. Majtheny sent a handful of women who happened to be at the post into the forage house near the corral for safety and detailed several men to guard the building. The raiders did not attack again that night. The next day they remained in small groups at various locations around the post but still did not attack. Finally they disappeared.[24]

The attack marked one of the few times when such a large force of Indians raided in the state and actually threatened a military post. Comanches and Kiowas, who made up the great majority of the party and almost all others who came into the North Texas area, did tend to raid in larger groups than Apaches and other tribes to the south. But parties of more than forty were exceptional.

Hutchins, meanwhile, led his patrol to Flat Top Mountain and set up observation posts at various points on it because the mountain overlooked trails frequently used by Indians. Finding nothing, the troops swung out to Fort Belknap then circled south, crossed the Trinity River, and approached Buffalo Springs. Three miles from the post they came across a large Indian trail. When Hutchins rode back into the post and received a report on the Indian attack, he immediately wrote the District of Texas headquarters, requesting a company of infantry and a light artillery piece for future defense of Buffalo Springs, as well as the equipment and horses his men lacked.[25]

Construction of the post at Buffalo Springs went on through the spring and summer and into the fall of 1867. Civilian masons and quarrymen worked through much of the summer.[26] Troops labored right beside them. A party of two noncommissioned officers and ten men on extra duty built the forage house in late spring.[27] One party cut logs in the nearest woods and hauled them into camp behind mule teams. Another detail of extra-duty men built a stockade around the existing corral with those logs. The stockade served as a powerful redoubt in case of another attack. A 250 by-200-foot rectangle, it consisted of logs rising ten feet above ground level and sharpened on the top. A double gate barred the main entry.[28]

At times the command had difficulty obtaining building materials. They faced such a problem in mid-summer when they began work on a post bakery, and the delay adversely affected the troops' diet, forcing them to eat hardtack instead of fresh bread.[29] Most construction materials had to come a considerable distance. Finished items such as windows came by wagon all the way from the port of Indianola on the Gulf Coast. Troops hauled stone and lumber almost twenty miles from a point along the West Fork of the Trinity River. To manufacture mortar, men operated a lime burner at Buffalo Springs. Laborers—soldiers and civilians—cut the stone and lumber used for the buildings by hand. Some stone walls had loopholes cut into them for defensive fire.[30]

The command at Buffalo Springs took action early to provide adequate housing for troops for the coming winter. In late August, the men began building winter quarters. Each company built its own huts out of pickets. During construction, a company had no regular garrison duty, so the work progressed rapidly. By winter, troops had settled snugly into their huts.[31]

Additional structures went up during the fall. The need for protection from another attack remained a primary concern in design. By early November the post already had a hospital. To make it more defensible, the command detailed eleven enlisted men to build a protective stockade around it.[32]

Construction benefited local citizens and the area economy significantly. During the summer of 1867, a large number of civilians worked on crews at the post. Masons and quarrymen made up the majority, but about twenty carpenters also lent their skills. In addition, blacksmiths, wheelwrights, common laborers, and other craftsmen served on the work force. The civilian payroll at Buffalo Springs for August totaled over $7000. All construction costs for the post amounted to approximately $100,000, virtually all of it going into the civilian economy.[33]

Officers and men at Buffalo Springs made efforts to improve the training of their fellow soldiers or at least to provide some mental diversion from the tedium of life at the remote post. Late in November, the command instituted a school of instruction for officers and noncommisioned officers three days every week.[34] In a less formal, unofficial approach, some troopers printed a one-page newspaper, writing the articles themselves and distributing the sheet to the rest of the men.[35]

Despite these efforts, morale at Buffalo Springs suffered during the summer and fall. Overwork sapped the men's spirits most of all. In addition to heavy manual labor, troops served on guard details, herding parties, and other garrison duties. Because of difficulties between the white population in North Texas and newly freed blacks, some soldiers from Buffalo Springs had to protect government officials attempting to register voters in the region. Others had to drive wagon teams as an extra-duty assignment when the army decided to dismiss the civilian teamsters at the post.[36]

Fortunately for the garrison, two new companies of the Sixth Cavalry arrived in the fall to reinforce them and share the workload.

The eight officers now at the post decided to name it Camp Tucker in honor of one of their recently deceased comrades in the regiment, Captain Henry Tucker.[37]

In October, while construction went forward on various post buildings, a serious shortcoming in the Buffalo Springs location became apparent to its commanding officer, Captain Hutchins. A stream that had provided plenty of fresh water when the post was established in April had stopped running because of a three-month drought beginning in July. Settlers reported that things had never been so dry before. Tanks and springs throughout the area dried up. Although troops dug wells, they did not provide as much water as desired.[38] Hutchins reported the problem to his superiors in San Antonio and made observations and recommendations regarding proper locations for military posts. He believed that a cavalry post should be placed next to a reliable stream of clear water that could supply post needs even in the driest years.[39]

Permanent water supplies proved much more vital to the army than to their opponents in North Texas for obvious reasons—military posts were stationary while Indian war parties seldom camped two days in the same spot. Raiders could keep moving until they found enough water to replenish their supplies. In the southwestern part of the state ten years later, military commanders such as Colonel Benjamin Grierson turned the region's limited water supplies into an advantage for the army, but in North Texas in the late 1860s the scarcity worked in favor of their enemies.

Hutchins recommended that construction at Camp Tucker/Buffalo Springs stop, at least temporarily, while an expert inspected the region for locations with permanent water and suitable in other respects for a large post. He knew only three sites where the army could establish a replacement for the camp. The first, a point near Red River Station twenty-five miles north, had a reputation as unhealthy. The second, on a stretch of the Wichita River, had no health drawbacks but lay so far west on the frontier line that it left settlements in the Buffalo Springs area without protection. The third site, Jacksboro, had the disadvantage of being thirty miles inside the frontier line, but it stood in the center of an area often hit by Indians. It also possessed abundant water, as well as grass, wood, and building stone. In case other good locations near Buffalo Springs had been overlooked before, Hutchins sent Captain Daniel Madden, Sixth Cavalry, on a scout through the vicinity to find them.[40]

Ironically, Hutchins, only two weeks after his first report, found an excellent, and apparently permanent, source of water for Buffalo Springs. Troopers dug out the spring, located not far from camp, to a diameter of fifteen feet. It yielded an hourly flow of one hundred gallons of excellent water.[41]

In mid-November, Major Robert M. Morris, Sixth Cavalry, relieved Hutchins as commanding officer of Buffalo Springs. Changes came quickly under Morris. He overhauled the guard details, and he ordered Captain Madden and C Company, Sixth Cavalry, to reoccupy Jacksboro permanently.[42]

Despite discovery of the new water source at Buffalo Springs, District of Texas headquarters in San Antonio determined to switch locations of the main post back to Jacksboro. Madden's company guarded civilians rebuilding that post, but by December three companies still occupied Buffalo Springs. Major Morris requested that they be allowed to remain through the winter because their quarters were comfortable and plenty of supplies were on hand.[43]

In early January, troops at Buffalo Springs saw some minor action. An Indian raid near Montague, northeast of the post, brought Morris and a small detachment to the settlement to investigate. Because the war party had left the vicinity several days earlier and he had few serviceable horses, Morris did not pursue them. He did leave several enlisted men there as a temporary guard, however.[44]

Within weeks, Captain Madden relieved Morris and assumed command of Buffalo Springs as well as Jacksboro. He switched his headquarters to Fort Richardson and ordered one of the three companies remaining at Buffalo Springs to join him and bring the post records with them. A question still existed about whether the army would completely abandon Buffalo Springs or keep it as a picket station.[45]

On February 23, 1868, Madden ordered the remaining two companies at Buffalo Springs to change station to Jacksboro and haul the quartermaster stores with them. A few men remained behind to serve as a picket station under the command of Lieutenant Thomas Tolman. The station remained active into the spring, sending out scouts in the vicinity. Finally, on April 15, the commanding officer of Fort Richardson deactivated Buffalo Springs.[46]

The post served most importantly as base for many scouting operations and patrols over the year of its existence. Indirectly, it benefited the Texas frontier because the Indian attack on the post during the summer of 1867 caused such concern among government officials that they established a camp near the reservations to monitor Indian activity. That camp in Indian Territory later became Fort Sill.[47]

When the army evacuated Jacksboro in April 1867, and sent two of the companies there to Buffalo Springs, the other four companies from the abandoned post headed west to occupy old Fort Belknap, one of the most important pre-Civil War forts in North Texas. The army intended to rebuild and reactivate the fort, if feasible, as it held a strategic location.[48]

Fort Belknap stood on a bluff a half-mile north and east of the Brazos River. Forty miles east lay Jacksboro. The old Butterfield Overland Mail route passed close to the fort. Most of the buildings had suffered from the weather and from local settlers scrounging for building materials during the years since United States troops abandoned the fort on the eve of the Civil War.[49]

As with Buffalo Springs, Fort Belknap had a water problem. Although situated on the Brazos, the post could not use it as a water source because of its terrible quality. Neither humans nor animals would drink it. Troops had dug a well at the fort, but it failed to provide a steady supply. Soldiers could haul water from streams in the area, but their distance from the post made that method extremely inconvenient. As a result, the four companies sent to Belknap received orders in July to change station thirty miles northwest, to the site that would become Fort Griffin. They abandoned Fort Belknap accordingly and headed west.[50] During the following years troops from Fort Richardson and, occasionally, Fort Griffin used Belknap at various times as a temporary camp or rendezvous point, as well as a mail escort relay station. The fort, however, never saw further use as a permanent outpost.[51]

One post that did see permanent duty began in May 1870, when James Oakes, veteran colonel of the Sixth Cavalry, commanding officer of Fort Richardson, sent Captain Curwen B. McLellan and K Company, Sixth Cavalry, to scout the Red River area south and west to the Brazos for Kiowa and Comanche raiding parties. Oakes ordered McLellan to establish a scouting camp near the Little Wichita River to use as a base until at least June 10. The colonel hoped to keep a company there all summer, if he had enough troops to meet his other commitments,[52] which included escorting herds on the cattle trails to California, scouting the state's north-central counties, and providing escort to a Professor Roessler exploring for minerals in the area.[53] An Indian attack that killed a stage driver near old Fort Belknap diverted Oakes' attention from the plan for a summer scouting camp and caused him to send McLellan's command after the war party. McLellan crossed the Red River and eventually recovered most of the mail taken in the raid, then turned south. On July 12, he fought a superior Indian force on the North Fork of the Little Wichita and suffered a defeat at the enemy's hands.[54]

McLellan, like Oakes, was an experienced frontier soldier. In fact, he had served as an enlisted man with Oakes in the Second Cavalry in the late 1850s.[55] McLellan's defeat made a deep impression on Colonel Oakes. In a report to his superiors in San Antonio, he expressed the army's frustration with the type of warfare in which they were engaged. Large patrols seldom caught or came to grips with Indian raiders, but, according to him, smaller columns lacked the strength to defeat most war parties. He suggested that a strong offensive expedition far into the Indians' home territory, possibly even onto the reservations, coupled with smaller defensive patrols through the Texas settlements, offered some chance of success. Even that tactic, however, might well fail because plentiful grass and water at the time gave Indian bands complete freedom of movement. In any event, Oakes had no opportunity to try what he had suggested because he lacked sufficient troop strength.[56] Nevertheless, his comments did make clear the inherent weakness of a strategy that employed defensive patrols alone and left the initiative entirely in the Indians' hands.

Not until September did officers at Fort Richardson have the opportunity to establish a semi-permanent scouting camp in the Little Wichita country. Early that month two companies of the Sixth Cavalry and one of the Eleventh Infantry set out for a spot on the East Fork of the Little Wichita, some ten miles northeast of Buffalo Springs. A third cavalry company planned to join them in a few days.[57]

Oakes believed that patrols from the new camp would be more effective than those from Richardson simply because the camp was in the immediate area to be scouted, rather than thirty or more miles away as Richardson was. He planned for the infantry to protect and garrison the camp while most of the cavalry engaged in constant patrols. Cavalry patrols out of Fort Richardson would cooperate with those from the scouting camp.[58]

In late September, Oakes and his superiors began considering the possibility of a new, permanent four-company post north or northwest of Richardson. They realized that adequate water was the most significant problem. Both the Little and Big Wichitas ran very low and sometimes even dry in certain months. Oakes charged Major R. M. Morris, commanding the scouting camp, with locating a suitable site for the proposed new post.[59]

Called Camp Wichita, the locale had ample water most of the time. Troops dammed a stream beside the camp to accumulate a supply and also utilized ponds close by. Oakes planned to keep the camp in operation through the fall and winter and ordered Morris to dig a well if necessary.[60]

For scouts out of Camp Wichita, Oakes laid down a strict policy. Any patrol coming across an Indian trail should follow it so long as the least hope of success remained. He reprimanded one officer who had given up a trail too easily. Scouts from Camp Wichita had responsibility to cover the area from the headwaters of the West Fork of the Trinity to the Red River and eastward, but Oakes expanded that area toward the northwest and the southeast.[61]

Because the army planned for Camp Wichita to be temporary, the command at Fort Richardson would not send materials such as doors and windows for structures at the camp. Troops lived in tents raised on pickets. Before they did any other building, they had to construct pole sheds for their animals. At Camp Wichita the need to stop costly Indian raids on the local settlements dominated every-thing else, especially comfort of the garrison.[62]

Troops from the camp clashed with Indians early in October 1870 and lost thirteen horses. That patrol, reinforced by another detachment under Captain McLellan, pursued the Indians but lost them. Fort Richardson sent additional scouts into the vicinity that month until five companies of cavalry were operating in the area, as well as the infantry company guarding the camp. Colonel Oakes ordered Morris to build a picket stockade for defense and promised to send a few Tonkawa Indian scouts as soon as possible.[63]

Oakes sent the Tonkawas, but trouble came of it. Two of them returned in November to Fort Richardson as military prisoners charged with minor violations. Both scouts had horses they had captured in a recent action against Comanches, and a corporal from Camp Wichita confiscated the animals when he saw the scouts being taken into custody at Fort Richardson. The two Tonkawas demanded the horses be returned because, customarily, Tonkawa scouts received any horses they captured from hostile Indians. Captain John Irwin, Sixth Cavalry, commanding Camp Wichita after Major Morris, had to investigate the matter.[64]

The frequent patrols out of Camp Wichita wore down the horses and by late November the command had to curtail scouting to rest and fatten their animals. Just days later, however, troopers mounted up once again in response to a raid along Denton Creek near Montague where two women were killed and five children captured.[65]

An exceptionally severe winter caused considerable hardship for men and animals at Camp Wichita. Travel to Fort Richardson became hazardous. Lieutenant Henry B. Mellen, Sixth Cavalry, attempted the trip in December in order to sit on a court-martial. In swimming his horse across the swollen West Fork of the Trinity during a blizzard, he tumbled down a bank and back into the icy water. He managed to make it to the bank again but then collapsed from the cold and lay for two days and nights in below-zero temperatures before a party of hunters found and rescued him. He recovered eventually, but lost a leg and the other foot to frostbite.[66]

By the middle of winter, Camp Wichita had almost exhausted its hay supply, and one cavalry company had to return to Fort Richardson. The remaining horses faced strict rationing.[67] On request of the commanding officer of the camp, Fort Richardson dispatched several wagons and teams, along with a number of scythes, to Camp Wichita for the purpose of cutting and gathering hay standing in open fields near the camp. Officers hoped it would carry the animals through the last few weeks of winter until spring grass began coming up.[68]

The end of the subpost at Camp Wichita came suddenly. In late winter orders arrived at Fort Richardson transferring the entire Sixth Cavalry out of the state. On March 10, 1871, all available wagons at Fort Richardson headed out for Wichita to bring in the three remaining companies under Major Abraham K. Arnold, Sixth Cavalry.[69]

✳ ✳ ✳

A number of less important picket stations and outposts, including Sherman, Pilot Grove, the government sawmill, Montague, Salt Creek, and others followed orders from Fort Richardson. A detachment from Richardson garrisoned Sherman, near the Red River, in early and mid-1868. It consisted of fifteen men under Lieutenant Edmund C. Hentig, Sixth Cavalry.[70] Eighteen miles southeast of Sherman, the community of Pilot Grove hosted a small outpost of Fort Richardson during 1868 and 1869. Lieutenant J. H. Sands, Sixth Cavalry, commanded the detachment there in the summer of 1868.[71] The post continued until August 10, 1869.[72]

Most forts established a sawmill to provide lumber for building purposes, and Fort Richardson did not deviate from that tradition. In fact, the fort had two sawmills associated with it. The first functioned under control of Buffalo Springs when that post was in operation. Troops set up the mill along the West Fork of the Trinity, about eighteen miles from Buffalo Springs.[73] A small detachment of enlisted men guarded the site and its civilian engineer and sawyer.[74]

Another mill stood on Big Sandy in Wise County east of the fort (in the same general area as the first mill) where six enlisted men guarded the civilians and government property. In November 1868, Fort Richardson sent an eight-man patrol under Lieutenant Moses Wiley, Sixth Cavalry, out after Indians raiding near the sawmill. Wiley attempted to get local citizens to join his detail in the pursuit. The following June, Lieutenant Isaac Walter, Sixth Cavalry, took charge of the operation with orders to run the mill as efficiently as possible and to keep a precise inventory of all lumber and shingles cut and sent to the fort.[75]

Although the sawmill escaped serious danger from Indians, a murder occurred in the vicinity in October 1869. Returning from detached service, Sergeant F. Socker, D Company, Sixth Cavalry, and a Private Hyland of the same regiment left the mill for Fort Richardson. At a spot approximately twenty miles short of the fort, Hyland apparently murdered the sergeant, who was known to be carrying a quantity of money. Officers at the fort arrested Hyland, but later released him for lack of evidence. He deserted immediately and fled to Weatherford, where he, in turn, was murdered.[76]

The town of Montague, forty miles northeast of the fort, held a temporary garrison more than once during the active years of Fort Richardson. Following a serious Indian raid in the area, Major R. M. Morris stationed ten enlisted men there for a short time in January 1868.[77] Again in July 1870, a large war party hit settlements near Montague, and commanders at Fort Richardson sent a detachment of about twenty men to guard the town temporarily.[78] In October further raids caused another detachment to stop in Montague for a few days.

For a number of weeks in late winter of 1871, Fort Richardson maintained a picket station at Salt Creek on the road running west toward Fort Griffin. When the Sixth Cavalry transferred north in March, troops abandoned the post.[79] The soldiers had dubbed that picket post "Borthwick's Station" after the lieutenant in command, William A. Borthwick.[80]

A few points in Fort Richardson's area of responsibility received small details of troops as guards. Colonel Ranald Mackenzie stationed such a detail at Whaley's Ranch on the extreme westward edge of the frontier in the spring of 1872. Whaley's Ranch stood on the Red River, seven miles below the mouth of the Big Wichita and fifteen miles north of the settlement at Henrietta.[81] The ranch often proved to be the target for Indian raids from north of the Red River. Whaley, a tall man and an ex-dragoon sergeant before the Civil War, sometimes sold grain to the military—for a lower price than was customary—because the army offered protection.[82]

A bizarre incident involving three troopers took place at the ranch three years later after most Comanches and Kiowas had been forced to give up their raids into Texas. The three had spent several days trailing thieves who had stolen horses from a Comanche camp. The wife of Jack Kilmartin, one of the soldiers, was house-keeper at Whaley's Ranch. Since the men happened to be nearby, they decided to spend the night there. Mrs. Kilmartin cooked supper for them but seemed furious at her husband. The next morning a gunshot woke the other two soldiers. To their horror they saw the woman holding a smoking pistol next to Kilmartin's body. The men reported the murder to Colonel Mackenzie when they returned, but he could do nothing about a violation of civil law.[83] In June 1872, Mackenzie planned to send a guard similar to the one at Whaley's Ranch to Van Hoozier's Ranch, but orders from the Department of Texas took those troops elsewhere.[84] Also at that time, a handful of soldiers guarded a hay camp for Fort Richardson.[85]

In addition to those outposts, commanders at Fort Richardson occasionally established temporary camps for special purposes. In May and June 1868, Lieutenant Thomas Tolman led a major scout of eighty-three men toward the Wichita Mountains in the south-western part of Indian Territory. He selected a supply depot on Beaver Creek to which wagons hauled rations and forage for his command. Tolman's scouting column carried its supplies on pack mules but could return to the depot when they ran low.[86] Tolman continued to use the camp for supplies and as a rendezvous point with additional detachments sent to reinforce him during the month of June.[87]

In the early spring of 1870, at the beginning of the raiding season, Lieutenant James Hill, Sixth Cavalry, and a twenty-two-man patrol under his command established a temporary scouting camp at Clear Creek in southwestern Cooke County. From that base they scouted Cooke, Montague, and Wise Counties for three weeks before working back to Fort Richardson by way of Buffalo

Springs. Lieutenant Frank Russell, Sixth Cavalry, with a similar patrol operated out of a scouting camp between Weatherford and Palo Pinto during the same period. Russell's command scouted Parker and Palo Pinto Counties for three and a half weeks then swung through old Fort Belknap and back to Richardson.[88]

During the decade of its existence, Fort Richardson used these subposts and small stations primarily as extensions of its power to spots closer to the forward edge of the frontier. The region around the fort remained dangerous into the early 1870s because of its proximity to the Kiowa and Comanche reservations, but at that time the army shifted its focus farther west into the Fort Griffin region as troops attempted to strike and defeat the last non-reservation bands on their home ground on the Staked Plains.

FORT GRIFFIN, ITS OUTPOSTS, AND SUPPLY CAMPS ON THE STAKED PLAINS

Fort Griffin held a pivotal position in the late 1860s and early 1870s as the post closest to the northern Staked Plains. Although many Comanche and Kiowa raids into Texas originated on the reservations in Indian Territory, the Staked Plains, or Llano Estacado, represented the untamed and undefeated elements of those tribes because the region had frustrated white efforts at exploration and settlement for decades. Both tribes had hunted on its vast, treeless expanses since the eighteenth century, and one band of Comanches still lived there, spurning government efforts to draw them to the reservation.

To improve protection of settlements, Fort Griffin's officers used several subposts and picket stations. In addition, on major military expeditions against Indians on the Staked Plains, commanders established advanced supply camps to enable their columns to persist in operations against hostile tribes without having to depend on supply lines stretching back to one of the major posts. Often Fort Griffin furnished the supply camps that served as a jumping-off point for offensive missions.

Fort Griffin began as a camp for four companies of the Sixth Cavalry who abandoned Fort Belknap for lack of water in late July 1867 and moved thirty miles southwest onto the Clear Fork of the Brazos. They made camp on low, soft ground near the river at first, but soon moved to a hill a quarter-mile from the water. For a time military authorities referred to the post as Camp Wilson, after Henry H. Wilson, a recently deceased lieutenant of the regiment.[1]

Still under that name, the post sent out a significant scout on October 13. Forty-five enlisted men and twenty-two Tonkawa scouts, under command of Sergeant W. A. T. Ahrberg, rode 160 miles through Shackleford, Stephens, and Palo Pinto Counties operating against Comanches. Unlike most patrols, this one found Indians. A war party had killed five settlers and stolen their horses when the troops appeared. Soldiers killed three warriors and captured an Indian woman, as well as nineteen horses and a mule.[2]

Shortly after that action, Camp Wilson received a new name, Fort Griffin, in honor of General Charles Griffin, commander of the Department of Texas for the previous two years, who had just died of yellow fever.[3]

The first commanding officer of Fort Griffin, Lieutenant Colonel Samuel D. Sturgis, had had a colorful career already. He came out of West Point a year early, in 1846, to take part in the Mexican War as a brevet second lieutenant. His regular commission came a year later. He served in dragoon and cavalry units from the beginning, won four brevets for gallantry in major battles in both the Eastern and Western Theaters in the Civil War, and ended that war as a brevet major general. Following his Texas service in the Sixth Cavalry, he won promotion to colonel of the Seventh Cavalry in May 1869. He remained in that position, commanding the regiment that his subordinate George Armstrong Custer so flamboyantly led in battle, until 1886, ten years after Custer's disaster at the Little Bighorn.[4]

Troops pitched tents for officers and men on the height soon named Government Hill. For Sturgis they transported a two-room log house from a nearby abandoned ranch up to the top of the hill. Within a few months, wooden huts housed the enlisted men, and

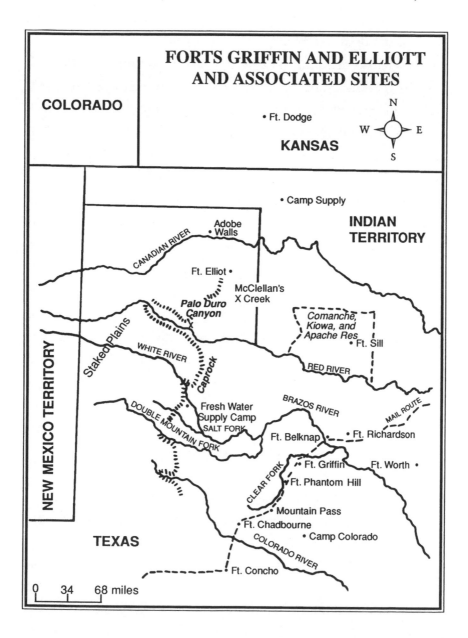

officers had separate living quarters with kitchens.[5] The command used lumber for most of the rest of the buildings, although a few important structures were built of stone. The builders, however, failed to allow their lumber to cure before using it. As a result, many of the boards warped and split after they were set in place, causing leakage and drafts in virtually every building.[6]

A civilian community of hard drinkers, gamblers, and buffalo hunters grew up on the flat land at the bottom of Government Hill. The hunters flocked to the region in large numbers in the early 1870s as a result of a new commercial process for tanning buffalo hides. Because of the new process and the resultant increase in demand for buffalo hides for industrial and commercial use, a huge, calculated slaughter of the bison began on the plains north and west of the post. Fort Griffin itself became a shipping and supply point for an army of hunters. At one point during the decade, six mail routes operated out of Fort Griffin to handle the traffic generated by the hide industry.[7]

Primarily in response to the slaughter of the buffalo, warriors from Kiowa, Comanche, and Cheyenne camps rose up in a desperate effort to sweep the hunters from the plains in the summer of 1874. In late June, several hundred braves hit a small band of buffalo hunters at Adobe Walls on the Canadian River and attempted to overrun the camp. The hunters with their long-range buffalo rifles and the advantage of crude fortifications managed to break every Indian charge and inflicted heavy casualties on the warriors. The action at Adobe Walls marked the beginning of the Red River War, in which the army finally broke the power of the southern Plains tribes.[8]

General Philip Sheridan and his subordinates planned a simultaneous offensive by five attacking columns against the Native Americans gathered on the Staked Plains. One column under

Colonel Nelson Miles moved south from Fort Dodge, Kansas, by way of Camp Supply, Indian Territory. Another under Major William Price advanced eastward from Fort Union, New Mexico. Lieutenant Colonel John Davidson, a Mexican War veteran and brevet major general during the Civil War,[9] headed west toward the Staked Plains from Fort Sill. Colonel Ranald Mackenzie led his troops north from Fort Concho. The final column, under Lieutenant Colonel George Buell, struck north and west from Fort Griffin between Davidson and Mackenzie.[10]

From previous experience, commanders of those columns knew that locating the Indian encampments would pose one of the greatest problems in the campaign. To aid in this undertaking, Miles employed twenty Delaware Indians as scouts, and Mackenzie used a number of Tonkawas from Fort Griffin, a few Lipan Apaches, and thirteen Seminole Negro scouts from Fort Clark. Those scouts performed extremely valuable service in locating bands of hostile Indians, especially the main Comanche village in Palo Duro Canyon.[11]

On September 28, 1874, Mackenzie struck that camp, which stretched for two or three miles down the bottom of the canyon. His men managed to descend into the gorge from above without giving the Indians more than a few minutes of warning. Once on the canyon floor, the troops mounted and charged through the huge village, scattering the Indians. Sporadic fighting continued for several hours as Mackenzie's men drove the Indians back from one point to another. After the fighting ended, he ordered the village and everything in it burned, and he had all but a few of the huge Indian horse herd that he had captured shot to prevent their recapture by the resourceful Comanches. Mackenzie's victory, coupled with relentless patrols and a severe winter that wore down and demoralized those Indians who chose to continue fighting proved decisive in bringing the war to an eventual conclusion early in 1875.[12]

From Texas to the Canadian border, attacking villages became one of the army's most successful tactics against Indians on the plains. Many people disputed the morality of such attacks because Indian women and children often became victims in the fighting, and entire villages faced exposure and starvation following the destruction. The army, however, had few options in bringing its power to bear. Although most units had the firepower and discipline to defeat and destroy virtually any Indian force not greatly superior in numbers, those units could seldom bring a war party to bay long enough to engage it in regular battle.[13]

Attacks on villages gave the army an opportunity to come to grips with its Indian opponents, as did winter campaigns. Both tactics neutralized the Plainsmen's superiority in mobility, the former by hitting them when they were hampered by family and possessions, the latter by striking when their horses had no green grass. In addition to those two methods, the army's use of Indian scouts to locate the enemy proved valuable and effective. Some officers advocated the further step of using larger units of Indian or frontiersman auxiliaries not only to hunt hostile bands, but also to conduct the actual attacks upon them.[14]

Despite the occasional large-scale offensive operation, the army more commonly followed a defensive strategy against Indians threatening the frontier, a strategy blessed by both General William T. Sherman and Sheridan. In other parts of the nation as well as in Texas, troops raised fort after fort, most of them to protect either routes of travel or settlements. Unfortunately, the army tried to man too many forts with too small a force.[15]

In any given year between 1867 and 1881, for example, Texas alone had twenty or more active posts but only a few understrength regiments to man them. This strategy of a network of many moderate or small posts attempted to provide defense for virtually every endangered spot. With so few troops, however, the garrison at each post could not adequately patrol its entire area of responsibility, and raiding parties slipped through the cordon with small chance of interference by the army.[16]

Despite its limitations, the use of many small posts did offer some benefits over the alternative of a few very large forts. Without being close enough to a trouble spot to respond quickly, troops provided no defense for it. Only a multitude of small posts could distribute soldiers to all the areas most likely to need them. If rail lines had covered the frontier earlier, they would have provided enough mobility to allow concentration of troops at a few large posts. In the event of trouble, trains could have rushed units to the scene rather quickly. That level of railroad coverage did not come until approximately 1880, however, and only then did the government begin turning to a policy of concentration rather than dispersal.[17]

Thus hampered by inadequate defensive capabilities, military commanders turned more and more to offensive operations designed to carry the fight to the Indian where he was most vulnerable and least mobile. In an effort to increase their own mobility during the Red River War and other offensive campaigns on the Staked Plains, officers such as Mackenzie made extensive use of supply camps. Such camps, used as bases of operations, enabled them to strike farther and pursue Indians more relentlessly because supplies were within much closer reach.

In his expedition against Comanches on the Llano Estacado following the Warren wagon train massacre in 1871, Mackenzie established a supply camp early in October, near the southeastern corner of present-day Crosby County. The camp stood not far from the mouth of Blanco, or Yellow House, Canyon at a stream known variously as Duck Creek or Catfish Creek. Army officers usually referred to it as the supply camp on the Freshwater Fork of the Brazos, that fork also being called the White River.[18]

Lieutenant Henry Lawton, Fourth Cavalry, took command of the supply post when Mackenzie led the main column onward seeking Comanche villages. Two companies of infantry stayed behind to guard the supply wagons there.[19] Lawton—who had a distinguished military career that lasted from Lincoln's call for volunteers after Fort Sumter until the very last days of the 1800s—worked out of the supply camp during the next five weeks, hauling rations, forage, and ammunition from Fort Griffin to Mackenzie's command.[20]

The following year (1872), Mackenzie again ventured out onto the Staked Plains, this time to operate not only against recalcitrant Indians, but also New Mexican Comancheros who supplied guns and other valuable items to the raiding Indians in exchange for stolen cattle and horses. The traders had established a good trail westward across the plains from their camps to settlements in New Mexico. The trail had good water and grazing all along its course.[21]

On orders from General C. C. Augur, commanding the Department of Texas, Mackenzie reestablished the camp on the Freshwater Fork of the Brazos in May.[22] Again he used it as a supply depot and base of operations against the Comanches as well as Comancheros. Mackenzie led major scouts as far as the headwaters of the Red River near Palo Duro Canyon and along the cattle thieves' road to New Mexico. Fort Griffin again served as the main point furnishing supplies to the wagons plying the trail out to the supply camp. Trains hauled forage on a regular schedule for the hundreds of horses and mules of Mackenzie's command and rations and ammunition for the men. A few supply trains bound for the camp also originated at Fort Concho.[23]

Mackenzie found no Indians on the Staked Plains during the initial phases of his 1872 campaign. He believed that they had gone farther north and scoured the countryside in that direction to find them. In preparation for operations, he made arrangements to have an alternate source of supply available closer to his proposed patrol area by ordering a considerable quantity of rations and forage to be laid up at Camp Supply in Indian Territory.[24] Nevertheless, he continued to use the Freshwater Fork camp as his base of supply, and his wagons continued to rely primarily on Fort Griffin from which to obtain supplies because of its proximity and the good quality of the connecting road.[25]

Mackenzie's move to the north yielded results in late September. His scouts located a large Comanche camp on the North Fork of the Red River a short distance above the mouth of McClellan's Creek. The command overran the village, killing over twenty braves and capturing 120 women and children as well as the Indian horse herd. That night Comanches succeeded in stampeding and recapturing the herd, but the captives remained, and Mackenzie's command returned to the supply camp and, eventually, their garrison forts.[26] During the same campaign, Lieutenant Colonel W. R. Shafter and troops from the Twenty-fourth Infantry operated out of the supply camp on the Freshwater Fork in conjunction with Mackenzie. While Mackenzie moved far to the north and west, Shafter scouted and mapped the country closer to camp, especially south of it. His command provided a mobile security force for the camp and returned to it for rest and fresh supplies when needed.[27]

Two years after that mission, Mackenzie again led a column onto the Staked Plains, this time for the last round of the Red River War. He operated again from his old supply camp on the Freshwater Fork of the Brazos. On September 2, 1874, Lieutenant Henry

Lawton, serving as quartermaster of the expedition, led an empty wagon train out of the camp back to Fort Griffin for more supplies. Lawton and his men made many more such trips, often under adverse weather conditions that caused the loss of animals and cargo. The trip covered almost 140 miles over the route blazed by Mackenzie in 1871 and commonly known as the Mackenzie Trail.[28]

As in the past, Mackenzie made plans for additional supply camps to serve his troops when they operated too far from the Freshwater post. He considered establishing one site at McClellan's Creek, spot of his 1872 victory.[29] Freshwater, however, remained the main, and by far the most important, camp during the campaign. From it, Lieutenant Lawton sent loaded wagons to Mackenzie's force and other units in the field, allowing them to continue operating for many weeks at a time without having to return to base.[30]

Troops evacuated the supply camp on January 10, 1875, and returned to Fort McKavett shortly thereafter.[31] Army units returned later that year, however, for a few more months. Lieutenant Colonel Shafter used the camp as his base of supply during mopping-up operations on the Staked Plains.[32] Captain Theodore A. Baldwin, Tenth Cavalry, also participated in those operations and led a long scout out of the supply depot in August 1875.[33]

While the supply camp operated independently, connected with Fort Griffin only because the supply route originated at that fort, other small posts existed as outposts of Griffin. Those included the subpost of Phantom Hill and the picket station at Mountain Pass.

Fort Phantom Hill had served as a major post in the early 1850s, but the army had pulled out in 1854. Fire destroyed the fort shortly afterward. In 1858, the Overland Mail began using one or two surviving stone buildings as a way station.[34] Not until well after the Civil War, however, did the army reoccupy the old fort. When the army did return to Phantom Hill, troops used it merely as a subpost of Fort Griffin. A small detachment garrisoned the site by the early summer of 1869. Conditions proved difficult for the men in that remote spot. They had no choice but to live in tents, because little remained of the fort's original buildings. Discomfort led to poor morale among some of the men and at least one desertion early in Phantom Hill's existence as a subpost.[35] Loneliness also plagued the garrison, especially in the early days. The detachment at Phantom Hill numbered just five privates with a corporal in charge. Their duties of guarding the mail station gave them little chance to see many other people and even less chance for entertainment.[36] Troops at the subpost found some degree of excitement in October 1869 when Indians attacked a stage a few miles west. A cavalry patrol from Fort Concho under Captain John Bacon, Ninth Cavalry, moved out in pursuit, operating in conjunction with another cavalry force under Lieutenant Peter H. Boehm. The two columns attempted but failed to catch the raiding party near Phantom Hill. Bacon's patrol trailed a party of a dozen Indians for a time before losing them and returning to the post by way of Phantom Hill.[37]

A manpower shortage threatened Phantom Hill's existence the following spring. Enlistments of so many soldiers at Fort Griffin were expiring that the possibility existed of having to close the subpost for lack of men to garrison it. The commanding officer at Griffin requested either reinforcements or that Fort Concho temporarily take responsibility for garrisoning Phantom Hill. In the event that neither of those possibilities worked out, he planned to man the subpost with a detachment of one noncommissioned officer, one private, and five of his Tonkawa scouts, although such an assignment placed the Tonkawas in great danger. Comanches had such hatred for the other tribe that they would have readily attacked an outpost if they found out their enemies were there.[38] A war party did engage troops from Phantom Hill a few days later, but the army soon closed the subpost.[39]

Orders from the Department of Texas the next May called for reestablishment of Phantom Hill. Detachments would serve one month before being relieved, and at least two officers and an infantry company would serve at the subpost at all times. A small cavalry detachment had responsibility for providing couriers to Fort Griffin and elsewhere as needed for rapid communications. The men would live in tents until they could build more permanent shelters, but department headquarters wanted as little money spent on such shelters as possible. Patrols from Phantom Hill had orders to ride to a point halfway to the subpost of Fort Concho at Fort Chadbourne to the south, at least once every month. The men at Phantom Hill received permission and even encouragement to hunt in the vicinity and, thus, to keep the area under regular surveillance.[40]

On June 13, 1871, Captain Lynde Catlin and F Company, Eleventh Infantry, plus six enlisted cavalrymen reestablished the subpost at Phantom Hill. Just a month later, however, the garrison withdrew to join in the campaign Mackenzie was beginning against the Kiowas.[41] The following January, a garrison similar to the one withdrawn, reoccupied Phantom Hill. Two Tonkawa scouts accompanied the detachment this time.[42] Finally, on August 26, 1872, the army withdrew from Phantom Hill because the mail line moved the route.[43] Troops never permanently garrisoned the post again, although trains did use Phantom Hill as a temporary supply depot, during the Red River War of 1874-1875.[44]

Troops from Fort Griffin operated a picket station, closely tied in with the subpost of Phantom Hill, at Mountain Pass, the next stop southwest on the mail route. The station at Mountain Pass stood near the eastern entrance to the pass over the Abercrombie range. Actually the pass resembled a gradual ascent to a large, flat tableland.[45] It had steep sides like a gorge through its entire one-mile length and offered excellent opportunities for ambushing any party traveling over it.[46]

The troops stationed at Mountain Pass lived in far-from-comfortable conditions. At times they stayed in tents. Early in 1872, the detachment made efforts to improve the situation. They requested building materials for troop quarters from Fort Griffin. At the time, the men lived in a one-room building with one door and no windows; the chimney did not carry off smoke efficiently, the building's picket walls let in plenty of cold air; the mud-and-hay roof leaked. Soldiers cooked in the stage station and stored their provisions in a tent. A spring provided good water, but lack of an established spot for a latrine threatened to pollute the water supply. Officers hoped to build a good two-room structure to quarter the detachment, but no record exists that it was ever completed.[47]

Troops at Mountain Pass skirmished a number of times with Indians during the three years of the post's existence. On February 15, 1870, a party of seventy-five raiders struck the mail station and fought an hour-long battle with the defenders. In the end, the Indians broke off the fight, taking five mules and a horse belonging to the stage company. Troops claimed three Indians dead.[48]

Three months later another war party ran off all the mail company's stock while the animals grazed some distance from the station.[49] In July, a party of forty recruits under Lieutenant Gilbert E. Overton, Sixth Cavalry, on the way to Fort Griffin from Concho, camped at the foot of a bluff a quarter-mile from the stage station. The party traveled in four wagons, and, because they were recruits, they had only six old breech-loading rifles among them. About fifty Indians chose that day to strike the horse and mule herd, a short distance from the station. Private John

Charlton, in immediate charge of the recruits, passed out the six rifles and told the remaining men to pick up tree branches approximately the size of guns. The Indians started to attack the soldiers' camp, but a few shots and the sight of what appeared to be a well-armed unit frightened them off. Lieutenant Overton returned to camp from the station just in time to see the Indians ride off. Charlton eventually became a sergeant,[50] while Overton would win a brevet captaincy four years later for leading a cavalry charge against hostile Indians at McClellan's Creek in the Texas Panhandle.[51]

As with Phantom Hill, the army withdrew its detail from Mountain Pass on August 26, 1872, when the mail line changed its route.[52] Other small camps under Fort Griffin's jurisdiction functioned temporarily during the main post's years of existence. None of them remained in operation for a significant period of time.

FORT ELLIOTT

Near the end of the bitter campaigns on the Staked Plains during the Red River War, Colonel Nelson A. Miles recommended the army establish a post in that region to protect new cattle trails from Texas to the north and to flank the reservations of the Plains tribes in Indian Territory.[1] Fort Griffin stood too far to the southeast to provide such immediate protection and presented no obstacle to Comanches, Kiowas, and Cheyennes attempting to move west from their reservations into the Texas Panhandle.

Troops set up a temporary camp in a key location on the North Fork of the Red River in September 1874.[2] On February 3, 1875, Major James Biddle, Sixth Cavalry, and eight companies of his regiment and the Fifth Infantry officially established a post there called Cantonment on the North Fork of the Red River. In addition to the 400 men under his command, Biddle had one mountain howitzer and a Gatling gun. He immediately put his force to work, sending Captain Adam Kramer, Sixth Cavalry, and a three-company scout to the southwest toward the Salt Fork of the Red River. Kramer's patrol covered 155 miles between February 15 and 27, when it returned to camp.[3]

Kramer was no amateur at soldiering. A German immigrant, he enlisted in the dragoons four years before the Civil War. During the war he attained noncommissioned officer rank, then a commission and ended the war as a captain. After a brief stay in the Second U.S. Colored Cavalry, he transferred to the Sixth and stayed there for the rest of his long career. Several years after his service in the Texas Panhandle, Kramer would win distinction in two actions against hostile Indians in Arizona Territory.[4]

The month after Kramer's scout from the new Cantonment, two companies went out on patrol. Another company built a corduroy crossing over the Canadian River bottomland on the road to Camp Supply, Indian Territory. Although the post employed a number of civilian workers at that time, they all worked in service jobs rather than construction. The army delayed any building until it could choose a permanent site for the post.[5]

Fort Elliott (The Center for American History, University of Texas at Austin).

In June, orders came to move the camp to a permanent location, and its garrison occupied a new spot near the head of Sweetwater Creek, thirty miles south of the Canadian River and about the same distance west of Indian Territory.[6] The new location lay approximately 200 miles north-northwest of Fort Griffin.

About 170 men of the Nineteenth Infantry and Fourth Cavalry garrisoned the Cantonment on the Sweetwater.[7] The troops immediately began construction of permanent buildings. Six civilian carpenters hired on during July. By the next month, sixty civilian workers were laboring at the post. The command hired eleven more carpenters and three masons in September, and the work progressed steadily. By November, the command had completed most construction and let the civilian workers go.[8]

Troops and civilians built barracks for six companies of enlisted men and quarters for a dozen officers plus a commanding officer's quarters. In addition, they constructed storehouses, a headquarters building, stables, a post hospital, and living quarters for the laundresses always present on an army post. The building materials came by wagon from Fort Dodge, Kansas.[9]

In February 1876, military authorities changed the name of the post to Fort Elliott, in honor of Major Joel Elliott, killed in action with hostile Indians during the Battle of the Washita on November 27, 1868.[10] During that fight a short distance east of the fort in Indian Territory, Lieutenant Colonel George A. Custer and elements of his Seventh Cavalry Regiment destroyed Chief Black Kettle's Cheyenne village in a winter attack. Custer detached Elliott and about twenty men to block Indian escape routes and watch the movements of other tribes in the vicinity. An overwhelming force of Indians caught Elliott's command and wiped them out.[11]

Fort Elliott's garrison performed a variety of missions. During its first few months, the fort served as a base for scouts against hostile Indians in the Panhandle. In addition, troops from the post protected not only the cattle trails north to Kansas, but even Indian parties with legal permission to hunt on the Staked Plains. As early as August 1875, patrols went in pursuit of cattle thieves, a task that continued to demand the garrison's attention at various times over the next few years. On October 20, a detachment arrived at the fort with five civilian prisoners, arrested in possession of a herd of government horses and mules. The troops took the prisoners on to Fort Sill a few days later to face charges.[12] Two months later thirteen cavalrymen set out from the post after thieves who had stolen horses from Kiowa Indians on their reservation.[13]

The Battle of the Little Bighorn in Montana, in which Custer and over 200 of his regiment died, affected the garrison at Fort Elliott to a limited extent. Captain Clarence Mauck, commanding the post and B Company, Fourth Cavalry, led that company out of Fort Elliott in July, a few days after the battle, bound for Cheyenne, Wyoming Territory.[14] In October, Lieutenant Alexander H. M. Taylor, Nineteenth Infantry, shepherded a party of recruits through the fort and on toward Fort Leavenworth, Kansas, to replenish the decimated Seventh Cavalry.[15]

Routine matters and local crises rather than the war against the Sioux dominated activities at Fort Elliott, however. With most of the cavalry away on detached service on the northern plains or closer to home, the predominantly infantry garrison improved the post and enforced law and order. The command dug a well to supplement the water supply at the beginning of 1877. In early spring a small infantry detachment and one civilian guide left the post in pursuit of the outlaw John Bottom and stolen government property in the possession of his gang. The patrol returned several days later after killing Bottom and traveling 260 miles.[16]

Indian problems had not disappeared entirely at Elliott by that time, despite the defeat of the southern Plains tribes three years earlier in the Red River War. On May 6, 1877, Indians reportedly burned a Mr. McKama's trading post on the Brazos near the town of Reynolds.[17] A sizable cavalry force returned to the post late in the summer, increasing its striking power in the event of a new outbreak of fighting, but the fort's howitzer and Gatling gun were taken to another location.[18]

In September, over eighty men of the Fourth Cavalry rode out of Fort Elliott to round up a band of hostile Cheyennes who had left their reservation. The detachment did not return until two months later. At the same time, an infantry company marched to the village of Clarendon about fifty miles southwest of the fort on detached service.[19]

Another factor tended to aggravate the Indian situation in Fort Elliot's region during the same period. Texas cattlemen began to

A scouting party ready to leave Fort Elliott on patrol (The Center for American History, University of Texas at Austin).

drive more and more of their herds north through the Panhandle rather than over the Chisholm Trail farther east. That shift placed a greater burden on the garrison at Fort Elliott to protect the herds and brought an increased possibility for trouble between civilian cattlemen and Indians.[20]

Fort Elliott stood in prime buffalo country. By the late 1870s, after hunters had virtually eliminated the buffalo, ranchers ran cattle on the Panhandle's open ranges. Indians from the Kiowa, Comanche, and Cheyenne reservations in Indian Territory still filtered across the boundary line into Texas to hunt and sometimes came into conflict with cattlemen and other whites.[21]

A party of Texas Rangers under Captain G. W. Arrington moved into the Panhandle in the winter of 1878-79 in response to reports of hostile Indian incursions. Troops out of Fort Elliott patrolled the plains at the same time with orders to protect whites from Indians but to allow legitimate Indian hunting parties to take game. One such patrol under Captain Nicholas Nolan, Tenth Cavalry, came upon Arrington's Rangers as they prepared to attack an Indian camp. The troops stopped the Rangers and allowed the hunting party to continue unmolested.[22] Nolan, a tough and experienced career soldier, had had the misfortune of leading a patrol of his Buffalo Soldiers a year earlier out onto the Staked Plains. That patrol had disintegrated after a hellish four days without water in the Texas summer, and Nolan carried the stigma of the ordeal for the rest of his life.[23]

Friction between the Rangers and troops from Fort Elliott continued into the summer of 1879, with similar incidents occurring. Finally, Lieutenant Colonel John W. Davidson, Tenth Cavalry, commanding officer at Elliott, reported the situation to Texas Governor O. M. Roberts. From that time on Rangers offered no more trouble to legitimate Indian hunting parties.[24]

Not all bands of Indians reported to be on the Staked Plains had permission to be off the reservation. Troops from Elliott engaged in two major scouts after such groups in the spring of 1879. In April, twenty men of the Tenth Cavalry covered the area as far as Clarendon and Palo Duro Canyon in search of hostile Indians. They found none.[25] The following month Captain Nolan and H Company of the same regiment went out in pursuit of a party of Comanches said to be moving toward the Staked Plains from Fort Sill. Nolan's men had an advantage that many earlier cavalry columns did not have. Grass was plentiful at the time, and they had

Nicholas Nolan
(The Center for
American History,
University of Texas
at Austin).

no need to carry much forage. Other supplies had to come in by wagon from Forts Concho and Griffin, however, so the patrol could not operate completely unhampered by a supply line.[26]

During the same spring, Fort Elliott maintained a small outpost at Symer's Ranch. A detachment of A Company, Tenth Cavalry, under a sergeant's command garrisoned the ranch. Quartermasters also used the ranch as a small forage depot for supplying patrols in the field.[27]

In order to deal with Indian hunting parties visiting the area more and more frequently, Lieutenant Colonel Davidson suggested to Department of the Missouri headquarters in June 1879 that funds be allocated for an interpreter. The post already had a civilian guide, but with an overall decrease in Indian raids in the region and growing familiarity with the area among his officers, Davidson believed that the guide's services were no longer essential. The government could save $75 per month by dispensing with the man and use that money toward the $100 monthly salary Davidson wished to pay an interpreter. The colonel proposed hiring George Fox for the new job. Department headquarters agreed to Davidson's proposal a few days later, and Fox hired on as post interpreter.[28] The command released William Dixon, experienced scout and buffalo hunter, from employment as guide. (Dixon had earned his place in history at the Battle of Adobe Walls several years earlier, when he had made his famous "long shot," knocking a Comanche off his horse at a range of three-quarters of a mile.) Two months after Dixon's termination, Captain Nolan, temporary commanding officer at Fort Elliott, requested that he be rehired.[29]

Demands from several quarters strained Fort Elliott's limited manpower in the fall. A detail of nine men worked with the United States marshal investigating thefts of livestock in Indian Territory. A detachment of thirty stayed busy for many weeks building a telegraph line connecting the fort to other posts. Only two officers and twenty enlisted men remained to carry out regular escort and patrol duties.[30]

In December, a new commanding officer, Captain Richard I. Eskridge, Twenty-third Infantry, rode out with a guide, an interpreter, and three enlisted men to investigate trouble along the boundary between Texas and Indian Territory. A cowboy had reported being attacked by Indians, but Eskridge found only a few small bands of Kiowas and Delawares hunting without permits in the area and could not determine if they were responsible for the attack. A larger party of Comanches did have a permit to hunt, and he took some of them to Fort Elliott to give them rations and

Comanche warrior Tabatosa (The Center for American History, University of Texas at Austin).

let them identify stock stolen from their reservation earlier and recovered by the marshal.[31]

As Indian troubles diminished further, troops at Fort Elliott concentrated more and more on improving roads and communications between other forts and on enforcing the law. One such construction effort saw Lieutenant Henry O. Flipper, Tenth Cavalry, build a telegraph line from Elliott to Fort Supply, Indian Territory.[32] Scouts continued, and detachments went out whenever reports of trouble came in, but those reports became fewer and fewer. In all of 1879, Indians had killed only one settler in the area and had stolen just a few horses and cattle.[33]

Although actual danger seldom threatened soldiers at Fort Elliott, duty there remained far from pleasant because of the remoteness of the site. The garrison regarded a visit by an officer from another post to be a special occasion worthy of a celebration.[34]

Commanding officers made a special effort to provide basic forms of recreation for the men under their command. A post library furnished various books and periodicals.[35] After the library and headquarters building mysteriously burned on February 27, 1879, the command took steps to replace it with a larger, better structure housing a school and chapel in addition to the library.[36] The post established a school for those men who wished to improve their education and detailed one member of the garrison to serve as teacher—Private Moncrief received the privilege of exemption from all roll calls except reveille in recognition of his service benefiting his fellow soldiers.[37] Additional efforts by the command to make life more pleasant for their men included providing better food. Toward that end the post included an orchard of 1000 peach trees.[38]

Fort Elliott remained an active post well after danger from the Indian tribes of the southern Plains had passed. The presence of troops in the Panhandle helped stabilize the area during its transition from wilderness to a settled ranching area. In that period Fort Elliott had the distinction of being virtually the only post in Texas to protect Indians from whites as well as whites from Indians. The garrison served as much in the role of a police force as it did a military force. The army closed the post in October 1890.[39]

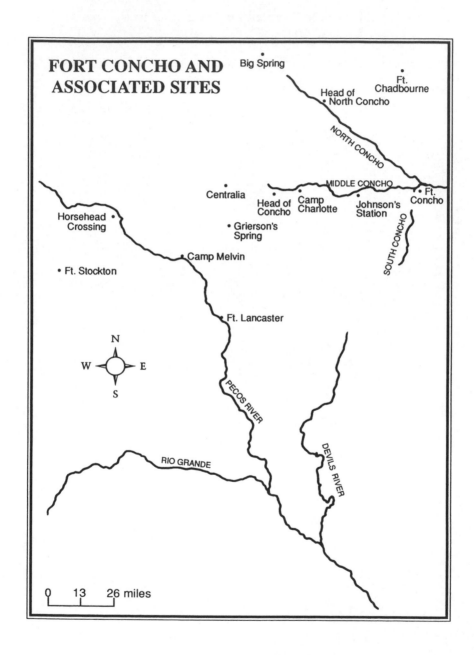

FORT CONCHO AND ASSOCIATED SITES

Big Spring

Ft. Chadbourne

Head of North Concho

NORTH CONCHO

MIDDLE CONCHO

Centralia

Head of Concho

Camp Charlotte

Johnson's Station

Ft. Concho

Horsehead Crossing

Grierson's Spring

SOUTH CONCHO

Camp Melvin

Ft. Stockton

Ft. Lancaster

N
W   E
S

PECOS RIVER

DEVILS RIVER

RIO GRANDE

0   13   26 miles

FORT CONCHO
AND ITS OUTPOSTS

Of all the posts on the Texas frontier, Fort Concho held the most central and strategic location. It stood within striking distance of the Staked Plains to the northwest and the arid trans-Pecos region of the Apache to the west, giving the garrison the opportunity to halt north-south Indian movement and thus interrupt raiding patterns of some of the most warlike of the tribes that menaced Texas settlements. The fort's locale also allowed it to protect a major portion of the mail route to the west.

As soon as the army returned to the Texas frontier after the Civil War, military commanders attempted to establish and maintain a fort within the general geographic area of the branches of the Concho River. At first, they chose to reoccupy Fort Chadbourne, a pre-war post on the mail route to El Paso. In the spring of 1867, elements of the Fourth Cavalry rode into the fort and pitched camp. Shortly over 300 men garrisoned the post.[1]

Problems soon arose over the fort's water supply, however, prompting district headquarters to choose a different location for the region's main post. Reports from scouting expeditions in the field and a study of the main transportation routes across West Texas convinced military leaders that a spot near the confluence of the different branches of the Concho River and its tributaries would prove to be the best site. The location ensured a permanent supply of water more than adequate to meet the needs of men and animals. In addition, it covered the crossroads of the San Antonio-El Paso road, the Overland Mail route, and the increasingly popular Goodnight-Loving Trail running northwest to New Mexico and Colorado.[2]

In late November 1867, a small detachment from Fort Chadbourne established the camp that became Fort Concho. A few days later the detachment officially transferred its headquarters from Chadbourne to the new post, which they named Camp Hatch in honor of Major John Hatch of the Fourth Cavalry. The following February, authorities changed the name to Fort Concho.[3]

Permanent buildings rose slowly. Remote as Concho was, construction materials had to come in by ox cart over a route hundreds of miles in length. To make matters worse, the army found that stone was the best construction material only after lengthy experimentation using adobe. Nevertheless, the fort eventually took shape.[4]

Troops stationed at Fort Concho sometimes came into conflict with a rough lot of civilians in the town of Saint Angela, which grew up across the river during the fort's early years. The situation became particularly troublesome during times when black troops garrisoned the fort. Late in 1877, Saint Angela witnessed a shooting spree by a party of Texas Rangers in one of the town's saloons. Angered that black soldiers were dancing with the same girls and drinking in the same room, the Rangers ran the unarmed troops out in a hail of bullets. No one suffered injury at the time. Colonel Benjamin H. Grierson, in command of Concho, called for an apology by the Rangers but never received one.[5]

A few months later a rowdy group of cowboys and buffalo hunters cut up a black sergeant's uniform, with him in it, at one of

Fort Concho (The Center for American History, University of Texas at Austin).

the local saloons. Several troopers armed themselves and returned to the bar. In the gunfight that followed, one man on each side died and three suffered wounds. The murder of a black soldier by a drunken rancher in Saint Angela three years later led to a major riot by troops and the threat of deadly force in retaliation by a Texas Ranger company dispatched to the trouble spot.[6]

Fort Concho did offer certain pleasures to its garrison, especially to officers and their families. Many of them enjoyed the dry, expansive countryside around the fort and its abundance of fish and game. At times throughout the year, soldiers and their families found opportunity to celebrate at weddings, holidays, and parties.[7]

A number of outstanding officers commanded Fort Concho. Those included Colonel Ranald Mackenzie, whom General Ulysses S. Grant had characterized as the most promising young officer in the army; Lieutenant Colonel W. R. Shafter, who would command the American force that fought the Spanish in Cuba in 1898; and Colonel Grierson, a former music teacher who later led two cavalry raids through Mississippi in the Civil War. The fort became a staging and support base for a number of offensive expeditions against hostile tribes, including Mackenzie's and Shafter's thrusts onto the Llano Estacado in the early and mid-1870s.

Fort Concho's role in protecting and pacifying the region around it proved more significant, however, than its contributions to those faraway campaigns. For that purpose it maintained a number of subposts and picket stations to extend its control far beyond the vicinity of the fort itself and to provide bases for far-ranging patrols in search of Indian marauders.

Troops from Fort Concho garrisoned several stations on or near the mail route during the early years of its existence. Those included Fort Chadbourne, Camp Colorado, Centralia Station, Johnson's Station, Head of the Concho, and old Camp Charlotte. During the late 1870s, the command established subposts at three points to serve as base camps for scouting operations and escorts and to control key water sources west of the post. Those subposts included the new Camp Charlotte, a scouting camp at the Head of the North Concho, and Grierson's Spring. In addition, the fort used temporary outposts at other points when necessary.

Fort Chadbourne had served as an important post on the frontier line before the Civil War but had lacked the permanent water supply necessary for retention as a major fort following the end of that conflict. Although its main garrison moved to Fort Concho in 1867, Chadbourne's location made it valuable as a picket post for a few men. The troops remaining there provided escorts and protection to the mail station and to the coaches that carried the mail.[8]

Fort Concho's picket stations usually held men on a temporary basis whenever circumstances made it necessary or desirable. In the fall of 1869, however, the command ordered that three of its stations, including Fort Chadbourne, be permanently garrisoned.[9]

Chadbourne's detachment consisted of one noncommissioned officer and six privates.[10] The size of the garrison fluctuated slightly over the next two years but remained small. In March 1871, the station included one corporal and three privates.[11]

At the end of May, however, new orders came through from the Department of Texas establishing Fort Chadbourne as a full-fledged subpost. An entire company of the Eleventh Infantry plus a cavalry detachment of seven men from the Fourth Cavalry made up the garrison.[12] Troops at Fort Chadbourne had responsibility for protecting the mail station and stages as before, but now had the additional task of patrolling the mail route for considerable distances on a regular schedule. Those patrols had to travel the route north to the picket station at Mountain Pass, a point halfway to Phantom Hill, at least once a month. A similar patrol from Phantom Hill covered the other half of the route from their subpost to Mountain Pass.[13] That arrangement did not last long, because Mackenzie's expeditions against the Kiowas and then the Comanches occupied most of the troops from the newly established subposts. From the summer of 1871 on, only small details of soldiers served at Fort Chadbourne on a temporary basis to guard the mail line.

Beginning in 1869, Fort Concho maintained a few troops at Camp Colorado, about eighty miles northeast of the fort and sixty miles due east of Fort Chadbourne. The camp stood upstream of Brownwood on Jim Ned Creek, a tributary of the Colorado River, in Coleman County. The army had established Camp Colorado before the Civil War, but after the war it never attained great importance as a military post. Some state forces, such as Texas Ranger units, also used the camp as a base of operations. During 1875, work details of soldiers linked Camp Colorado to Forts Concho and Griffin by a military telegraph line.[14]

Centralia Station stood on the mail route to El Paso about seventy miles west and up on the southern reaches of the Staked Plains. Troops under Major Joseph Rendelbrock, Fourth Cavalry, established a picket station there in the summer of 1868. Ben Ficklin, running the mail line in that part of the state, helped supply the picket post during its early weeks of operation.[15]

Fort Concho or its outposts kept small details of men at Centralia Station much of the time over the next years. At least as late as 1880, detachments guarded the station and the mail coaches that used it. Only when the Indian danger had definitely passed did the army permanently withdraw its men.[16]

The mail relay point at Johnson's Station (sometimes referred to as Johnston's Station) had much in common with Centralia. Troops garrisoned it during the same period, and it functioned as a picket station for guarding the mail line. The same order that established a permanent military presence at the picket post of Fort Chadbourne in late 1869 applied to Johnson's Station as well. The small garrison built permanent quarters—a building with a pole roof covered with mud or unformed adobe—for themselves. From that vantage point a sentry could watch both the military stable and the mail-company corral.[17]

Johnson's Station stood on the south bank of the Middle Concho River at a point on the mail route about twenty-five miles west of Fort Concho.[18] By December 1869, the garrison there consisted of one noncommissioned officer and four privates. A band of Indians on a small winter raid hit the station just before Christmas. They ran off five cavalry horses named Tobe, Texas, Joe, Bill, and Billy.[19] The raid provoked a quick reaction. Fifty troopers rode out of Fort Concho in pursuit on Christmas Day. On the administrative side, a board of survey convened to determine who was officially responsible for the loss and if there were any financial accountability. To forestall further raids, the command later dispatched heavy reinforcements to Johnson's Station. A lieutenant with two sergeants, two corporals, and twenty-three privates of E Company, Ninth Cavalry, plus a hospital attendant, headed for the site. They planned to stay for at least a month, scouting the region vigorously for hostile bands.[20] The command at Fort Concho continued to keep small details at Johnson's Station through the mid-1870s. Sometimes the men remained there for thirty days, but occasionally they stood duty of sixty days or more.[21]

The mail station known as Head of the Concho stood on the mail route at the head of the Middle Concho River almost exactly between Johnson's Station to the east and Centralia Station to the west, and about twenty-eight miles from each.[22] Beginning in late April 1868, one company from Fort Concho occupied the station for a three-month period. Other units continued to garrison Head of the Concho on a temporary basis through the next few months until orders came through making the station permanent.[23]

To house the permanent garrison, troops built a fortified stone structure thirty feet long by ten feet wide. The building had two rooms, one for the men and the other to serve as a stable.[24] One sergeant, one corporal, six infantry privates, and two mounted cavalry privates manned the station. The men had plenty of ammunition in case of a serious fight—one hundred rounds each, plus another thousand as a general reserve in the station building. They served a forty-day tour at Head of the Concho before being relieved.[25] Captain George Gamble, commanding Fort Concho in the fall of 1868, had the option of stationing up to twenty-five additional cavalrymen at the picket post to scout actively after Indians in the vicinity.[26] Troops continued to occupy the mail station at Head of the Concho through 1879.[27] They suffered from Indian raids on some occasions, especially night attacks targeting the animals of the garrison and the stage company.[28] Larger forces periodically used Head of the Concho as a base camp for extensive scouts when conditions required.[29]

Camp Charlotte began as a picket station of Fort Concho on the mail route and eventually became a regular subpost. Troops from the fort established Camp Charlotte in April 1868 on the south bank of the Middle Concho just below the mouth of Kiowa Creek. They built an impressive log stockade measuring 190 feet by 115 feet, bastioned at each corner, around the stables. Tents inside the stockade housed the enlisted men, while officers' quarters and the guard house stood outside the walls.[30]

Units at Camp Charlotte protected the mail line but also served in other capacities. Even before the army officially established the camp, troops used it as a base from which they escorted cattle herds moving west into the trans-Pecos country and on to New Mexico.[31] Huge numbers of cattle passed through the region in the late 1860s and the 1870s, presenting a tempting target to hostile Indians. Often Comanche war parties stole cattle and drove them to secret meeting points on the Staked Plains where they traded them to New Mexican Comancheros for guns and ammunition. Sometimes Indian bands managed to run off the remuda (or horse herd) of a cattle outfit on the trail or even the horses of the military escort guarding the herd. One such attack in the fall of 1872 took troopers by surprise just three miles from Camp Charlotte.[32] Although most hostile activity by Comanches and their allied tribes in the north had stopped by the mid-1870s, attacks from Apaches and, occasionally, Kickapoos from the south and west increased in the latter years of the decade. Because of the attacks, the army posted more troops to Camp Charlotte and other points west of Fort Concho, particularly Grierson's Spring and the Head of the North Concho River.

Between 1878 and 1882, Camp Charlotte functioned primarily as a subpost of Fort Concho for thorough scouting and patroling of the region. On one such typical scout, Lieutenant Millard Fillmore Eggleston, Tenth Cavalry, rode out with fifteen enlisted men and a civilian guide named Monroe to find a party of Indians who had stolen livestock from a nearby ranch. Monroe found the Indians' trail an hour after the command reached the site of the attack, though the Indians had tried to obliterate it. The troops marched forty-five miles in pursuit that first day.[33]

The next day a few cowboys joined the command. Eggleston thought the Indians, seven or eight Apaches, were bound for the Head of the North Concho, so he sent word to the detachment there to watch for the war party. The Indians slipped past during the night. Eggleston had the soldiers follow the Indians while he angled across to the west to cut off the hostiles from Fort Stanton and the Sand Hills. Somehow the Apaches eluded both columns, and Eggleston's command returned to Camp Charlotte a few days later after their rations had run out. They had marched 241 miles in seven days.[34]

In addition to grueling and usually unsuccessful scouts and pursuits, men at Camp Charlotte spent a great deal of time and energy building roads and telegraph lines to link the various posts in the region. Road building involved not only clearing and grading new routes through the rocky, arid countryside, but also shortening existing roads and improving them. Troops used blasting powder with great effect to decrease steep grades and remove boulders. Sheer muscle power sufficed to clear out smaller rocks, rubble, and stumps. Because many of the original roads had far more curves than necessary, working parties reduced travel distances between points by cutting corners, straightening out those routes wherever possible. Where runoff tended to wash soil and gravel across a roadway, men used the native stone for low retaining walls. Eventually, these improvements resulted in roads suitable for fully loaded wagons.[35]

Troops made similar improvements in telegraph lines and, where no previous lines existed, built new ones. They cut wire into half-mile lengths at the camp and hauled it by wagon to the stretch of road where it was to be used. Men dug holes for the poles by hand, normally three and one-half to four feet deep.[36] By the early spring of 1881, the line ran from San Antonio through Fort Concho, Camp Charlotte, and Grierson's Spring to Fort Stockton and beyond. Grierson's Spring had a station and an operator; Camp Charlotte had neither.[37] Such work on road and telegraph probably did more to remove the Indian threat in the region than the more active measures of scouting and pursuit. By the late summer of 1882, little need remained for Camp Charlotte. With the threat of Indian attack in the area virtually gone, the Department of Texas ordered the outpost abandoned.[38]

Between 1879 to 1882, troops from Fort Concho maintained a subpost at the Head of the North Concho River (not to be confused with the picket station known as Head of the Concho on the Middle Concho River). Patrols camped on or near the site at least as early as 1872, but units from Fort Concho did not establish a permanent outpost until later. Local settlers sometimes referred to the outpost as Camp Elizabeth.[39] In response to repeated Indian incursions west of Fort Concho, D Company, Tenth Cavalry, established the subpost at the Head of the North Concho near the end of July 1879. The company had orders to scout north, west, and south for hostile Indians and to spare neither men nor horses in pressing a vigorous pursuit of any Indians seen.[40]

The army kept troops at Head of the North Concho continuously from 1879 until 1881.[41] In midsummer 1881, a new, more subtle danger threatened the men at Head of the North Concho when a trader named Jackson set up a camp next to the subpost and began to sell whiskey and tobacco to the garrison. Lieutenant Calvin Esterly stepped in quickly to eliminate this threat to good order and discipline at his outpost. He placed an armed sentry between the military camp and Jackson's site to stop any traffic between the two. He also reported the trader's activities to Colonel Benjamin Grierson, who passed on the information to the county sheriff.[42]

During the subpost's three most active years, the command continually tried to make it more comfortable for the garrison. They replaced some of the crude picket shelters with small stone houses that stayed drier and had fewer bugs.[43] Fort Concho supplied shingles and lumber for roofing the temporary buildings.[44] For better meals the garrsion brought in a field oven.[45]

Head of the North Concho served primarily as a cavalry base camp.[46] Troops often rotated between it, Camp Charlotte, and the subpost at Grierson's Spring. In late fall 1881, the Department of Texas shifted the supply point providing forage for the cavalry horses at North Concho to the growing town of Big Spring, making it much easier to supply the subpost.[47] Shortly after the supply shift, however, military authorities decided to abandon Head of the North Concho. Grierson favored such a move because he believed the subpost's usefulness had passed with the virtual end of Indian raids in the area.[48] Finally, in November 1882, the last troops there permanently evacuated the post and returned to Fort Concho.[49]

The arid country west of Fort Concho contained numerous springs, but their location often remained a mystery to the white man unless accident or dogged exploration revealed them. In May 1878, two cattlemen discovered a flowing spring in a small canyon on a direct line between Camp Charlotte and Pecos Bridge. The two men, W. L. Riggs and M. N. Wilkins, shared their information with Lieutenant Mason M. Maxon, Tenth Cavalry, a few days later, and Maxon noted the location of the water hole for military use. Eventually, the site acquired the name, Grierson's Spring, after the man in charge of the army's District of the Pecos.[50]

Colonel Grierson realized that control of the water sources in that dry area could prove decisive in making it safe from Indian raids. To that end, he ordered his patrols out of Fort Concho to make every effort to locate and record all water holes that they came across.[51] Grierson's Spring, located twenty-eight miles southwest of the stage station at Head of the (Middle) Concho, stood in a perfect location for providing water to travelers following a direct line between that point or Camp Charlotte and the Pecos Bridge near Fort Lancaster. No road existed, but Grierson's troops built one, along with many others connecting virtually all of the army's far-flung outposts in the region.[52] Thus, Grierson's Spring combined the two essential elements of the colonel's strategy for pacification of the region—control of all water sources and connection of all military posts by a series of roads. Troops erected permanent stone buildings at Grierson's Spring over an extended period. During the summer of 1879, Lieutenant James Pratt, Twenty-fifth Infantry, directed the construction of quarters ten feet by thirty feet, suitable for officers or enlisted men.[53] The following winter and spring, soldiers at Grierson's Spring completed a stone corral and stables as well as a guard house. The guard house had two rooms, each twelve feet square. All buildings had thatched roofs. The command obtained timber for the construction in Lancaster Canyon, twelve miles to the south.[54]

Other construction efforts occupied a considerable part of the garrison's energies. Troops continually repaired wagon roads leading to other sites and worked to reduce the distance between points by straightening routes. Lieutenant Pratt, in addition to his work on buildings, installed a large water pump to make better use of the flow from the spring.[55] Many soldiers at Grierson's Spring helped build and repair military telegraph lines. In the spring of 1879, working parties rerouted the line that had followed the stage road between Head of the Concho and the Pecos River to a new run from Camp Charlotte southwest to the Pecos via

James Pratt (Fort Davis National Historic Site).

Grierson's Spring. By changing the route, they cut the length from seventy-two miles to fifty-eight miles.[56]

The area around Grierson's Spring proved to be dangerous on occasion, more from the weather than from hostile Indians. The spring itself formed the head of a watershed from the Staked Plains. The small canyon where the spring surfaced caught water draining from the limestone plateau above it.[57] The watershed frequently channeled a flash flood in periods of heavy rain. One officer in the region lost his family to such a torrent, and many scouting columns had animals and camp equipage washed away. Other forms of violent weather also struck the area at times. In 1879, a savage hail storm hit Grierson's Spring just as the animals of the command finished watering. Although soldiers held each animal securely by the bridle, the hail came down so hard and heavy that the frightened horses and mules broke free and stampeded down the canyon. The men had to follow on foot. They recovered all of the animals, but only after a miserable and dangerous night and morning of hard work.[58] Another severe storm hit in July of the following year. Rushing water damaged the cisterns at the spring and washed out sections of the road nearby, and high winds blew down walls on some of the buildings.[59]

Scouting for hostile Indians remained the primary responsibility of units stationed at Grierson's Spring throughout its existence. Troops from the subpost covered the area west to the Pecos, south to Fort Lancaster, and north to Centralia Station and Castle Gap.[60] Those units did their work well and relentlessly closed off the area from Indian incursions. By the spring of 1882, Grierson recommended that the subpost be abandoned. It was no longer needed. That fall, the last troops transferred out of Grierson's Spring.[61]

At the same time, the colonel also recommended closing Fort Concho itself. If that did not happen, he suggested establishing a subpost near the new railroad line that crossed the region. Deep Creek, sometimes called Calvert's Creek, seemed best among the possible locations for that two-company post. The site lay 110 miles northwest of Fort Concho and twenty miles above Colorado City. He recommended that an additional one-company outpost be located at Gold Greek, some forty miles northwest of the railroad. Both spots had good grass, water, and timber, and would give the army excellent central locations from which to patrol the surrounding region. As it turned out, however, the Department of Texas decided against the new outposts. Fort Concho itself lingered on for a few years but finally closed in 1889.[62]

The outposts of Fort Concho proved more effective in countering the Indian threat than those of most other Texas forts. Concho's picket stations performed no better than similar stations elsewhere in guarding mail stops and stagecoaches; however, the main subposts in the late 1870s and early 1880s achieved a degree of success rare on the state's frontier.

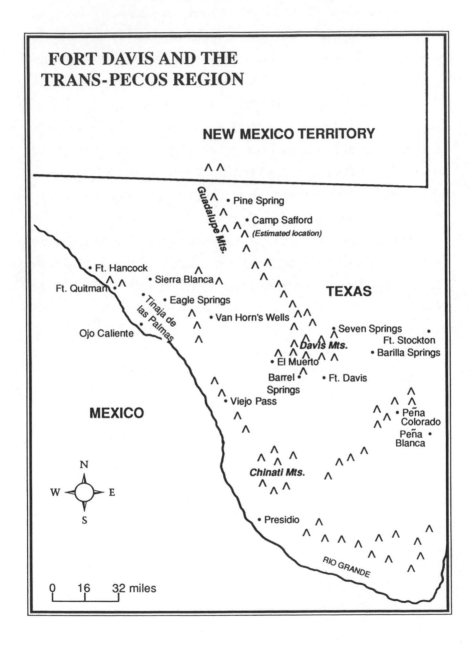

FORT DAVIS AND THE TRANS-PECOS REGION

NEW MEXICO TERRITORY

Λ Λ

Guadalupe Mts.

• Pine Spring

• Camp Safford
Λ *(Estimated location)*

Λ

• Ft. Hancock

Ft. Quitman •
Λ Λ

• Sierra Blanca Λ

TEXAS

• Tinaja de las Palmas

• Eagle Springs

Ojo Caliente •
Λ

• Van Horn's Wells

• Seven Springs

Davis Mts.

Ft. Stockton •

• Barilla Springs

• El Muerto

MEXICO

Barrel • Springs

• Ft. Davis

Λ
Λ Λ
Λ • Peña Colorado

Peña • Blanca

• Viejo Pass

Chinati Mts.

N

W E

S

• Presidio

RIO GRANDE

0   16   32 miles

FORT DAVIS
AND ITS OUTPOSTS

Whereas the army located most of its major posts along the edge of the frontier facing toward unpacified territory and with settlements behind, it placed Fort Davis in the very middle of the Apaches' domain. A person riding out of the fort faced great danger for a hundred miles or more in every direction. For that reason, Fort Davis stood as a citadel of protection for ranchers and travelers.

The United States Army had built Fort Davis in the 1850s but evacuated it on the eve of the Civil War. On July 1, 1867, the military returned. Lieutenant Colonel Wesley Merritt led four companies of the Ninth Cavalry back onto the post, the first federal troops there for seven years. Sheer cliffs and steep, rocky mountains overshadowing the fort on two sides caused Merritt to remark on the potential danger from Indians posted on those heights.[1] Nearby Limpia Creek provided a permanent source of good water to the post.

Merritt had one of the most distinguished careers of any American soldier of the period. After graduation from West Point, he began active service in the dragoons a year before the outbreak of the Civil War. He remained in mounted units for the rest of his regimental service. His citations and promotions for gallantry during the war are almost too numerous to list, the first being a brevet majority on the field at Gettysburg. Ending the war as a major general, he reverted to lieutenant colonel of the Ninth Cavalry. In 1876 he received promotion to colonel and command of the Fifth Cavalry. He finally attained the permanent rank of major general in 1895, five years before his retirement.[2]

Merritt and his troops enjoyed the scenery and healthy climate at Fort Davis, but other conditions made their situation difficult. The command had to rebuild the fort, most of which had been burned during the Civil War. In addition, the lack of fresh vegetables caused a major outbreak of scurvy among the garrison in 1868. Merritt had to train his troops virtually from scratch. Also, because the majority of the regiment's enlisted men had little education, a great shortage existed in soldiers capable of handling paperwork and administrative duties.[3]

The companies at Fort Davis had little trouble from Indians during the first year.[4] For the next three years after that, raids and small-scale attacks increased, drawing the army's attention to the Big Bend area in particular. Vigorous action by Lieutenant Colonel William R. Shafter and units from Fort Davis and the posts to the east, however, forced an end to the worst depredations by the end of the summer of 1871.[5]

Much of the work of troops at Fort Davis consisted of patrol and protection of the mail route running past the fort from San Antonio and Fort Stockton to El Paso and points farther west. Although the Comanche War Trail passed through much of the region covered by Fort Davis, the majority of Indian raids on isolated ranches and on coaches along the mail route came from small bands of Apaches native to the trans-Pecos area and south-eastern New Mexico. Eventually, military forces headquartered at the post had to wrest control of the region from those bands and break their power permanently in order to make the countryside safe. After a decrease in such raids for several years following Shafter's campaigns, Apaches stepped up their hit-and-run attacks on stagecoaches and wagon trains west of the Pecos in 1877. The attacks increased in both severity and frequency the next year as war parties threatened settlements as well as travelers.[6]

The Apache chief, Victorio, of the Warm Springs, or Ojo Caliente, band, proved to be the most difficult adversary for units at Fort Davis and nearby posts. Victorio united them with the Mescalero band in a war against both the United States and Mexico that combined small-scale fights with pursuits and patrols covering tremendous distances. Victorio and his followers left their New Mexico reservations several times in 1879, the final time in late summer. They vowed never to return and never to surrender. From that time on, they played a constant game of cat-and-mouse with American and Mexican troops sent to hunt them down. Appearing and disappearing at will, Victorio's raiders crossed the international boundary a number of times, making it next to impossible for the armies of either nation to pursue them effectively.[7]

Strained relations between the two countries added to the difficulty and made concerted action against the common enemy extremely difficult. Troops under Colonel Edward Hatch in New Mexico engaged in long, futile pursuits of Victorio's band as 1880 began. Then in May, a detachment of Indian scouts under Henry K. Parker found and attacked the Apaches on the Palomas River, driving them into Mexico.[8]

General E. O. C. Ord, commanding the Department of Texas, had placed Colonel Benjamin H. Grierson in command of the District of the Pecos, comprising the western part of the state, in 1878, when troubles with the Apaches were starting to increase. Grierson realized the futility of attempting to run small bands of

Apaches to ground when the Indians possessed intimate knowledge of the countryside and military commanders did not. He determined to gain a thorough familiarity with the arid region in extreme West Texas, especially with its few, precious water sources. Once he had located them through the diligent mapping efforts of every patrol he sent out in 1878 and 1879, he began to establish outposts at those water sources. With his troops in control of the only water in the region, Grierson could force the Apaches to fight on his terms.[9]

Grierson knew that Victorio would likely cross into Texas once Mexican troops came too close to his hiding places, and the colonel wanted to be ready for him. After deploying his units to cover the most probable routes that the Apaches would take into the United States, he rode with a small escort toward Eagle Springs, west of Fort Davis on the mail route. On the way, he received dispatches from patrols along the Rio Grande that Victorio had crossed the river and headed north. Grierson led his force of less than a dozen

Fort Davis (The Center for American History, University of Texas at Austin).

Tinaja de las Palmas (Fort Davis National Historic Site).

men to Tinaja de las Palmas, fifteen miles west of Eagle Springs and the only water source for a considerable distance to the north.[10]

Victorio and his band also made for Tinaja de las Palmas on their way north, but Grierson and his small escort managed to hold them off until reinforcements arrived and forced the Apaches to retire below the Rio Grande. Several days later, in early August, Grierson again beat Victorio to water, this time at Rattlesnake Springs in the Sierra Diablo. After a stiff fight for possession of the water hole, the Indians broke off the engagement and again crossed into Mexico.[11] Although small bands of renegade Apaches continued to menace travelers and ranchmen in the Fort Davis region, Victorio never again did so. Two months after the fight at Rattlesnake Springs, Mexican troops surrounded and destroyed Victorio's force in the hills of northern Chihuahua.[12]

Grierson assumed command of Fort Davis after all Apache raiding in the region had virtually ceased and remained at the post for three years until 1885 when he and the Tenth Cavalry transferred out of the state. The fort remained active, but largely unnecessary, until 1891.[13]

Between 1866 to 1886, Fort Davis maintained a large number of outposts to aid in controlling and protecting its region. Those posts fell into one or both of two main categories. The first included picket stations at points along the mail route. Posts in the second category covered important water holes and served as scouting camps. Three posts—Fort Quitman, Camp Peña Colorado, and Fort Hancock—made up a third group related to Fort Davis, but they fit more properly into a separate category of minor independent forts. Yet another outpost, referred to as the Pinery, functioned as a sawmill and furnished lumber to Fort Davis.

From east to west along the mail route to El Paso, Fort Davis garrisoned stage stations at Barilla (or Varilla) Springs, Barrel Springs, El Muerto, Van Horn's Wells, and Eagle Springs. Fort Davis stood between Barilla Springs to the east and Barrel Springs to the west.

Some troopers liked duty at picket stations on the mail lines. It gave them a break from the routine of garrison duty at the fort. It had certain drawbacks, however, and a greater element of danger. The danger came from the fact that only a handful of troops usually stayed at a picket station, and from the constant presence of horses and mules in the station's corral—tempting prizes for Indian raiders. In addition, civilian employees of the mail lines often mistreated military guards, especially black soldiers who comprised Fort Davis' complement during much of its existence. Sometimes stage drivers refused to allow offgoing black station guards to ride coaches back to the main fort if white passengers were aboard.[14]

Barilla Springs stage station consisted of a two-room building surrounded by a high adobe wall and an adobe corral.[15] Troops stationed there lived in a building similar to the stage station. The quarters had adobe walls, a mud roof and floor, and no bunks or furniture. The soldiers cooked in the open fireplace. Few trees grew in the immediate vicinity, and the men had to cut and haul firewood from three miles away.[16]

The terrain at El Muerto (Fort Davis National Historic Site).

Shortly after the army reoccupied posts in southwestern Texas following the Civil War, Colonel Edward Hatch recommended a full company garrison for Barilla Springs and several other stations on the mail route.[17] A shortage of troops, however, made a garrison of that size impossible, and the stations had to manage with a handful of soldiers. In mid-September 1868, the corporal in command at Barilla Springs reported a night attack by an undetermined number of Indians. Troops from Fort Stockton rode out in pursuit of the raiders, but retaliation proved fruitless. Such attacks and such unsuccessful pursuits became commonplace at Barilla Springs and the other picket stations on the mail route.[18]

Raids increased in 1871. In June of that year an estimated force of sixty Indians struck a military wagon train camped at Barilla Springs and ran off forty mules. Forts Davis and Stockton sent troops to follow the raiders.[19] A few days after the attack, a combined force of eighty men under Lieutenant Colonel W. R. Shafter left Barilla Springs and pursued the Indians onto the Staked Plains. After a nine-day march, the troops caught and attacked a party of Apaches, capturing one and recovering sixteen animals.[20] Indians continued to attack Barilla Springs throughout the 1870s, primarily for its livestock. Sometimes they managed to make off with mules or horses, but at other times the garrison or civilian employees drove off the attackers and inflicted losses on them.[21]

During the height of the Victorio campaign in mid-1880, a troublesome incident arose concerning one of the soldiers on guard at Barilla Springs. Private George Taylor rode as escort on many of the stages that passed from the station to other points on the mail line. He had the habit of cursing the drivers and almost came to blows with some. Despite orders from Fort Davis designed to keep soldiers from arguing with civilian employees of the stage line, Taylor persisted. Finally, all of the drivers on that stretch of the line

refused to permit him to ride their coaches, preferring the greater
risk of Indian attack to Taylor's personality.[22]

Barilla Springs and the other picket stations on the mail line
retained their military guards as long as danger from the Apaches
remained. By the mid-1880s, however, the need for military protection at each station had practically ceased, except along the
immediate Mexican border, and the army pulled its pickets back
into Fort Davis and the other larger posts.

The mail route ran through Barilla Springs to Fort Davis and
then through a station known as Barrel Springs. That station stood
twenty-two miles southwest of the fort. It consisted of a forty-by-sixty-
foot corral made of stone slabs stacked about eleven feet high, and two

Victorio (Fort
Davis National
Historic Site).

adobe rooms. The rooms stood on either side of the one gate to the corral and against its outside wall. That arrangement gave the station the appearance of a small fortress and provided a stout defensive position for the inhabitants. The spring itself lay in a ravine a quarter-mile from the station and furnished a modest source of permanent water.[23]

The first troops to guard Barrel Springs, a detachment of twelve men of the Forty-first Infantry, transferred to the station from Fort Davis on June 30, 1868. In December of that year, Colonel Wesley Merritt at Fort Davis reduced the garrison to seven enlisted men, a number he considered sufficient to protect the station itself, the animals having been withdrawn by the stage

A typical Mescalero Apache (Fort Davis National Historic Site).

company to another location. Fresh troops from the fort relieved the detail approximately every two months.[24]

Friction existed at times between the military and the stage employees. During the army's first year at Barrel Springs, a stage driver there named John Clark aided a fugitive from justice. Colonel Merritt reported the incident to district headquarters, commenting on the lack of respect for government and military authority evident in so many of the ex-Confederate civilians in Texas.[25]

Barrel Springs never faced a determined Indian attack, possibly because of its proximity to Fort Davis or because it often had no horses or mules to attract a raiding party. Nevertheless, Apaches sometimes did threaten. In September 1877, F. C. Godfrey, agent at the Mescalero Agency at South Fork, New Mexico Territory, requested that Fort Davis send out patrols to Barrel Springs and other points to intercept groups of Mescaleros who had recently left the reservation to join other Apaches in raiding.[26] In June 1880, during Victorio's last summer, men presumed to be Indians shot at the station keeper at Barrel Springs but did not attack the station.[27] That incident marked the last action by hostile Indians at the post.

The mail road swung northwest again past Barrel Springs and ran almost fourteen miles before it reached Dead Man's Hole station, more commonly referred to as El Muerto. The station there consisted of a stone corral, fifty-two by forty-four feet, and two adobe buildings on the outside wall. One of the buildings had loopholes in the wall it shared with the corral, allowing men inside to fire into the corral, apparently a measure designed to counter raids on the station's livestock. A spring a half-mile away provided water.[28]

On December 11, 1867, the first troops ordered to guard El Muerto, a twelve-man detachment of the Ninth Cavalry, rode to the station. Infantry replaced the cavalry six months later.[29] In September 1869, Captain William Bayard, Ninth Cavalry, commanding Fort Davis, sent a force over twice as large to El Muerto but found that the spring could not supply enough water for all of the animals and men. Bayarde reduced the garrison to ten men.[30]

Indians struck El Muerto on occasion. In the early summer of 1869, a band ran off the mail company's mules.[31] A lull in Indian activity over the next few years caused the army to reduce the size of the detail at El Muerto and other stations on the line continually until, by the summer of 1877, only two soldiers guarded each picket station. Additional troops rode escort on the stages, a practice some army leaders found completely unnecessary.[32]

After Apache raids increased in the late 1870s, Fort Davis doubled its guard details at El Muerto and other stations from two men to four. Soldiers still rode escort on the stages.[33] As with the other picket stations on the mail route, the army found it unnecessary to continue guarding El Muerto after Indian raids stopped in the early 1880s.

The mail route continued from El Muerto thirty-two miles to Van Horn's Wells, located in the foothills of the Van Horn Mountains. The mail company had constructed station buildings of adobe and stone, surrounded by a corral. Water came to the surface near the station and formed an oasis of permanent pools and willow trees.[34] A small guard occupied Van Horn's Wells. Through the late 1870s, they lived in tents rather than solid structures.[35] When Apache raids intensified in 1877, coaches along the route near Van Horn's Wells suffered as much as any. One stage driver, William Mitchell, lent a new tailor-made shirt to another driver. A few days later, travelers found the other driver dead, shot full of arrows while wearing Mitchell's new shirt.[36] Such attacks prompted the army to reinforce the detail at Van Horn's Wells, but not to any large degree.[37] Van Horn's Wells remained a small picket station until danger from the Apaches ended.

Edward Hatch (Fort Davis National Historic Site).

Eagle Springs, last of the mail route picket stations, lay twenty miles northwest of Van Horn's Wells. The station itself stood in a narrow canyon in the Eagle Mountains. It had a huge corral, 115 feet long by forty-three feet wide, with thick limestone slab walls. The springs seeped out of rock a quarter-mile to the west. Indians attacked Eagle Springs station more than any other spot on the mail route, probably because they could approach it unseen from one of several directions and, of course, because of the reliable supply of water.[38] Realizing the danger, Colonel Edward Hatch sent F Company, Ninth Cavalry, under Captain Henry Carroll to Eagle Springs from Fort Davis in December 1867.[39] A few weeks later Hatch inspected the area himself to determine the extent of the Indian problem around the station. After his inspection Hatch recommended that the District of Texas station a full company at Eagle Springs.[40]

By June 1868, I Company, Ninth Cavalry, under Captain
Theodore Boice garrisoned Eagle Springs. Stretched across
hundreds of miles of frontier, however, the regiment could not
continue to keep that much of its strength at one picket station,
regardless of its importance as a water source or its danger. Military
authorities continually reduced the garrison until only a sergeant
and four privates remained by late 1871.[41]

Eagle Springs and the other water holes provided a fairly
dependable supply for small detachments and stage animals, but the
quantity often proved inadequate for larger bodies of troops moving
through the area. Cavalry units usually had to travel in staggered
groups one or more days apart in order to allow enough time for
springs to fill up again after men and animals had drunk. Some
officers suggested blasting out the springs to enlarge them and eliminate the problem, and at a few locations that was accomplished.[42]

When Apache raids increased in 1878, the command at Fort
Davis began sending larger detachments to Eagle Springs, not to
guard the station, but to scout the surrounding country. In effect,
Eagle Springs shifted from picket station to subpost with the
increase in garrison and change in responsibilities. In June of 1878,
Captain L. H. Carpenter, Tenth Cavalry, led a large force to Eagle
Springs with orders to patrol the area, locate all water sources, find
any Indian trails, and determine the availability of grass and timber
with the object of establishing scouting camps at the best spots.[43]

The additional troops placed a strain on the water supply at
Eagle Springs. As early as the fall of 1878, units based there had to
keep most of their men out on patrol to avoid overtaxing the
springs.[44] By the summer of 1880, the situation had grown worse.
For a time, Captain Carpenter had to move his command to another
location in order to provide water for his animals.[45] Despite water
shortages, troops from Eagle Springs had several successes against

Indian raiders during the late 1870s and early 1880s. In late July 1879, Captain Michael L. Courtney, Twenty-fifth Infantry, with one company of that regiment and a few men from the Tenth Cavalry, left Eagle Springs in pursuit of a band of Apaches. Courtney's patrol stuck to the trail as it headed northeast toward New Mexico Territory. The troops finally caught up with the war party near Sulphur Springs, a short distance south of the New Mexico boundary, and engaged them. In the skirmish Courtney's men killed two Apaches and captured ten horses.[46]

The most important fight involving troops at Eagle Springs was the engagement between Grierson's small command and Victorio's raiders at Tinaja de las Palmas in late July 1880. Grierson, with reinforcements, denied the Apaches much-needed water after a fight lasting several hours. The Indians fled south to Mexico.[47]

Troops continued to use Eagle Springs as a base for scouts of the surrounding area long after Mexican soldiers finally destroyed Victorio's band in the fall of 1880. At the end of June 1882, however, the last troops pulled out of Eagle Springs, and the picket station ceased to exist.[48]

The town of Presidio, on the Rio Grande approximately a hundred miles southwest of Fort Davis, served as a subpost during the late 1870s and early 1880s. Problems from Mexican revolutionaries as well as Indians first prompted Americans in the town to request troops. Colonel George L. Andrews, Twenty-fifth Infantry, and a company from Fort Davis occupied Presidio briefly in the summer of 1872 during a revolutionary disturbance.[49]

In September 1875, Thomas G. Williams, special U.S. Indian commissioner in the area, suggested that General E. O. C. Ord, commanding the Department of Texas, close Fort Davis and transfer its garrison to Presidio to guard the region better against depredations by Mescalero Apaches.[50] Two months later, J. W. Clarke, a

United States customs official, asked for military protection at Presidio. Although two officers sent from Fort Davis to assess the situation recommended a force be stationed at Presidio, a shortage of troops and problems with civilian officials prevented the command at Davis from taking action.[51] In December 1876, however, Mexican revolutionaries took an American citizen hostage, and a sizable detachment of troops from Fort Davis under Colonel Andrews moved toward the town to effect his release. They hauled a field gun with them. When the detachment arrived at Presidio, Andrews fired two shells from the field gun into the Mexican town of Ojinaga as a threat to make the Mexicans release the captive. A few days later the man made his way across the Rio Grande to safety.[52]

The troops occupied a location known as Spencer's Rancho at Presidio.[53] In February 1877, five soldiers from the subpost and a number of civilian volunteers pursued a party of Indians who had run off livestock from a nearby ranch. The patrol followed the Indians' trail forty miles to a point near Eagle Springs but gave up the pursuit.[54]

Troops continued to operate out of Presidio for the next few years, scouting the border region and pursuing Indians and Mexican outlaws. At times, several companies used the subpost as a base of operations.[55] By 1883, a railroad from El Paso to Chihuahua had already taken most of the trade that previously passed through Presidio. In addition, lack of a clear government title to the subpost's land and unsatisfactory quarters for the soldiers convinced the government to close it. The army abandoned the site in 1883.[56]

In the late spring of 1878, Colonel Grierson had ordered Lieutenant Mason Maxon to establish a permanent scouting camp at Peña Blanca, at the head of San Francisco Creek. The camp stood many miles south of Fort Stockton in the Big Bend region, and

Mason Maxon (Fort Davis National
Historic Site).

Colonel Benjamin Grierson (Fort
Davis National Historic Site).

authority alternated between Stockton and Davis. From Peña
Blanca, patrols scouted the surrounding area during the summer
for Indians, water sources, and wagon routes to link the posts and
settlements of the region. Lieutenant Calvin Esterly of Maxon's
command made a number of excellent maps of the water holes and
other natural features found during the scouts.[57]

Maxon lost no time in establishing a strict military routine for
his new camp. He promulgated a daily schedule that had troops up
before sunrise and feeding and grooming their animals before a
six o'clock breakfast. He ordered a formal inspection of the entire
command to be made weekly. All men would bathe at least three
times per week unless excused by the post surgeon.[58]

In August 1878, Maxon left Peña Blanca for Fort Stockton,
but his troops remained.[59] Early in October, an Indian raid from

Mexico into Kerr County prompted Grierson's headquarters to warn the command at Peña Blanca to watch for the war party.[60] The garrison saw little if any action against Indians, however, and road building remained their most important duty. The following year, a company of the Twenty-fifth Infantry occupied Peña Blanca and worked on the road to the post at Peña Colorado, near the town of Marathon.[61] Afterward, army units no longer occupied Peña Blanca.

During Grierson's tenure as commander of the District of the Pecos (1878-1881), Fort Davis maintained a subpost at Pine Spring, sometimes called Bull Spring. The spring lay at the summit of Guadalupe Pass in the range of that name and had served as a stage station for many years.[62] Troops had used the spring as a rendezvous point and temporary camping place on some occasions in earlier years, such as when a sizable detachment of the Ninth Cavalry from Fort Davis and Fort Stockton passed through on a scout in the Guadalupes in April 1870.[63] Permanent use only came during the Apache trouble in the late 1870s.

Elements of the Tenth Cavalry established the subpost at Pine Spring during the first eight months of 1878, and patrols scoured the surrounding country in all directions.[64] The post stood in a strategic location to block Apache movement because of its position astride the route from Fort Stanton and southeastern New Mexico to the Rio Grande. Grierson ordered constant patrols out from Pine Spring to watch for Indian war parties over the next three years.[65] A detachment from one such patrol, under Lieutenant R. E. Safford, Tenth Cavalry, pursued a small party of Indians near Wild Horse Tanks on April 12, 1879. The troops captured the Indians' horses, but the Apaches escaped on foot.[66]

Lieutenant Safford died of illness a short time later while he and his men were camping at Manzanita Springs on the eastern slope of the Guadalupes. On May 9, 1880, Lieutenant Mason Maxon established a semi-permanent scouting camp at the spot and named it Camp Safford in the young officer's memory. From Safford, Maxon and his men engaged in several scouts, on one of which they rode all the way to El Paso and back.[67]

Another subpost existed during the same period at Seven Springs on a branch of the east fork of Toyah Creek.[68] The post stood about twenty miles north of Fort Davis.[69] The springs, all within a one-mile circle, issued from the base of lava mountains north of the main road leading to Toyah. Each flowed above ground for a short distance, none for more than 200 yards, before returning underground. If dug out and enlarged, the largest source of water had the capability of supplying a company of cavalry.[70]

Colonel Grierson placed an infantry company at Seven Springs in the early summer of 1878 to prevent Indians from using the water, to keep them from passing through the surrounding area, and to protect the stage road from Barilla Springs to Limpia Canyon. The army was already using the point as a supply depot for passing cavalry units. Foot soldiers served to guard those supplies.[71]

In addition to the infantry, a small cavalry detachment occupied the subpost. Infantry patrols went out from the post regularly, and smaller daily scouting parties covered the vicinity to a distance of fifteen miles. If any patrol came across Indian sign, one man would return to the camp and alert the cavalry detachment, which would start out on the trail immediately. The cavalrymen kept six days' rations packed and ready constantly for that purpose.[72] Grierson kept units stationed at Seven Springs for most of the next two years, scouting and patrolling the roads in an effort to keep hostile Indians out of the area.[73]

From the mid-1870s through 1880, the army periodically stationed troops at Faver's Ranch, sometimes known as the scouting camp in the Chinati Mountains. The outpost stood about twenty-five miles north of Presidio.[74] Faver's Ranch became a favorite target of Indian raiders after the Civil War. Attacks in 1866 and 1867 resulted in several ranchmen dead and hundreds of head of livestock stolen. Conditions did not improve with time. In March 1870, Indians killed another man and stole 400 head of sheep.[75] Five years later they struck the ranch again with similar results. The army responded by stationing a detachment of troops there.[76]

During the hunt for Victorio, a significant force operated out of the camp, scouting the Chinati Mountains and keeping close watch on the fords of the Rio Grande. Troops of the Tenth Cavalry

William R. Shafter (Fort Davis National Historic Site).

and the First Infantry occupied Faver's Ranch during that period. Lieutenant Colonel W. R. Shafter, commanding the newly formed District of the Bravo, made his headquarters there for a time.[77]

Although the garrison at Faver's Ranch did not engage in a major action against Victorio or any other large party of hostile Indians during the period, they sometimes had to deal with small bands of raiders. In the spring of 1880, a handful of Apaches on foot hit a Mexican family near the Russell Ranch. They killed one boy, took another captive, and stole a horse. The Indians then fled the area, pursued by the boys' father and several other Mexicans. A unit of Seminole Negro scouts and a cavalry detachment joined in the chase, but the Apaches killed the horse and vanished on foot without leaving a trail over the rocky ground.[78]

Briefly during the Victorio campaign of 1880, a detachment of troops held Viejo Pass, a gap in a series of mountain ranges paralleling the Rio Grande. The pass, ten miles west of the present town of Valentine and sixty miles west of Fort Davis, provided a natural avenue for the Apaches through the rugged country along the Mexican border. In addition, a permanent spring furnished water year round.[79]

In early June 1880, a small detail of Pueblo Indian scouts with Lieutenant Frank Mills, Twenty-fourth Infantry, and a few troops camped in Viejo Pass on the way from El Paso to the Fort Davis area. Despite advice from the Pueblos, the lieutenant insisted on camping in an exposed position surrounded by rocky heights. The next morning, a band of Apaches hidden in the rocks above opened fire on the camp, killing Simon Olgin, head of the scouts, and scattering the troops. The remaining scouts returned fire and eventually drove the Apaches away.[80] Captain Louis Carpenter and his company of the Tenth Cavalry at Eagle Springs immediately rode to the site and took up the trail. Although they failed to catch the Apaches, Carpenter's men occupied Viejo Pass, denying the raiders further use of the pass and its water supply for the remainder of the campaign.[81]

Viejo Pass continued to be one of the most strategic points in the region southwest of Fort Davis. Grierson kept elements of the Tenth Cavalry operating in the area well into 1883, long after any major Apache threat had disappeared. He recommended purchasing the site for use as a permanent post, but shortly after that recommendation, the army transferred him and his regiment to Arizona, and nothing came of his suggestion.[82]

For a short time during the Victorio campaign, troops out of Fort Davis maintained a small picket station to watch the Rio Grande at Ojo Caliente, northwest of Viejo Pass and southwest of Van Horn's Wells and the Eagle Mountains. The most costly engagement for Grierson's soldiers in the entire campaign in Texas occurred there on October 28, 1880.[83]

A small detachment of two noncommissioned officers and ten privates formed the picket at Ojo Caliente. Their company commander had detached the men on a scout down the river several days before the fight, and, on October 27, the patrol established a camp at Ojo Caliente for surveillance of the Rio Grande crossing. The next morning a band estimated at between a dozen and fifty Apaches who had earlier broken off from Victorio's party struck the soldiers by surprise. The Indians killed four or five of the troops and captured their animals and much of their equipment. Although cavalry units closed on the spot from three directions, the Apaches vanished into Mexico. From that time on, the army used Ojo Caliente as a temporary picket station.[84]

Of all the outposts of Fort Davis, one had construction rather than combat as its object, and that outpost was referred to as the pinery. Actually, a number of pineries existed during the fort's active years because the supply of timber at one location lasted for a limited time. Soon after companies of the Ninth Cavalry under Lieutenant Colonel Wesley Merritt's command reoccupied Fort Davis, a detail of troops from that regiment began sawmill operations at a site close by to provide materials for new construction.[85] Another pinery, established in October 1870, stood approximately sixteen miles northwest of Fort Davis. Troops from the Twenty-fifth Infantry garrisoned the site to help in the work and to provide protection from Indian attack.[86] The command at Fort Davis pulled out the troops after a few months, but more than a dozen civilians remained to continue work at the mill. Soon they transferred the machinery to a new site, twenty-five miles from the fort where abundant timber stood. In early March 1871, Indians threatened the outpost, causing the civilians to request a detachment of troops or a supply of arms with which to defend themselves.[87]

The pace of operations at the pineries depended upon the amount of construction at Fort Davis. In 1870 and 1871 new buildings went up at the fort, requiring a large amount of lumber. As a result, work at the pinery went forward rapidly. Lumber cut there for new construction included two-by-fours, two-by-sixes, two-by-eights, one-by-sixes, for flooring, and shingles, plus other sizes.[88] Teamsters hauled the timber back to Fort Davis on mule-drawn wagons.[89] Wagons required roads in the Davis Mountain region, and some troops spent a great deal of time building or repairing routes that linked the pineries with the fort. Producing a roadway with a gentle enough grade for heavily laden wagons proved difficult and extremely tiresome. Some soldiers refused to work on the roads. A detail of infantry under Lieutenant Charles R. Ward, Tenth Cavalry, came to the point of mutiny over such a situation and had to be threatened with working under guard before they finally returned to the job.[90]

A new round of construction at Fort Davis and the minor post of Peña Colorado south of the fort in the early 1880s caused the pineries to go into production again. In July 1881, Lieutenant Colonel Shafter sent a company of infantry with the steam sawmill from Fort Davis to an old pinery site thirty miles north in Limpia Canyon, where much timber was still standing. The troops worked feverishly and were shipping thousands of board feet of lumber back to the fort by the end of September.[91]

Lack of funds for repairs at Fort Davis kept the pinery in operation through early 1884, even in the absence of major new construction. The sawmill provided lumber necessary to keep up the fort when the command had no money to purchase wood from civilian contractors.[92] By June, however, the pinery began to close down operations as the men cut the last standing timber in the vicinity. The garrison dismantled the mill's equipment and abandoned the pinery at the end of the month.[93]

CHAPTER 11

FORT QUITMAN, CAMP PEÑA COLORADO, AND FORT HANCOCK

Three minor independent forts in the rugged mountain region south and west of Fort Davis figured prominently in the pacification of West Texas from 1866 to 1886. Fort Quitman, Camp Peña Colorado, and Fort Hancock each functioned as subposts of Fort Davis during certain periods, but they attained their highest levels of importance as independent forts.

In the summer of 1858, the army built Fort Quitman as an independent post guarding the San Antonio-El Paso road at the point where that road first reached the Rio Grande from the east. The post overlooked the river at a location approximately 120 miles west of Fort Davis. Authorities named it after the late Governor John A. Quitman of Mississippi, a general of volunteers in the Mexican War.[1]

Following the Civil War, troops returned to Fort Quitman only after an increase in hostile Indian activity endangered travelers along the San Antonio-El Paso road. On January 1, 1868, F Company, Ninth Cavalry, reactivated the deserted post. Two more companies soon joined the original garrison, bringing the total force to 280 men.[2] In May and June elements of Quitman's garrison guarded Eagle Springs, thirty-seven miles east on the road to Fort Davis. For that brief period Eagle Springs functioned as a subpost of Fort Quitman, but afterward it came under the jurisdiction of Fort Davis.[3]

Troops from Quitman engaged in numerous scouts of the surrounding countryside as summer continued. Indian raids on the mail route increased because of an abundance of good grass and water for the warriors' ponies, and the command at the fort responded by providing more escorts to travelers and mail carriers and sending out additional patrols.[4]

Officers at Quitman faced two problems that had little to do with fighting Indians. First, a number of people on both sides of the border chose to press claims against the United States government for losses incurred before or during the war. Certain Mexican residents of San Lorenzo, a village across the river from the fort, demanded $100,000 for wood and grass supposedly taken by American troops in 1861.[5] The garrison did a great deal of business with the citizens of San Lorenzo and other nearby towns in Mexico, buying fresh vegetables and frequenting saloons and brothels there, but the fort's officers looked on the damage claims as nothing but blatant attempts to swindle the United States government.[6]

Secondly, the buildings at Quitman had lost windows, doors, and even roofs during the years of disuse between 1861 and 1868. Constructed of adobe, some of the structures fell in on their occupants during heavy rains. Many soldiers had to live in tents because of the poor condition of barracks and officers' quarters. As a result of the living conditions, a large percentage of the garrison suffered from illnesses such as dysentery, fever, and bronchitis. The army considered building new structures or overhauling old ones but never put those plans into action. The buildings at Fort Quitman did eventually become more habitable but only because troops made the repairs themselves.[7]

Garrison life at Fort Quitman continued without any great variation or excitement through the early and middle 1870s. At times the post held considerable firepower in the form of two Gatling guns and a pair of three-inch field guns, but the command never had occasion to use them against Indians. Patrols went out frequently, often as far as the Guadalupe Mountains, and sometimes they found Apache war parties or camps. The skirmishes that resulted seldom caused more than one or two casualties on either side. The most exciting event of the fort's tenure involved nature rather than Indian fighting. On the night of February 9, 1873, an earthquake shook the fort for a few seconds, breaking windows and bottles but causing no injuries. Fort Quitman's existence as an independent post came to an end when the Department of Texas deactivated it on January 5, 1877.[8] The army reoccupied Quitman again three years after its deactivation, although as a subpost of Fort Davis rather than an independent fort. Captain L. H. Carpenter visited the abandoned post in early 1880 to determine whether the army should reactivate it for use against Victorio's Apaches. The government decided against full restoration, but Colonel Benjamin Grierson, commanding the District of the Pecos, stationed company-sized detachments there throughout the Victorio campaign.[9]

The pace of operations at Quitman reached its maximum during July and August 1880. At the end of July, troops from Quitman helped Grierson and a small detachment at Tinaja de las Palmas, east of the subpost, turn Victorio's band back from water and force them to cross the Rio Grande.[10] A few days later, conditions reached their most critical point around Fort Quitman. Apaches killed James J. Byrne, a Civil War major general and a railroad employee in 1880, during an attack on a stagecoach near the fort on August 9. Two days later the commanding officer at Quitman reported that Indians had the fort under virtual siege.[11]

The crisis diminished over the next few days as Grierson's units again forced the Apaches into Mexico. With Victorio's defeat and death at the hands of Mexican troops in the fall of 1880, the major threat from hostile Indians in the region ended. A detachment remained at Quitman, but the troops spent most of their time guarding strategic points or providing escorts for parties working on the Texas & Pacific Railroad. The command even maintained a small outpost of its own at Carrizo Pass during the summer of 1881. By the following summer, lack of a real Indian threat nearby caused military authorities to transfer the remaining troops at Quitman. On July 10, 1882, the last soldiers marched out of the post and started for Camp Rice, farther up the Rio Grande.[12]

Far to the east of old Fort Quitman, the army established the second minor independent post in the region at Peña Colorado, near present-day Marathon. Colonel Grierson ordered two companies to the site in late 1879, when troubles with Apaches in the region were increasing. The presence of a military force there denied water from Maravillas Creek and Rainbow Springs to Indians operating southeast of Fort Davis. Equally important, troops at Peña Colorado, or Rainbow Cliffs, began building a long section of a new military road linking San Antonio with El Paso. The new road provided a shorter, more direct route east and west, and Peña Colorado stood in the middle of one of its longest segments.[13]

Located approximately fifty miles southeast of Fort Davis and sixty miles southwest of Fort Stockton, Camp Peña Colorado had good communications with both. It served as a subpost of Davis during much of the early part of its existence but attained independent status in mid-1884.[14] The camp lay in a small valley ringed by hills, which protected it from surrounding desert.[15]

Stone provided the first and most logical building material for the structures at the post. Troops quarried the stone from a small hill less than a mile from the camp and constructed small huts to serve as quarters. Lack of wood forced the soldiers to roof their huts with mud and grass, a poor material during the area's brief but dramatic rain storms. Over a long period, the command at Peña Colorado replaced their cruder dwellings with more substantial structures.[16] Fort Davis supplied hinges, windows, and other materials; the pinery provided rafters, poles, and wooden slabs for roofing the stables. On one trip, five wagons from Peña Colorado hauled almost 300 slabs from the pinery for that purpose.[17]

The layout of Camp Peña Colorado resembled that of the major forts on the frontier, except on a smaller scale. Two enlisted barracks stood on one of the long sides of a rectangle facing three small officers' quarters across the parade ground. Storage and utility buildings occupied the short east side of the parade ground, and the post hospital stood on the west. The camp maintained a remote sentry post approximately one-half mile to the east.[18] Troops dug a well at the springs to provide an abundant source of water, and guardhouse prisoners had the task of hauling that water to camp every day in a water cart. Private contractors provided some firewood, but the government also maintained a mule-driven treadmill saw to cut cordwood.[19]

Camp Peña Colorado began as an infantry post, its garrison well suited to the command's primary mission of road building. Cavalry units came there eventually, however, and the troopers engaged in scouting and the pursuit of hostile Indians. No important actions took place between troops from the post and Apache war parties, but the garrison did contribute to the pacification of the region by its regular patrols.[20] Peña Colorado also helped pacify its portion of the trans-Pecos area by maintaining several outposts. Those included Collins Spring, Andrews Gap, Willow Springs, and Nevill's Spring. In March 1880, F Company, Twenty-fifth Infantry, occupied Collins Spring. In April they moved camp six miles to Andrews Gap and remained there on detached service until the middle of May, when the outpost closed permanently.[21]

The command at Peña Colorado also maintained a scouting post at Nevill's Spring, deep in the Big Bend country. In response to the murder of a family named Petty by renegade Indians in the area in November 1884, the army established a scouting camp at Willow Springs, a spot destitute of water and wood despite its name.[22] A detachment of Seminole Negro scouts and ten enlisted men of the Tenth Cavalry formed the first garrison.[23] A few weeks later the garrison transferred to a better location at Nevill's Spring, where it remained for many years.[24] Seminole Negro scouts continued to form the primary force operating out of Nevill's Spring during its entire existence, but those men traveled to their headquarters at Fort Clark periodically to be paid. In the absence of the scouts, details from Peña Colorado garrisoned Nevill's Spring and maintained surveillance of the area.[25]

Camp Peña Colorado outlasted Fort Davis as an active military post. The army abandoned Davis in 1891, but Peña Colorado remained for two more years as the army's main post in the Davis Mountain-Big Bend area.[26]

The third minor independent post in the region, Fort Hancock, stood on the Rio Grande fifteen miles upstream from Fort Quitman.[27] Originally known as Camp Rice, the post received the name Fort Hancock on May 14, 1886, in memory of Major General Winfield Scott Hancock.[28] Camp Rice began as a camp on the Southern Pacific Railroad approximately thirty-seven miles

The officers' quarters at Fort Hancock (Fort Davis National Historic Site).

northwest of Sierra Blanca, Texas. An army scouting party sent out to locate a spot for a new post to replace Fort Quitman in late April 1882 selected a site near the railroad camp. Plentiful wood and water existed at the new location, and it provided an excellent vantage point from which troops could monitor Rio Grande crossings in the area.[29] In early July, Quitman's garrison transferred to their new post.[30]

High water threatened the camp shortly after its establishment and forced the garrison to shift its location a short distance away to higher ground in August.[31] The men had few comforts at the new fort. They lived in tents for the first few months, and only in November did the command take steps to procure lumber for temporary quarters. The weather had turned cold by that time, and the troops suffered considerably from the lack of adequate shelter. No one among the garrison had training in carpentry, so the command had to beg the services of a skilled carpenter along with the building materials.[32] Improvements came very slowly. By the following September, the men still had canvas roofs over their quarters, and those roofs had started to leak badly.[33] Adequate living quarters at Camp Rice remained a problem for a long time.

Despite uncomfortable conditions, the garrison at Camp Rice provided an active deterrent to Indian raiders and occasional groups of Mexican bandits operating along the Rio Grande. Small patrols from the fort combed the area north of the river on a monthly basis during the first two years of the post's existence. By 1884, the garrison began to reduce its scouting activity because a large number of ranches had been established in the region, and increased settlement had helped diminish the danger from raiders.[34]

That same year, Camp Rice became an independent post, no longer under the control of Fort Davis. Under its new name, Fort Hancock, it outlasted both Davis and Peña Colorado, remaining an active military post until 1895.[35]

The three minor forts aided in the pacification of their section of the frontier as much by the outgrowths of their presence as by the actual military force they brought to bear against the Apaches. Those outgrowths included road building, in the case of Camp Peña Colorado, and protection of the railroad by Fort Hancock. All three posts, by their mere presence, encouraged settlement by growing numbers of ranchers. As the country became more populated, hostile Indians found it more difficult and dangerous to continue raiding in the trans-Pecos region. Thus, just as they had done elsewhere on the frontier, the dual forces of settlement and military power worked together to pacify far West Texas.

POSTSCRIPT

Few signs of the outposts remain today. Some of the more prominent ones, such as Grierson's Spring, have historical markers standing near the ruins. Stone walls and foundations last, but those of wood and adobe have disappeared over time. Of course, by their very nature outposts were designed to be temporary. Human beings made use of them for a few months or a few years then moved on.

It is only in connection with those people who lived, worked, and fought there that the outposts still have any significance. The heritage and the sacrifices of those men deserve recognition. For two decades following the Civil War they were there in the most remote reaches of the Texas frontier, standing in the gap.

CHAPTER 1

1. B. Hutchins to Assistant Adjutant General, District of Texas, May 18, 1867, Records of Fort Richardson, Texas, Record Group 393, National Archives (hereafter cited as RFRT) (Microfilm in possession of Texas Parks and Wildlife Department, Austin).

2. R. M. Morris to Louis Caziare, February 14, 1869, RFRT; James Oakes to C. E. Morse, May 15, 1869, RFRT.

3. W. H. Wood to Acting Assistant Adjutant General, Department of Texas, January 2, 1873, and January 12, 1873, RFRT. See Thomas T. Smith, *The U.S. Army and the Texas Frontier Economy* (College Station: Texas A&M University Press, 1999), for a discussion on how the army procured horses in Texas.

4. George Gamble to Post Adjutant, Fort Stockton, August 2, 1867, Headquarters Records of Fort Stockton, Record Group 393, National Archives (hereafter cited as HRFS) Microfilm M-1189.

5. Don Rickey, Jr., *Forty Miles a Day on Beans and Hay: The Enlisted Soldier Fighting the Indian Wars* (Norman: University of Oklahoma Press, 1963), 244-45.

6. John R. Hutto, "Pioneering of the Texas and Pacific," *West Texas Historical Association Year Book* 12 (July 1936): 125-27.

7. Robert Wooster, *The Military and United States Indian Policy 1865-1903* (New Haven: Yale University Press, 1988), 123-24. Further information on the use of railroads to supply the army in Texas is found in Smith, *U.S. Army*, 44-45.

8. Emmett M. Essin, III, "Mules, Packs, and Packtrains," *Southwestern Historical Quarterly* 74 (July 1970): 53.

9. Ibid., 53, 62.

10. W. Turrentine Jackson, *Wagon Roads West: A Study of Federal Road Surveys and Construction in the Trans-Mississippi West 1846-1869* (Berkeley: University of California Press, 1952), 44-45.

11. Arlen L. Fowler, *The Black Infantry in the West 1869-1891* (Westport, Connecticut: Greenwood Publishing Corporation, 1971), 24.

12. Frank M. Temple, "Colonel B. H. Grierson's Administration of the District of the Pecos," *West Texas Historical Association Year Book* 38 (October 1962): 89-94.

13. House, *Report of the Secretary of War*, 41st Cong., 1870, H. Exec. Doc. 1, pt. 2, 41.

14. L. Tuffly Ellis, ed., "Lieutenant A. W. Greely's Report on the Installation of Military Telegraph Lines in Texas, 1875-1876," *Southwestern Historical Quarterly* 69 (July 1965): 71.

15. Ibid., Map following page 76; House, *Report of the Secretary of War*, 44th Cong., 2d sess., 1876, H. Exec. Doc. 1, pt. 2, Map 49 (Copy in "United States Military Telegraph Records," box 3H137, Center for American History, University of Texas at Austin).

16. Temple, "Grierson's Administration," 93. See Smith, *U.S. Army*, 166-69, for additional information on the establishment of the military telegraph network in Texas.

17. Roy Eugene Graham, "Federal Fort Architecture in Texas during the Nineteenth Century," *Southwestern Historical Quarterly* 74 (October 1970): 166-67.

18. A. B. Bender, "Opening Routes across West Texas, 1848-1850," *Southwestern Historical Quarterly* 37 (October 1933):128-29.

19. Robert Wooster, *Soldiers, Sutlers, and Settlers: Garrison Life on the Texas Frontier* (College Station: Texas A&M University Press, 1987), 8.

20. Graham, "Federal Fort Architecture," 167.

21. Ibid.

22. W. Eugene Hollon, *Beyond the Cross Timbers: The Travels of Randolph B. Marcy, 1812-1887* (Norman: University of Oklahoma Press, 1955), 116, 122.

23. Rupert N. Richardson, *The Frontier of Northwest Texas 1846 to 1876* (Glendale, California: The Arthur H. Clark Company, 1963), 71-72.

24. Wooster, *Soldiers, Sutlers, and Settlers*, 9-10.

25. Ibid., 10.

26. Graham, "Federal Fort Architecture," 169.

27. B. W. Aston, "Federal Military Reoccupation of the Texas Southwestern Frontier, 1865-1871," *Texas Military History* 8 (1970): 125-26.

28. Ibid., 126-27.

29. Ibid., 127-30.

30. W. C. Holden, "Frontier Defense, 1865-1889," *Panhandle-Plains Historical Review* 2 (1929): 50-53.

31. Francis Paul Prucha, *A Guide to the Military Posts of the United States 1789-1895* (Madison: The State Historical Society of Wisconsin, 1964), 73, 77-78.

32. Holden, "Frontier Defense, 1865-1889," 53.

33. Graham, "Federal Fort Architecture," 176-83.

34. Wooster, *Soldiers, Sutlers, and Settlers*, 10-11.

35. Graham, "Federal Fort Architecture," 176-77.

36. Ibid., 183.

37. House, *Report of the Secretary of War*, 42d Cong., 2d sess., 1871, H. Exec. Doc. 1, pt. 2, 37; Robert M. Utley, *Frontier Regulars: The United States Army and the Indian 1866-1891* (New York: MacMillan Publishing Company, 1973), 46-47.

38. Utley, *Frontier Regulars*, 46-47.

39. Ibid.

40. House, *Report of the Secretary of War*, 1871, 65. A thought-provoking analysis of the army's methods and tactics and its use of forts in Texas, both before and after the Civil War, can be found in Thomas T. Smith, "Fort Inge and Texas Frontier Military Operations, 1849-1869," *Southwestern Historical Quarterly* 96 (July 1992): 1-26. Further information on the subject, covering an expanded time period, is presented in Thomas T. Smith, "U. S. Army Combat Operations in the Indian Wars of Texas, 1849-1881," *Southwestern Historical Quarterly* 99 (April 1996): 501-32.

41. House, *Report of the Secretary of War*, 42d Cong., 3d sess., 1872, H. Exec. Doc. 1, pt. 2, 54-55.

42. Commanding Officer, Fort Richardson, to Adjutant General, United States Army, June 29, 1872, RFRT.

CHAPTER 2

1. T. N. Campbell and William T. Field, "Identification of Comanche Raiding Trails in Trans-Pecos Texas," *West Texas Historical Association Year Book* 44 (October 1968): 129.

2. James Parker, *The Old Army: Memories 1872-1918* (Philadelphia: Dorrance and Company, 1929), 32.

3. Campbell and Field, "Identification of Comanche Raiding Trails," 129-30.

4. Ibid., 130.

5. Ibid., 130-34.

6. Ibid., 132-34.

7. Roscoe P. Conkling and Margaret B. Conkling, *The Butterfield Overland Mail 1857-1869* (Glendale, California: The Arthur H. Clark Company, 1947), vol. 2, 13-16.

8. Edward Hatch to A. H. M. Taylor, July 7, 1867, Headquarters Records of Fort Stockton, Record Group 393, National Archives (hereafter cited as HRFS) (microfilm M-1189).

9. Francis B. Heitman, *Historical Register and Dictionary of the United States Army, from its Organization, September 29, 1789, to March 2, 1903* (Washington: Government Printing Office, 1903), 510. A fuller treatment of Hatch's Civil War exploits is contained in Charles L. Kenner, *Buffalo Soldiers and Officers of the Ninth Cavalry 1867-1898: Black and White Together* (Norman: University of Oklahoma Press, 1999), 30-41.

10. Edward Hatch to A. H. M. Taylor, July 13, 1867, HRFS.

11. Ibid.

12. Edward Hatch to George Gamble, September 13, 1867, HRFS; for Gamble see, Heitman, *Historical Register and Dictionary of the United States Army*, 444. Gamble had risen through the ranks in an Illinois cavalry regiment during the Civil

War. He received a captain's commission in the Ninth shortly after the war's end.

13. Edward Hatch to Acting Assistant Adjutant General, District of Texas, September 16, 1867, HRFS.

14. Edward Hatch to A. H. M. Taylor, October 24, 1867, HRFS.

15. Edward Hatch to C. E. Morse, November 18, 1867, HRFS.

16. Ibid.

17. Wesley Merritt to Acting Assistant Adjutant General, Department of Texas, February 14, 1872, HRFS.

18. Heitman, *Historical Register and Dictionary of the United States Army*, 897.

19. Francis Moon to Fred Smith, July 30, 1867, HRFS.

20. M. M. Maxon, "Twenty Years in the Saddle: Reminiscences of His Military Experience 1869 to 1889," Maxon Family Papers, Fort Davis National Historic Site.

21. Mrs. O. L. Shipman, *Taming the Big Bend: A History of the Extreme Western Portion of Texas from Fort Clark to El Paso* (n.p.: n.p., 1926), 43.

22. Frohock had seen extensive combat in the Civil War and received brevets for gallantry at Shiloh and the siege of Vicksburg. He served as colonel in command of a black infantry regiment through most of 1864 and ended the war as a brevet brigadier general of volunteers. Heitman, *Historical Register and Dictionary of the United States Army*, 438. More information on Frohock can be found in Kenner, *Buffalo Soldiers and Officers*, 80-81.

23. W. F. Frohock to John Land, December 27, 1867, HRFS.

24. Ibid.

25. Ibid.

26. William H. Leckie, *The Buffalo Soldiers: A Narrative of the Negro Cavalry in the West* (Norman: University of Oklahoma Press, 1967), 85.

27. Ninth Cavalry Regimental Returns, October 1867, RG 94, National Archives (Microfilm M744, roll 87). Thomas T. Smith, *The U.S. Army and the Texas Frontier Economy 1845-1900* (College Station: Texas A&M University Press, 1999), 158-61, contains a useful description of the stagecoach and mail systems on the frontier.

28. Clayton W. Williams, *Texas' Last Frontier: Fort Stockton and the Trans-Pecos, 1861-1895*, edited by Ernest Wallace (College Station: Texas A&M University Press, 1982), 98.

29. John Loud to Commanding Officer, Fort Stockton, January 10, 1870, HRFS.

30. Michael Corney to Patrick Cusack, November 15, 1870, HRFS.

31. James H. Carleton to H. Clay Wood, December 23, 1870, HRFS.

32. H. Clay Wood to Commanding Officer, Fort Stockton, April 27, 1871, HRFS.

33. E. D. Townsend to Commanding Officer, Fort Stockton, August 16, 1871, HRFS.

34. Don Rickey, Jr., *Forty Miles a Day on Beans and Hay: The Enlisted Soldier Fighting the Indian Wars* (Norman: University of Oklahoma Press, 1963), 119.

35. J. F. Wade to Assistant Adjutant General, Department of Texas, June 24, 1871, HRFS.

36. Ninth Cavalry Regimental Returns, February 1868. For a discussion of the need for fruits and vegetables in the diet of troops on the frontier, see Michael L. Tate, *The Frontier Army in the Settlement of the West* (Norman: University of Oklahoma Press, 1999), 164-65.

37. Louis Johnson to Post Adjutant, Fort Stockton, December 1, 1871, HRFS.

38. A German immigrant like many soldiers of the period, Johnson had proved to be an able officer during the Civil War. Meritorious service in battles at Mill Springs and Missionary Ridge had brought him promotion, including command of a black infantry regiment in 1864. After the war, he reverted to the rank of lieutenant in the Forty-first Infantry, also a black regiment. Heitman, *Historical Register and Dictionary of the United States Army*, 576.

39. Louis Johnson to Post Adjutant, Fort Stockton, December 13, 1871, HRFS.

40. "Inspection Report of Fort Stockton Texas for the Month of November 1871" (extract), HRFS.

41. John S. Loud to Commanding Officer, Company G, Twenty-fourth Infantry, January 2, 1872, HRFS.

42. W. R. Shafter to M. M. Blunt, telegram, April 12, 1879, HRFS. For a narrative of Shafter's career, including extensive coverage of his years on the Texas frontier, see Paul H. Carlson, *Pecos Bill: A Military Biography of William R. Shafter* (College Station: Texas A&M University Press, 1989).

43. Joseph Worsh to M. M. Blunt, April 15, 1879, HRFS.

44. After serving as a company commander of black infantry during the Civil War, Bullis won a regular commission in the Forty-first Infantry. Over the next fourteen years he was cited for gallantry in no less than four engagements with hostile Indians in Texas and Mexico. Heitman, *Historical Register and Dictionary of the United States Army*, 261. Detailed narratives of the history of the Seminole Negro Indian scouts appear in Kevin Mulroy, *Freedom on the Border: The Seminole Maroons in Florida, the Indian Territory, Coahuila, and Texas* (Lubbock: Texas Tech University Press, 1993); Frank N. Schubert, *Black Valor: Buffalo Soldiers and the Medal of Honor, 1870-1898* (Wilmington, Delaware: SR Books, 1997); and Kenneth Wiggins Porter, "The Seminole Negro-Indian Scouts," *Southwestern Historical Quarterly* 55 (January 1952): 358-77. A more concise history is in Ron Tyler, et al., *The New Handbook of Texas*, vol. 1, 571-73. See also Edward S. Wallace, "General John Lapham Bullis, the Thunderbolt of the Texas Frontier, I," *Southwestern Historical Quarterly* 54 (April 1951): 452-61, about Bullis' early life in New York and his Civil War record; Edward S. Wallace, "General John Lapham Bullis, the Thunderbolt of the Texas Frontier, II," *Southwestern Historical Quarterly* 55 (July 1951): 77-85, for his experiences in Texas; and Tyler, *The New Handbook of Texas*, vol. 1, 823-24.

45. Heitman, *Historical Register and Dictionary of the United States Army*, 698.

46. Thomas Vincent to District Commander, Fort Stockton, telegram, April 30, 1879, HRFS.

47. Williams, *Texas' Last Frontier*, 98.

48. Edward Hatch to George Gamble, July 1, 1868, HRFS.

49. Roscoe P. Conkling and Margaret B. Conkling, *The Butterfield Overland Mail 1857-1869*, vol. 3 (Glendale, California: The Arthur H. Clark Company, 1947), sheet 1.

50. Rudolfo Gausetsky to E. Dimmick, October 1, 1868, HRFS.

51. James Wade to C. E. Morse, June 16, 1869, HRFS.

52. Post Adjutant, Fort Stockton, to Commanding Officer, K Company, Twenty-fifth Infantry Regiment, November 8, 1873, HRFS.

53. Lieutenant Thomas Davenport, "Journal of the March of a Detachment of Company M, Ninth Cavalry, from Fort Stockton to Independence Creek," February 1874, HRFS.

54. Charles Gallagher to Commanding Officer, Fort Stockton, April 15, 1878, HRFS; B. H. Grierson to Commanding Officer, Fort Stockton, telegram, April 15, 1878, HRFS.

55. Robert G. Smither to Commanding Officer, Fort Stockton, July 25, 1879. HRFS; John Wright to Adjutant, Fort Stockton, August 24, 1879, HRFS.

56. George A. Armes, *Ups and Downs of an Army Officer* (Washington: n.p., 1900), 519-21.

57. "Scout of Detachment of Company M, Ninth Cavalry" March 1874, HRFS.

58. Ibid.

59. Robert Smither to Commanding Officer, Fort Stockton, telegram, June 4, 1879, HRFS. Information on daily routine and living conditions at Camp Santa Rosa is available in Marcos E. Kinevan, *Frontier Cavalryman: Lieutenant John Bigelow with the Buffalo Soldiers in Texas* (El Paso: Texas Western Press, 1998), 204-07.

60. House, *Report of the Secretary of War*, 46th Cong., 2d sess., 1879, H. Exec. Doc. 1, pt. 2, 113.

61. Calvin Esterly to Acting Assistant Adjutant General, District of the Pecos, September 10, 1879, HRFS.

62. Heitman, *Historical Register and Dictionary of the United States Army*, 408, 677.

63. John Bigelow to Adjutant General, Department of Texas, December 9, 1879, HRFS.

64. George Armes to Adjutant, Fort Stockton, June 5, 1879, HRFS.

65. Ibid., June 16, 1879, HRFS.

66. T. M. Vincent to Commanding Officer, Fort Stockton, June 14, 1879, HRFS.

67. Ibid., June 21, 1879, HRFS. For a thorough account of the early life and later military career of the contentious Captain Armes, see Bruce Dinges, "The Irrepressible Captain Armes: Politics and Justice in the Indian-Fighting Army," *Journal of the West* 32 (April 1993): 38-53.

68. Wesley Merritt to Louis Johnson, March 19, 1872, HRFS.

69. Louis Johnson to Post Adjutant, Fort Stockton, March 26, 1872, HRFS.

70. Ninth Cavalry Regimental Returns, April 1872. A native of Prince Edward Island in Canada, Vincent had come to Missouri and spent the Civil War in the state militia. He served in the Ninth Cavalry from 1867 until his death. Heitman, *Historical Register and Dictionary of the United States Army*, 987.

71. Ira Trask to Louis Johnson, June 4, 1868, HRFS.

72. Louis Johnson to Ira Trask, June 14, 1868, HRFS.

73. A description of the bridge and its function can be found in Tate, *Frontier Army*, 61-62.

CHAPTER 3

1. Fort Clark Post Returns, December 1866, RG 94, National Archives (Microfilm M-617, Roll 214).

2. Ibid., March 1867, April 1868.

3. House, *Report of the Secretary of War*, 40th Cong., 3d sess., 1868, H. Exec. Doc. 1, 711.

4. Paul H. Carlson, "William R. Shafter, Black Troops, and the Opening of the Llano Estacado, 1870-1875," *Panhandle-Plains Historical Review* 47 (1974): 3.

5. Charles M. Robinson, *Frontier Forts of Texas* (Houston: Lone Star Books, 1986), 48.

6. Don E. Alberts, *Brandy Station to Manila Bay: A Biography of General Wesley Merritt* (Austin: Presidial Press, 1980), 207.

7. Mrs. Orsemus Bronson Boyd, *Cavalry Life in Tent and Field* (1894; reprint, with an introduction by Darlis A. Miller, Lincoln: University of Nebraska Press, 1982), 292-93.

8. For a detailed account of the raid against the Kickapoos, see Ernest Wallace, *Ranald S. Mackenzie on the Texas Frontier* (Lubbock: West Texas Museum Association, 1964), 92-104. Excellent narratives of Mackenzie's outstanding, but sad, career are in Michael D. Pierce, *The Most Promising Young Officer: A Life of Ranald Slidell Mackenzie* (Norman: University of Oklahoma Press, 1993); and Charles M. Robinson, III, *Bad Hand: A Biography of General Ranald S. Mackenzie* (Austin: State House Press, 1993).

9. James Parker, *The Old Army: Memories 1872-1918* (Philadelphia: Dorrance and Company, 1929), 44-45.

10. Robinson, *Frontier Forts*, 47.

11. Leon C. Metz, *Border: The U.S.-Mexico Line* (El Paso: Mangan Books,

1989), 162. Further information on the raid and the role played by the Seminole Negro scouts in it is contained in Ernest Wallace and Adrian Anderson, "R. S. Mackenzie and the Kickapoos: The Raid into Mexico in 1873," *Arizona and the West* 7 (summer 1965): 105-26; and in Kevin Mulroy, *Freedom on the Border: The Seminole Maroons in Florida, the Indian Territory, Coahuila, and Texas* (Lubbock: Texas Tech University Press, 1993), 117-21, 162-63. For a discussion of the diplomatic ramifications of such cross-border raids, see Robert Wooster, "The Army and the Politics of Expansion: Texas and the Southwestern Borderlands, 1870-1886," *Southwestern Historical Quarterly* 93 (October 1989): 151-68.

12. Mrs. O. L. Shipman, *Taming the Big Bend: A History of the Extreme Western Portion of Texas from Fort Clark to El Paso* (n.p., 1926), 43.

13. Alex L. ter Braake, *Texas: The Drama of Its Postal Past* (State College, Pennsylvania: The American Philatelic Society, 1970), 256. Additional information can be found in *The New Handbook of Texas*, "Camp Hudson," by Julia Cauble Smith.

14. Alberts, *Brandy Station*, 189.

15. Fort Hudson Post Returns, June 1867, RG 94, National Archives, (Microfilm M617, Roll 495).

16. Francis B. Heitman, *Historical Register and Dictionary of the United States Army, From Its Organization, September 29, 1789, to March 2, 1903* (Washington, Government Printing Office, 1903), 179. Bacon capped his service with promotion to brigadier general of volunteers during the war with Spain in 1898.

17. Ibid., 376. The highlight of Dodge's army career came in the fall of 1879 when, still in command of D Company of the Ninth, he led his unit to rescue hard-pressed troops under Major Thomas T. Thornburgh near the White River Agency in Colorado. For his gallantry in the desperate, three-day fight with hostile Indians, Dodge won the Congressional Medal of Honor.

18. Ninth Cavalry Regimental Returns, July 1867, RG 94, National Archives (Microfilm M744, Roll 87).

19. Ibid., October-November 1867.

20. Fort Hudson Post Returns, October-December 1867.

21. Ibid., February 1868.

22. Fort Clark Post Returns, April 1868.

23. Ibid., May 1871. Pettie had served most of the preceding ten years in the infantry, winning distinction in the Battle of Gettysburg. Heitman, *Historical Register and Dictionary of the United States Army*, 786.

24. Allen Lee Hamilton, *Sentinel of the Southern Plains: Fort Richardson and the Northwest Texas Frontier, 1866-1878* (Fort Worth: Texas Christian University Press, 1988), 65-83. Sherman was inspecting the frontier in response to reports that Indians from north of the Red River were decimating settlements in the northwestern Texas frontier zone.

25. Fort Clark Post Returns, June 1871-January 1872.

26. Ibid., February 1872.

27. Wesley Merritt to Louis Johnson, March 19, 1872, Headquarters Records of Fort Stockton, Record Group 393, National Archives (hereafter cited as HRFS) (microfilm M-1189).

28. Paul H. Carlson, "William R. Shafter: Military Commander in the American West" (Ph.D. diss., Texas Tech University, 1973), 186-88.

29. James Wade to C. E. Morse, June 16, 1869, HRFS.

30. Grover C. Ramsey, "Camp Melvin, Crockett County, Texas," *West Texas Historical Association Year Book* 37 (October 1961): 137.

31. Edward Hatch to George Gamble, July 1, 1868, HRFS.

32. Ira Trask to Robert Neely, August 31, 1868, HRFS. For more information on this outpost, which became known as Camp Melvin, see *The New Handbook of Texas*, s.v. "Camp Melvin," by Julia Cauble Smith.

33. Rudolfo Gausetsky to E. Dimmick, October 1, 1868, HRFS.

34. S. E. Armstrong to E. D. Dimmick, October 10, 1868, HRFS.

35. James Wade to C. E. Morse, June 16, 1869, HRFS.

36. E. D. Judd to H. C. Wood, November 11, 1869, HRFS.

37. Ramsey, "Camp Melvin," 139. Information on Pecos Bridge can be found in Michael L. Tate, *The Frontier Army in the Settlement of the West* (Norman: University of Oklahoma Press, 1999), 61-62.

38. Robert G. Smither to Commanding Officer, Fort Stockton, August 16, 1880, HRFS.

39. Ramsey, "Camp Melvin," 141-44.

40. L. E. Edwards to Commandant [sic] of Fort Stockton, March 22, 1873, HRFS.

41. Post Adjutant, Fort Stockton, to Commanding Officer, K Company, Twenty-fifth Infantry Regiment, November 8, 1873, HRFS.

42. Ninth Cavalry Regimental Returns, November 1867; Shipman, *Taming the Big Bend*, 43.

43. Fort Hudson Post Returns, December 1867.

44. Ninth Cavalry Regimental Returns, April 1868.

45. Ibid., December 1868.

46. John Loud to Commanding Officer, Fort Stockton, January 10, 1870, HRFS.

47. Shipman, *Taming the Big Bend*, 46-47.

48. Fort Clark Post Returns, March 1876.

49. J. H. Taylor to Commanding Officer, Fort Stockton, March 23, 1876, HRFS.

50. James B. Gillett, *Six Years with the Texas Rangers 1875 to 1881*, M. M. Quaife, ed. (New Haven: Yale University Press, 1925), 86-87.

51. R. F. O'Beice to Adjutant General, Department of Texas, July 11, 1880, HRFS.

52. Fort Clark Post Returns, February 1881.

53. Ibid., April-July 1881.

54. Ibid., August-December 1881.

55. George A. Armes, *Ups and Downs of an Army Officer* (Washington: n.p., 1900), 520-21.

56. Allan A. Stovall, *Nueces Headwater Country: A Regional History* (San Antonio: The Naylor Company, 1959).

57. Fort Clark Post Returns, May-December 1871.

58. R. F. O'Beice to Adjutant General, Department of Texas, July 11, 1880, HRFS.

59. Fort Clark Post Returns, March 1873-February 1876.

60. Ibid., May 1878-February 1881.

61. Fort Hudson Post Returns, November 1867.

62. Ibid., January 1868.

63. Wesley Merritt to Louis Johnson, March 19, 1872, HRFS.

64. Fort Clark Post Returns, May 1878.

65. Ibid., September 1872-December 1881; Special Orders No. 21, Fort McKavett, February 1, 1872, Fort McKavett Post Records, Record Group 393, National Archives (microfilm in possession of Texas Tech University).

66. Gillett, *Six Years*, 207-208.

CHAPTER 4

1. Jerry M. Sullivan, *Fort McKavett: A Texas Frontier Post* (Austin: Texas Parks and Wildlife Department, n.d.), 27-28. Beaumont had graduated from West Point just weeks after the battle at Fort Sumter and gained an immediate assignment with the First Cavalry. A few months later the army transferred him to the Fourth Cavalry, where he served for almost two years. He distinguished himself in numerous engagements throughout the war, including an attack that he led against a rebel battery at the Harpeth River in Tennessee, which resulted in capture of the battery. Beaumont received the Congressional Medal of Honor for that action. At the conclusion of the war he rejoined the Fourth Cavalry for several years' service. By the end of his career, he had risen to the rank of lieutenant colonel of the Third Cavalry. Francis B. Heitman, *Historical Register and Dictionary of the United States Army, From Its Organization, September 29, 1789, to March 2, 1903* (Washington: Government Printing Office, 1903), 204.

2. Sullivan, *Fort McKavett*, 28.

3. Boehm had entered the service in 1858 as a private and continued in that rank until just weeks before Lee's surrender at Appomattox. Finally gaining a

commission in a New York regiment, he became aide-de-camp to General George A. Custer with the Army of the Potomac. A month later, at the end of March 1865, he won the Congressional Medal of Honor for rallying a retreating unit and holding his position in the face of a determined Confederate attack. Heitman, *Historical Register and Dictionary of the United States Army*, 227.

4. E. B. Beaumont to J. A. Potter, August 31, 1868, Records of Fort McKavett, Texas, Record Group 393, National Archives (hereafter cited as RFMT) (microfilm in possession of Texas Tech University, Lubbock, and Texas Parks and Wildlife Department, Austin).

5. Sullivan, *Fort McKavett*, 28-30.

6. H. B. Clitz to Assistant Adjutant General, Department of Texas, September 13, 1875, RFMT. In his thirty years of commissioned service to that time, Clitz had faced his share of difficult situations. Graduating from West Point just in time for the Mexican War, he received a brevet to first lieutenant for heroism at Cerro Gordo on Winfield Scott's route to Mexico City. Three additional citations for gallantry came during the Civil War, one leading to temporary promotion to brigadier general. Heitman, *Historical Register and Dictionary of the United States Army*, 311.

7. Sullivan, *Fort McKavett*, 37-38; Fort McKavett Post Returns, March 1880, Record Group 94, National Archives (Microfilm M-617, Roll 688).

8. Fort Clark Post Returns, January-February 1872, Record Group 94, National Archives (Microfilm M-617, Roll 214).

9. Sullivan, *Fort McKavett*, 35.

10. Special Orders No. 6, Fort McKavett, April 21, 1868, RFMT; H. B. Clitz to Assistant Adjutant General, Department of Texas, July 17, 1877, RFMT.

11. Special Orders No. 6, Fort McKavett, April 21, 1868, RFMT.

12. R. S. Mackenzie to H. Clay Wood, July 14, 1869, RFMT.

13. Ibid.

14. Henry Carroll to C. E. Morse, June 29, 1869, RFMT.

15. R. S. Mackenzie to H. Clay Wood, July 14, 1869, RFMT.

16. Post Adjutant, Fort McKavett, to J. L. Bullis, July 25, 1869, RFMT.

17. R. S. Mackenzie to R. F. Ficklin, August 1, 1869, RFMT.

18. R. S. Mackenzie to H. Clay Wood, August 23, 1869, RFMT.

19. Special Orders No. 123, Fort McKavett, November 12, 1869, RFMT.

20. John M. Carroll, ed., *The Black Military Experience in the American West* (New York: Liveright, 1971), 403-04. For more detailed information on Emanuel Stance's rowdy military career, see Charles L. Kenner, *Buffalo Soldiers and Officers of the Ninth Cavalry 1867-1898: Black and White Together* (Norman: University of Oklahoma Press, 1999), 159-63, 172-73; and Frank N. Schubert, *Black Valor: Buffalo Soldiers and the Medal of Honor, 1870-1898* (Wilmington, Delaware: SR Books, 1997), 9-26.

21. Post Adjutant, Fort McKavett, to H. B. Chamberlain, April 1, 1874, RFMT.

22. Thomas M. Anderson to Assistant Adjutant General, Department of Texas, October 22, 1876, RFMT.

23· H. B. Clitz to Assistant Adjutant General, Department of Texas, July 17, 1877, RFMT.

24. E. B. Beaumont to J. A. Potter, August 31, 1868, RFMT.

25. Special Orders No. 101, Fort McKavett, September 29, 1868, RFMT.

26. Special Orders No. 100, Fort McKavett, September 15, 1869, RFMT.

27. Special Orders No. 128, Fort McKavett, November 20, 1869, RFMT. Heyl had entered the army in 1861 and served in a Pennsylvania cavalry regiment for most of the war. He eventually transferred into the Fourth Cavalry and later worked for the inspector general, but some of his most exciting duty came with the Ninth Cavalry on his scouts in the region of Fort Terrett. He received citations for gallantry in three separate actions against hostile Indians in West Texas between June and September 1869, during the last of which he was badly wounded. Heitman, *Historical Register and Dictionary of the United States Army*, 527. More detailed information on Heyl, especially about his ill-treatment of black enlisted men and their subsequent revolt, is in Kenner, *Buffalo Soldiers and Officers*, 72-79.

28. H. Clay Wood to Medical Director, Department of Texas, May 27, 1871, Headquarters Records of Fort Stockton, Record Group 393, National Archives (Microfilm M-1189).

29. Post Adjutant, Fort McKavett, to D. H. Kelton, September 8, 1876, RFMT.

30. Carroll's military career spanned almost forty years, from enlistment as a private in the regular army two years before the Civil War to retirement in 1899 as colonel of the Seventh Cavalry. He served through most of the Civil War as an enlisted man in the artillery but received a cavalry commission in 1864. After the war, he served many years on the frontier, winning citations for bravery for actions against hostile Indians in Texas and New Mexico. During the Spanish-American War he received temporary appointment as brigadier general of volunteers. See Heitman, *Historical Register and Dictionary of the United States Army*, 286.

31. Special Orders No. 190, Fort McKavett, November 13, 1872, RFMT.

32. B. W. Aston, "Federal Military Reoccupation of the Texas Southwestern Frontier, 1865-1871," *Texas Military History* 8 (1970): 126-27.

33. Fort McKavett Post Returns, April 1868.

34. Post Adjutant, Fort McKavett, to G. W. Budd, April 14, 1869, RFMT; Acting Post Adjutant, Fort McKavett, to W. W. Tyler, May 9, 1869, RFMT.

35. Henry Carroll to C. E. Morse, July 1, 1869, RFMT.

36. Special Orders No. 129, Fort McKavett, November 21, 1869, RFMT.

37. A German immigrant, Clous joined the army before the Civil War. He spent part of his first three years in the army as a member of the Ninth Infantry's band. He began the war as an enlisted man but won a commission in 1862. Clous fought at Gettysburg and won two brevets for gallantry there. After his regimental service on the frontier following the war, he spent most of the rest of his

career working for the judge advocate General. Heitman, *Historical Register and Dictionary of the United States Army*, 311-12.

38. Fort McKavett Post Returns, May 1871-May 1872.

39. Ibid., June 1872, July 1872.

40. Ibid., May 1871, November 1871.

41. Heitman, *Historical Register and Dictionary of the United States Army*, 327; Fort McKavett Post Returns, January-April 1872; Special Orders No. 10, Fort McKavett, January 12, 1872, RFMT.

CHAPTER 5

1. B. W. Aston, "Federal Military Reoccupation of the Texas Southwestern Frontier, 1865-1871," *Texas Military History* 8 (1970): 125-26.

2. Fort Brown Post Returns, November 1866, Record Group 94, National Archives (Microfilm M-617, Roll 152).

3. Fort Brown Post Returns, February 1869.

4. Ibid., July 1870.

5. Brit Allan Storey, ed., "An Army Officer in Texas, 1866-1867," *Southwestern Historical Quarterly* 72 (October 1968): 243-44; House, *Report of the Secretary of War*, 40th Cong., 2d sess., 1867, H. Exec. Doc. 1, 378.

6. Fort Brown Post Returns, May 1871; Storey, "Army Officer," 243.

7. Ibid.

8. Francis B. Heitman, *Historical Register and Dictionary of the United States Army, from Its Organization, September 29, 1789, to March 2, 1903* (Washington: Government Printing Office, 1903), 336.

9. Fort Brown Post Returns, March 1872.

10. Ibid., March 1873.

11. Ibid., August-September 1874.

12. House, *Report of the Secretary of War*, 42d Cong., 3d sess., 1872, H. Exec. Doc. 1, pt. 2, 57-58.

13. Heitman, *Historical Register and Dictionary of the United States Army*, 610.

14. Fort Brown Post Returns, April 1872.

15. Ibid., October 1872.

16. Ibid., December 1872-February 1873.

17. Ibid., April-November 1873.

18. Ninth Cavalry Regimental Returns, November 1873, Record Group 94, National Archives (Microfilm M744, Roll 88).

19. Ibid., July 1874.

20. Fort Brown Post Returns, August 1875-June 1879.

21. Ibid., June-October 1879.

22. Ibid., January 1880-December 1886.

23. Ibid., June 1872.

24. Ibid., October 1872. Wilson, a native Virginian who fought for the Union, never achieved promotion beyond captain, despite a citation for gallantry at Gettysburg. Six years after his brief tour at Penitas, he died when a gun accidentally exploded. Heitman, *Historical Register and Dictionary of the United States Army*, 1048.

25. Ninth Cavalry Regimental Returns, May 1873-July 1874.

26. House, *Report of the Secretary of War*, 45th Cong., 3d sess., 1878, H. Exec. Doc. 1, pt. 2, 82.

27. House, *Report of the Secretary of War*, 46th Cong., 2d sess., 1879, H. Exec. Doc. 1, pt. 2, 111. Hard cavalry service was nothing new to Kauffman. He entered the army in 1847 and served the next sixteen years as an enlisted man. Receiving a commission in 1863 in a Missouri cavalry regiment, he rose to the rank of major by the end of the Civil War. Then, like virtually all officers who managed to remain in the service after the war, he took a reduction in rank, becoming a first lieutenant in the Eighth Cavalry. Additional cavalry service rounded out his forty-five-year military career. He retired in 1892, a major in the Fourth Cavalry. Heitman, *Historical Register and Dictionary of the United States Army*, 586.

28. House, *Report of the Secretary of War*, 46th Cong., 3d sess., 1880, H. Exec. Doc. 1, pt. 2, 117, 127, 143-44.

29. Fort Brown Post Returns, September 1881.

30. Ibid., January 1871-January 1877.

31. Aston, "Federal Military Reoccupation," 126.

32. Ringgold Barracks Post Returns, January-March 1872, Record Group 94, National Archives (Microfilm M-617, Rolls 1020-21).

33. House, *Report of the Secretary of War*, 1872, 57.

34. House, *Report of the Secretary of War*, 44th Cong., 1st sess., 1875, H. Exec. Doc. 1, pt. 2, 94-95.

35. House, *Report of the Secretary of War*, 1880, 113.

36. Ringgold Barracks Post Returns, October 1868.

37. Ibid., May-June 1873.

38. Ibid., July 1873-August 1875.

39. Ibid., November 1874.

40. Ibid., August 1875-October 1879.

41. Ibid., September 1875-September 1884.

42. Ibid., September 1870.

43. Ninth Cavalry Regimental Returns, November 1873.

44. Ringgold Barracks Post Returns, December 1873, January 1874.

45. Ninth Cavalry Regimental Returns, February 1874.

46. House, *Report of the Secretary of War*, 44th Cong., 1st sess., 1875, H. Exec. Doc. 1, pt. 2, 106.

47. "Telegraphic," *Denison Daily Cresset*, April 2, 1875.

48. Ringgold Barracks Post Returns, May 1875.

49. Ibid., July 1876.

50. Ibid., May-September 1884.

51. Ibid., May 1868-February 1869.

52. Ibid., October 1877, April 1878. Thompson had begun the Civil War as a private, then commanded companies of black troops later in the war and on the frontier, and finally commanded a regiment by the turn of the century. Heitman, *Historical Register and Dictionary of the United States Army*, 957.

53. Ringgold Barracks Post Returns, November 1878, March 1879.

54. Ibid., June 1873, October 1873, November 1873-September 1874; Ninth Cavalry Regimental Returns, March 1874.

55. Ringgold Barracks Post Returns, March 1872-January 1875; Aston, "Federal Military Reoccupation," 126; House, *Report of the Secretary of War*, 40th Cong., 3d sess., 1868, H. Exec. Doc. 1, 714.

56. House, *Report of the Secretary of War*, 42d Cong., 3d sess., 1872, H. Exec. Doc. 1, pt. 2, 58.

57. House, *Report of the Secretary of War*, 46th Cong., 2d sess., 1879, H. Exec. Doc. 1, pt. 2, 107-08; House, *Report of the Secretary of War*, 46th Cong., 3d sess., 1880, H. Exec. Doc. 1, pt. 2, 140-42.

58. House, *Report of the Secretary of War*, 1879, 108-09.

59. Fort Duncan Post Returns, March 1868, Record Group 94, National Archives (Microfilm M-617, Roll 336); M. L. Crimmins, "Old Fort Duncan: A Frontier Post," *Frontier Times* 15 (June 1938), 379.

60. Fort Duncan Post Returns, April-September 1868.

61. Heitman, *Historical Register and Dictionary of the United States Army*, 876.

62. James Parker, *The Old Army: Memories 1872-1918* (Philadelphia: Dorrance and Company, 1929), 100-01. For more complete information on Shafter's long and eventful career, consult Paul H. Carlson, *Pecos Bill: A Military Biography of William R. Shafter* (College Station: Texas A&M University Press, 1989).

63. Rosella R. Sellers, "The History of Fort Duncan, Eagle Pass, Texas," (master's thesis, Sul Ross College, 1960), 24.

64. Fort Duncan Post Returns, May 1873.

65. Ibid., June-December 1875.

66. House, *Report of the Secretary of War*, 1878, 83-84.

67. Fort Duncan Post Returns, July 1879-April 1880.

68. Francis Paul Prucha, *A Guide to the Military Posts of the United States 1789-1895* (Madison: The State Historical Society of Wisconsin, 1964), 73.

69. Fort Duncan Post Returns, February 1872, June 1873. For additional information, see *The New Handbook of Texas*, s.v. "Camp Shafter," by Richard A. Thompson.

70. Paul H. Carlson, "William R. Shafter: Military Commander in the American West" (Ph.D. diss., Texas Tech University, 1973), 133-35; Carlson, *Pecos Bill*, 68-69.

71. Fort Duncan Post Returns, June 1874.

72. Ibid., February-October 1876.

CHAPTER 6

1. Allen Lee Hamilton, *Sentinel of the Southern Plains: Fort Richardson and the Northwest Texas Frontier 1866-1878* (Fort Worth: Texas Christian University Press, 1988), 15-19. Information on the regiment's activities in Texas can be found in William H. Carter, *From Yorktown to Santiago with the Sixth U. S. Cavalry* (Austin: State House Press, 1989), 131-56.

2. Donald W. Whisenhunt, "Fort Richardson: Outpost on the Texas Frontier," *Southwestern Studies* 5, no. 4 (1968): 8.

3. House, *Report of the Secretary of War*, 40th Cong., 3d sess., 1868, H. Exec. Doc. 1, 211-12.

4. Francis B. Heitman, *Historical Register and Dictionary of the United States Army, from Its Organization, September 29, 1789, to March 2, 1903* (Washington: Government Printing Office, 1903), 964; Daniel Madden to Assistant Adjutant General, District of Texas, February 27, 1868, Records of Fort Richardson, Texas, Record Group 393, National Archives (hereafter cited as RFRT) (microfilm in possession of Texas Parks and Wildlife Department, Austin); Major, Sixth Cavalry, (no signature) to Adjutant General, United States Army, March 24, 1868, RFRT; Commanding Officer, Fort Richardson, to C. E. Morse, June 17, 1868, RFRT.

5. R. M. Morris to Louis Caziare, February 14, 1869; James Oakes to C. E. Morse, May 15, 1869, RFRT. Information on how the army obtained horses for its units in Texas appears in Thomas T. Smith, *The U.S. Army and the Texas Frontier Economy 1845-1900* (College Station: Texas A&M University Press, 1999), 112-15.

6. Rupert N. Richardson, *The Frontier of Northwest Texas 1846 to 1876* (Glendale, California: The Arthur H. Clark Company, 1963), 270. For comparison with the situation in North Texas during the Civil War, when Texas had no regular troops guarding the frontier, see David Paul Smith, *Frontier Defense in the Civil War: Texas' Rangers and Rebels* (College Station: Texas A&M University Press, 1992).

7. Commanding Officer, Fort Richardson, to C. E. Morse, November 7, 1868, RFRT.

8. Commanding Officer, Fort Richardson, to Mr. H. Horton and Mr. R. H. Hopkins, November 11, 1868, RFRT.

9. James Oakes to C. E. Morse, May 29, 1869, RFRT.

10. Hamilton, *Sentinel*, 79-80. For concise information on the raid, see *The New Handbook of Texas*, "Warren Wagontrain Raid," by Allen Lee Hamilton.

11. Hamilton, *Sentinel*, 99-119.

12. Ibid., 126-34.

13. Robert G. Carter, *The Old Sergeant's Story: Fighting Indians and Bad Men in Texas from 1870 to 1876* (New York: Frederick H. Hitchcock, 1926; reprint, Mattituck, New York, and Bryan, Texas: J.M. Carroll and Company, 1982), 86.

14. Hamilton, *Sentinel*, 135.

15. J. W. Davidson to D. M. Key, July 3, 1877, RFRT.

16. Hamilton, *Sentinel*, 169-71.

17. H. H. McConnell, *Five Years a Cavalryman; or, Sketches of Regular Army Life on the Texas Frontier, Twenty Odd Years Ago* (1888; reprint, Freeport, New York: Books for Libraries Press, 1970), 62-63.

18. Ibid., 85.

19. Hutchins had entered the army as a private in April 1861, when President Lincoln called for volunteers in response to the capture of Fort Sumter. He quickly rose to commissioned rank and finished the war as lieutenant colonel of the First New Hampshire Cavalry. Heitman, *Historical Register and Dictionary of the United States Army*, 560.

20. B. Hutchins to Assistant Adjutant General, District of Texas, May 18, 1867, June 20, 1867, RFRT.

21. McConnell, *Five Years a Cavalryman*, 93-94.

22. Headquarters, Buffalo Springs, to Assistant Adjutant General, District of Texas, July 24, 1867, RFRT.

23. McConnell, *Five Years a Cavalryman*, 94-96.

24. Headquarters, Buffalo Springs, to Assistant Adjutant General, District of Texas, July 24, 1867, RFRT.

25. B. Hutchins to Assistant Adjutant General, District of Texas, July 23, 1867, RFRT.

26. McConnell, *Five Years a Cavalryman*, 85.

27. Special Orders No. 10, Buffalo Springs, May 28, 1867, RFRT.

28. Special Orders No. 34, Buffalo Springs, July 28, 1867, RFRT; McConnell, *Five Years a Cavalryman*, 103.

29. B. Hutchins to W. A. Rafferty, June 29, 1867, RFRT.

30. Theronne Thompson, "Fort Buffalo Springs, Texas Border Post," *West Texas Historical Association Year Book* 36 (1960): 160-61.

31. Special Orders No. 40, Buffalo Springs, August 26, 1867, RFRT; R. M. Morris, to Assistant Adjutant General, District of Texas, December 19, 1867, RFRT.

32. Special Orders No. 73, Camp Tucker Buffalo Springs, November 5, 1867, RFRT.

33. Thompson, "Fort Buffalo Springs," 174.

34. Special Orders No. 88, Camp Tucker Buffalo Springs, November 24, 1867, RFRT.

35. McConnell, *Five Years a Cavalryman*, 172-73.

36. B. Hutchins to Assistant Adjutant General, District of Texas, August 10, 1867, RFRT.

37. B. Hutchins to Adjutant General, United States Army, September 8, 1867; B. Hutchins to Assistant Adjutant General, District of Texas, September 21, 1867; B. Hutchins to John Tucker, September 28, 1867, RFRT.

38. B. Hutchins to Assistant Adjutant General, District of Texas, October 11, 1867, RFRT.

39. Ibid.

40. Ibid. Madden was an English immigrant. Enlisting in the United States Army in 1850, he served in the dragoons for more than ten years. He continued in the cavalry during the war and won distinction for his part in the final campaign against Lee in Virginia. Then he received his captaincy in the regular army in May 1867. By the time of his retirement in 1887, he would be a major in the Seventh Cavalry. Heitman, *Historical Register and Dictionary of the United States Army*, 683.

41. B. Hutchins to Assistant Adjutant General, District of Texas, October 24, 1867, RFRT.

42. Special Orders No. 80, Camp Tucker Buffalo Springs, November 15, 1867; Special Orders No. 81, Camp Tucker Buffalo Springs, November 16, 1867; Special Orders No. 84, Camp Tucker Buffalo Springs, November 19, 1867, RFRT. Morris was an old soldier, having entered the U.S. Military Academy in 1841, and earning a commission in time to participate in the Mexican War. He won three brevets for gallantry in that conflict, including one for the storming of Chapultepec. In 1863, he received promotion to major in the Sixth Cavalry and stayed there until retirement in 1873. Heitman, *Historical Register and Dictionary of the United States Army*, 728.

43. R. M. Morris to Assistant Adjutant General, District of Texas, December 19, 1867, RFRT.

44. R. M. Morris to C. E. Morse, January 16, 1868, RFRT.

45. Daniel Madden to Assistant Adjutant General, District of Texas, February 11, 1868, RFRT.

46. H. P. Eakin to Commanding Officer, Buffalo Springs, February 23, 1868, RFRT; Post Adjutant, Fort Richardson, to Thomas Tolman, April 4, 1868, RFRT; House, *Report of the Secretary of War*, 40th Cong., 3d sess., 1868, H. Exec. Doc. 1, 714.

47. Hamilton, *Sentinel*, 25.

48. McConnell, *Five Years a Cavalryman*, 62.

49. Ibid., 62-67.

50. Charles M. Robinson, III, *The Frontier World of Fort Griffin: The Life and Death of a Western Town* (Spokane, Washington: The Arthur H. Clark Company, 1992), 34.

51. General Orders No. 2, Headquarters, District of the Upper Brazos, May 22, 1877, RFRT.

52. James Oakes to Commanding Officer, Fort Sill, May 18, 1870, RFRT.

53. James Oakes to H. Clay Wood, June 2, 1870, RFRT. Oakes had seen plenty of similar frontier duty before the Civil War. He had graduated from West Point at the beginning of the Mexican War and had served with distinction in the dragoons. In 1855, he gained a captaincy in the Second Cavalry and campaigned there with many officers destined to win fame and honor in the Civil War. Although high rank eluded him in that war, he did gain command of the Sixth Cavalry in 1866. Heitman, *Historical Register and Dictionary of the United States Army*, 754.

54. James Oakes to H. Clay Wood, July 8 and July 17, 1870, RFRT.

55. McLellan won four brevets in his career for various actions in the Civil War and against hostile Indians in Indian Territory and New Mexico in the years following the war. When he reached retirement in 1893, he was lieutenant colonel of the First Cavalry. Heitman, *Historical Register and Dictionary of the United States Army*, 676.

56. James Oakes to H. Clay Wood, July 17, 1870, RFRT.

57. Ibid., September 10, 1870.

58. Ibid.

59. Ibid., September 26, 1870.

60. Ibid.

61. Post Adjutant, Fort Richardson, to R. M. Morris, October 4, 1870, RFRT.

62. Ibid., October 10, 1870.

63. Ibid., October 11, 1870; Mrs. Orsemus Bronson Boyd, *Cavalry Life in Tent and Field* (1894; reprint, with an introduction by Darlis A. Miller, Lincoln: University of Nebraska Press, 1982), 330. The army used scouts from various tribes with great effect in tracking hostile Indians. Sometimes the information a scout could glean from trivial signs along a trail seemed unbelievable to military officers. A few animal and human tracks, some discarded food, and particular signs of grazing could tell a scout about the people and horses in a party of Indians.

64. Post Adjutant, Fort Richardson, to John A. Irwin, December 1, 1870, RFRT.

65. Post Adjutant, Fort Richardson, to Commanding Officer, Camp Wichita, November 30, 1870; Post Adjutant, Fort Richardson, to Commanding Officer, Camp Wichita, December 8, 1870, RFRT.

66. R. G. Carter, *On the Border with Mackenzie; or Winning West Texas from the Comanches* (New York: Antiquarian Press, Ltd., 1961), 115.

67. Post Adjutant, Fort Richardson, to Commanding Officer, Camp Wichita, January 18, 1871, RFRT.

68. Ibid., January 25, 1871. For a brief discussion of the army's usual methods of obtaining forage for its animals in Texas, see Smith, *U.S. Army and the Texas Frontier Economy*, 74-77.

69. James Oakes to Assistant Adjutant General, Department of Texas, March 10, 1871, RFRT.

70. Harrison Holt to E. C. Hentig, June 22, 1868; Headquarters, Fort Richardson, to J. H. Sands, July 28, 1868, RFRT.

71. Headquarters, Fort Richardson, to J. H. Sands, July 28, 1868, RFRT.

72. Medical Histories of Posts, Fort Richardson, Record group 94, National Archives, RFRT.

73. McConnell, *Five Years a Cavalryman*, 93.

74. Special Orders No. 85, Camp Tucker Buffalo Springs, November 20, 1867, RFRT.

75. Special Orders No. 100, Fort Richardson, June 23, 1868; Special Orders No. 182, Fort Richardson, November 2, 1868; Special Orders No. 88, Fort Richardson, June 14, 1869, RFRT.

76. James Oakes to Lieutenant Richardson, Judge Advocate General, Jefferson, Texas, October 16, 1869; James Oakes to H. Clay Wood, December 4, 1869, RFRT.

77. R. M. Morris to C. E. Morse, January 16, 1868, RFRT.

78. James Oakes to H. Clay Wood, July 17, 1870, RFRT.

79. Post Adjutant, Fort Richardson, to Sergeant George Johnston, February 14, 1871; James Oakes to Assistant Adjutant General, Department of Texas, March 10, 1871, RFRT.

80. Carter, *On the Border*, 49.

81. R. S. Mackenzie to Assistant Adjutant General, Department of Texas, May 9, 1872; R. S. Mackenzie to G. W. Schofield, June 4, 1872, RFRT.

82. Carter, *The Old Sergeant's Story*, 126-27.

83. Ibid., 123-25.

84. R. S. Mackenzie to Mr. Loving, Weatherford, Texas, June 4, 1872.

85. Post Adjutant, Fort Richardson, to Commanding Officer, K Company, Eleventh Infantry, June 14, 1872, RFRT.

86. Special Orders No. 86, Fort Richardson, May 30, 1868, RFRT.

87. Special Orders No. 91, Fort Richardson, June 12, 1868, RFRT.

88. Special Orders No. 54, Fort Richardson, March 21, 1870, RFRT.

CHAPTER 7

1. Charles M. Robinson, III, *The Frontier World of Fort Griffin: The Life and Death of a Western Town* (Spokane, Washington: The Arthur H. Clark Company, 1992), 33-35.

2. House, *Report of the Secretary of War*, 40th Cong., 3d sess., 1868, H. Exec. Doc. 1, 712.

3. Carl Coke Rister, *Fort Griffin on the Texas Frontier* (Norman: University of Oklahoma Press, 1986), 65; Robinson, *Frontier World*, 35.

4. Francis B. Heitman, *Historical Register and Dictionary of the United States Army, from Its Organization, September 29, 1789, to March 2, 1903* (Washington: Government Printing Office, 1903), 934.

5. Rister, *Fort Griffin*, 65.

6. Robinson, *Frontier World*, 39.

7. Mari Sandoz, *The Buffalo Hunters: The Story of the Hide Men* (New York: Hastings House, 1954), 96; Alex L. ter Braake, *Texas: The Drama of Its Postal Past* (State College, Pennsylvania: The American Philatelic Society, 1970), 263.

8. Lonnie J. White, "Indian Battles in the Texas Panhandle, 1874," *Journal of the West* 6 (April 1967): 282-83. A detailed account of the fight at Adobe Walls, its background, and its aftermath is contained in T. Lindsay Baker and Billy R. Harrison, *Adobe Walls: The History and Archaeology of the 1874 Trading Post* (College Station: Texas A&M University Press, 1986), 3-110.

9. Heitman, *Historical Register and Dictionary of the United States Army*, 355.

10. White, "Indian Battles," 283-84.

11. Michael L. Tate, "Indian Scouting Detachments in the Red River War, 1874-1875," *Red River Valley Historical Review* 3 (1978): 207-16.

12. White, "Indian Battles," 300-02. For a detailed treatment of the Red River War, see James L. Haley, *The Buffalo War: The History of the Red River Indian Uprising of 1874* (Garden City, New York: Doubleday, 1976; reprint, Norman: University of Oklahoma Press, 1985). More personal accounts of the fighting can be found in Robert H. Steinbach, "The Red River War of 1874-1875: Selected Correspondence between Lieutenant Frank Baldwin and His Wife, Alice," *Southwestern Historical Quarterly* 93 (April 1990): 497-518; Robert H. Steinbach, *A Long March: The Lives of Frank and Alice Baldwin* (Austin: University of Texas Press, 1989), 60-96; and Richard Henry Pratt, *Battlefield and Classroom: Four Decades with the American Indian, 1867-1904*, edited and with an introduction by Robert M. Utley (New Haven: Yale University Press, 1964), 63-73.

13. Robert M. Utley, "A Chained Dog: The Indian-Fighting Army," *American West* 10 (July 1973): 22-23.

14. Ibid., 22-24. For interesting insights on some aspects of the relations between the army and its Indian scouts, see Thomas W. Dunlay, *Wolves for the Blue Soldiers: Indian Scouts and Auxiliaries with the United States Army, 1860-90* (Lincoln: University of Nebraska Press, 1982), 104-07, 122-23.

15. Robert M. Utley, *Frontier Regulars: The United States Army and the Indian 1866-1891* (New York: Macmillan, 1973), 46-47.

16. Ibid.

17. Ibid., 47.

18. Rister, *Fort Griffin*, 88-89; William H. Leckie, *The Military Conquest of the Southern Plains* (Norman: University of Oklahoma Press, 1963), 158-59; Allen Lee Hamilton, *Sentinel of the Southern Plains: Fort Richardson and the Northwest Texas Frontier, 1866-1878* (Fort Worth: Texas Christian University Press, 1988), 109.

19. Hamilton, *Sentinel*, 109.

20. Ibid., 117-19. Lawton was an infantryman throughout the Civil War and the years following it. In 1871, he transferred to the Fourth Cavalry. After seventeen years in that regiment, he went to work for the inspector general. His awards included brevets for gallantry in the Civil War. In one action outside Atlanta, Georgia, in 1864, he led a daring attack that captured a series of Confederate rifle pits, then held the position against two grim counterattacks. Lawton got back into combat during the Spanish-American War. Finally, in December 1899, he was killed in action by Filipino rebel forces near San Mateo during the Philippine Insurrection. Heitman, *Historical Register and Dictionary of the United States Army*, 620.

21. House, *Report of the Secretary of War*, 42d Cong., 3d sess., 1872, H. Exec. Doc. 1, pt. 2, 55-56. For background information and a discussion of the trade between Comancheros and Plains Indians, see Charles L. Kenner, *The Comanchero Frontier: A History of New Mexican-Plains Indian Relations* (Norman: University of Oklahoma Press, 1969, 1994).

22. House, *Report of the Secretary of War*, 42d Cong., 3d sess., 1872, H. Exec. Doc. 1, pt. 2, 55-56.

23. W. R. Shafter to W. H. Wood, August 10, 1872, Records of Fort Griffin, Texas, Record Group 393, National Archives (hereafter cited as RFGT) (Microfilm in possession of Texas Parks and Wildlife Department).

24. Ernest Wallace, ed., *Ranald S. Mackenzie's Official Correspondence Relating to Texas, 1871-1873* (Lubbock: West Texas Museum Association, 1967), 100-01.

25. Ibid., 111-12.

26. Ibid., 141-45.

27. Paul H. Carlson, "William R. Shafter, Black Troops, and the Opening of the Llano Estacado, 1870-1875," *Panhandle-Plains Historical Review* 47 (1974): 10-13.

28. Rister, *Fort Griffin*, 113-14.

29. Joe F. Taylor, ed. and comp., *The Indian Campaign on the Staked Plains, 1874-1875: Military Correspondence from War Department Adjutant General's Office, File 2815-1874* (Canyon, Texas: Panhandle-Plains Historical Society, 1962), 118.

30. Rister, *Fort Griffin*, 118-19.

31. Fort McKavett Post Returns, January 1875, Record Group 94, National Archives (Microfilm M-617, roll 688).

32. Paul H. Carlson, "William R. Shafter, Black Troops, and the Finale to the Red River War," *Red River Valley Historical Review* 3 (Spring 1978): 250-51.

33. "Letters and Reminiscences of Gen. Theodore A. Baldwin: Scouting after Indians on the Plains of West Texas," L. F. Sheffy, ed., *Panhandle-Plains Historical Review* 2 (1938): 11-12. Baldwin had served as an enlisted infantryman from 1862 until the end of the Civil War. Gaining a commission in 1865, he received promotion to captain just two years later. He began his cavalry service with a transfer to the Tenth in 1870 and moved back and forth between that regiment and the Seventh Cavalry for the remainder of his long career, commanding the Seventh for four years and retiring as a brigadier general in 1903. Heitman, *Historical Register and Dictionary of the United States Army*, 186.

34. Charles M. Robinson, III, *Frontier Forts of Texas* (Houston: Lone Star Books, 1986), 44.

35. Post Adjutant, Fort Griffin, to Commanding Officer, F Company, Fourth Cavalry, July 2, 1869, RFGT; Rister, *Fort Griffin*, 68.

36. Fort Griffin Post Returns, September 1869, Record Group 94, National Archives (Microfilm M-617, Roll 429).

37. Commanding Officer, Fort Griffin, to J. F. Hill, October 17, 1869; Special Orders No. 2, Headquarters, Sub-District of the Brazos, October 15, 1869, RFGT.

38. Commanding Officer, Fort Griffin, to Commanding Officer, Sub-District of the Brazos, April 27, 1870, RFGT.

39. Commanding Officer, Fort Griffin, to Acting Assistant Adjutant General, Sub-District of the Brazos, May 2, 1870, RFGT.

40. H. Clay Wood to Commanding Officer, Fort Griffin, May 27, 1871; Special Orders No. 105, Headquarters, Department of Texas, May 26, 1871, RFGT.

41. Commanding Officer, Fort Griffin, to Assistant Adjutant General, Department of Texas, June 13, 1871; R. S. Mackenzie to Commanding Officer, Fort Griffin, July 13, 1871, RFGT.

42. Special Orders No. 3, Fort Griffin, January 5, 1872, RFGT.

43. W. H. Wood to Acting Assistant Adjutant General, Department of Texas, September 2, 1872, RFGT.

44. Taylor, *Indian Campaign*, 127.

45. Roscoe P. Conkling and Margaret B. Conkling, *The Butterfield Overland Mail 1857-1869* (Glendale, California: The Arthur H. Clark Company, 1947), vol. 1, 332-34.

46. R. G. Carter, *On the Border with Mackenzie or Winning West Texas from the Comanches* (New York: Antiquarian Press, 1961), 62.

47. Post Adjutant, Fort Griffin, to Post Quartermaster, Fort Griffin, October 11, 1870; Commanding Officer, Subpost of Phantom Hill, to Post Adjutant, Fort Griffin, January 20, 1872; Rufus Cloud to Commanding Officer, Subpost of Phantom Hill, January 20, 1872, RFGT.

48. Commanding Officer, Fort Griffin, to J. F. Hill, February 20, 1870, RFGT.

49. Commanding Officer, Fort Griffin, to Acting Assistant Adjutant General, Subdistrict of the Brazos, May 2, 1870, RFGT.

50. John B. Charlton, *The Old Sergeant's Story: Winning the West from the Indians and Bad Men in 1870 to 1876*, Robert G. Carter, ed. (New York: Frederick H. Hitchcock, 1926), 68-69.

51. Heitman, *Historical Register and Dictionary of the United States Army*, 763.

52. W. H. Wood to Acting Assistant Adjutant General, Department of Texas, September 2, 1872, RFGT.

CHAPTER 8

1. M. L. Crimmins, "Fort Elliott, Texas," *The West Texas Historical Association Year Book* 23 (October 1947): 4-5.

2. Francis Paul Prucha, *A Guide to the Military Posts of the United States 1789-1895* (Madison: The State Historical Society of Wisconsin, 1964), 73.

3. Fort Elliott (Cantonment on North Fork of Red River) Post Returns, February 1875, Record Group 94, National Archives (Microfilm M-617, Roll 346). Biddle was a soldier of vast experience. He had served as an officer throughout the Civil War in both infantry and cavalry units. He commanded a volunteer cavalry regiment for a period, and picked up brevets for gallantry in battles at Richmond, Kentucky, and Nashville, Tennessee. He ended the war as a brevet brigadier general of volunteers. His service after the war was just as varied. From 1865 until his retirement in 1896 he served in three infantry and four cavalry regiments, the last assignment being command of the Ninth Cavalry. Francis B. Heitman, *Historical Register and Dictionary of the United States Army, from Its Organization, September 29, 1789, to March 2, 1903* (Washington: Government Printing Office, 1903), 217.

4. Ibid., 608. More detailed information about Kramer's life and military career are available in Constance Wynn Altshuler, *Cavalry Yellow and Infantry Blue: Army Officers in Arizona Between 1851 and 1886* (Tucson: Arizona Historical Society, 1991), 195-96.

5. Fort Elliott (Cantonment on the Sweetwater) Post Returns, March 1875.

6. Crimmins, "Fort Elliott, Texas," 5.

7. Fort Elliott (Cantonment on the Sweetwater) Post Returns, June 1875.

8. Ibid., July-November 1875.

9. Crimmins, "Fort Elliott, Texas," 5.

10. Fort Elliott Post Returns, March 1876.

11. Crimmins, "Fort Elliott, Texas," 6.

12. Fort Elliott Post Returns, July-October 1875.

13. Ibid., December 1875.

14. Ibid., July 1876.

15. Ibid., October 1876.

16. Ibid., November 1876-April 1877.

17. *Panhandle News*, June 2, 1877.

18. Fort Elliott Post Returns, August 1877.

19. Ibid., September-November 1878.

20. Homer K. Davidson, *Black Jack Davidson, A Cavalry Commander on the Western Frontier: The Life of General John W. Davidson* (Glendale, California: The Arthur H. Clark Company, 1974), 225.

21. James Parker, *The Old Army: Memories 1872-1918* (Philadelphia: Dorrance & Company, 1929), 64-65.

22. Davidson, *Black Jack Davidson*, 227. The Texas Rangers had a reputation for aggressive action against any Indians they suspected of posing a danger to the frontier. Arrington had been a sergeant until the end of 1877. Perhaps the two rapid promotions, to lieutenant then captain, made him more eager to attack the Indian hunting party, or maybe aggressiveness had been the reason for his quick promotions in the first place. Special Order 54, Adjutant General, State of Texas, to Major John B. Jones, Captain Pat Dolan, Lieutenant G. W. Arrington, and Captain Caldwell, December 29, 1877, Special Orders of Adjutant General of Texas (August 1870-April 2, 1897), Adjutant General's Record Group (RG 401), Archives Division, Texas State Library.

23. Detailed accounts of Nolan's ill-fated expedition are contained in H. Bailey Carroll, "Nolan's 'Lost Nigger' Expedition of 1877," *Southwestern Historical Quarterly* 44 (July 1940): 55-75; and W. Curtis Nunn, "Eighty-six Hours Without Water on the Texas Plains," *Southwestern Historical Quarterly* 43 (January 1940): 356-64.

24. Davidson, *Black Jack Davidson*, 228-29.

25. Fort Elliott Post Returns, April 1879.

26. Ibid., Special Orders No. 93, Headquarters, Fort Elliott, May 17, 1879.

27. George Read to Post Quartermaster, April 26, 1879, Records of Fort Elliott, Texas, Record Group 393, National Archives (hereafter cited as RFET) (Microfilm in possession of Panhandle-Plains Historical Museum, West Texas A&M University, Canyon, Texas).

28. J. W. Davidson to Assistant Adjutant General, Department of the Missouri, June 12, 1879, RFET; Charles Cooper to Post Quartermaster, Fort Elliott, June 25, 1879, RFET.

29. Nicholas Nolan to Assistant Adjutant General, Department of the Missouri, August 18, 1879, RFET. T. Lindsay Baker and Billy R. Harrison, *Adobe Walls: The History and Archaeology of the 1874 Trading Post* (College Station: Texas A&M University Press, 1986) has additional information on Billy Dixon's life.

30. Nicholas Nolan to Assistant Adjutant General, Department of the Missouri, October 10, 1879, RFET.

31. R. I. Eskridge to Assistant Adjutant General, Department of the Missouri, December 8, 1879, RFET. Eskridge would eventually be a forty-year man in the

army, enlisting as a private in 1861 and ending his career as colonel of the Twenty-seventh Infantry in 1901. He had won a brevet captaincy in 1867 for charging a large group of Indians who were fortified in the Infernal Caverns along the Pitt River in California. Heitman, *Historical Register and Dictionary of the United States Army*, 408.

32. Henry O. Flipper, *Black Frontiersman: The Memoirs of Henry O. Flipper, First Black Graduate of West Point*, Theodore D. Harris comp. and ed. (Fort Worth: Texas Christian University Press, 1997), 30-31.

33. R. I. Eskridge to Assistant Adjutant General, Department of the Missouri, January 8, 1880; January 11, 1880; January 23, 1880, RFET. Edward Hatch to Assistant Adjutant General, Department of the Missouri, April 5, 1880, RFET.

34. Parker, *Old Army*, 65-66.

35. Charles Cooper to Quartermaster General, United States Army, May 27, 1879; Nicholas Nolan to Quartermaster General, United States Army, October 10, 1879, RFET.

36. Edward Hatch to Assistant Adjutant General, Department of the Missouri, February 27, 1879; W. A. Nichols to O. L. Wirting, November 18, 1879, RFET.

37. George Read to E. S. Liscum, March 18, 1879, RFET.

38. S. Allen Byrd to Quartermaster General, United States Army, October 11, 1879, RFET.

39. Crimmins, "Fort Elliott, Texas," 11. A great deal of controversy often erupted when the government announced plans to close a post such as Fort Elliott. Although civilians usually claimed the continuing need for military protection as the reason they wanted a post to remain open, many government officials believed those civilians had profit in mind rather than protection. Government purchases of local goods and agricultural produce helped augment the limited frontier economy. For a discussion of these questions as they related to Fort Elliott's closing, see Michael L. Tate, *The Frontier Army in the Settlement of the West* (Norman: University of Oklahoma Press, 1999), 111-13.

CHAPTER 9

1. B. W. Aston, "Federal Military Reoccupation of the Texas Southwestern Frontier, 1865-1871," *Texas Military History* 8 (1970): 127.

2. Ibid., 128. For detailed information on Texas as one of the occupied military districts during Reconstruction, see William Richter, *The Army in Texas During Reconstruction, 1865-1870* (College Station: Texas A&M University Press, 1987). Thomas T. Smith, *The Old Army in Texas: A Research Guide to the U. S. Army in Nineteenth Century Texas* (Austin: Texas State Historical Association, 2000) provides a wealth of information on the organization of the army in Texas from the highest levels of command down to small units and the posts they garrisoned.

3. J. Evetts Haley, *Fort Concho and the Texas Frontier* (San Angelo, Texas: *San Angelo Standard-Times*, 1952), 128-31.

4. Ibid., 136-43.

5. Ibid., 274. An excellent source of information on Grierson's career and life is William H. Leckie and Shirley A. Leckie, *Unlikely Warriors: General Benjamin H. Grierson and His Family* (Norman: University of Oklahoma Press, 1984).

6. Ibid., 274-82. Susan Miles, "The Soldiers' Riot," *Fort Concho Report* 13 (Spring 1981): 1-20, offers a detailed narrative of the entire drama, while an investigation of the incident's economic and political roots and ramifications can be found in Bruce J. Dinges, "The San Angelo Riot of 1881: A Reassessment," paper read to the Texas State Historical Association, Houston, Texas, March 5, 1993, copy in "Riots-Fort Concho" file, Museum Research Library and Archives, Fort Concho National Historic Landmark, San Angelo, Texas.

7. Shirley A. Leckie, ed., *The Colonel's Lady on the Western Frontier: The Correspondence of Alice Kirk Grierson* (Lincoln: University of Nebraska Press, 1989), 86-87.

8. Haley, *Fort Concho*, 156.

9. Ibid., 157.

10. Special Orders No. 145, Fort Concho, November 22, 1869, Records of Headquarters, Fort Concho, Texas, Record Group 393, National Archives (hereafter referred to as RHFCT) (Microfilm in possession of Fort Concho National Historic Landmark).

11. Special Orders No. 76, Fort Concho, March 25, 1871, RHFCT.

12. Special Orders No. 129, Fort Concho, May 31, 1871, RHFCT.

13. H. Clay Wood to Commanding Officer, Fort Griffin, May 27, 1871, Records of Fort Griffin, Texas, Record Group 393, National Archives (Microfilm in possession of Texas Parks and Wildlife Department, Austin).

14. Haley, *Fort Concho*, 157-58; Special Orders No. 156, Fort Concho, August 1, 1875, RHFCT.

15. Haley, *Fort Concho*, 157. Rendlebrock was a Prussian by birth and carried on that nation's military tradition in his new home in the United States. He had enlisted in 1851 and served as a noncommissioned officer until early in the Civil War, when he received a commission. Breveted three times for gallantry in the war, he went on to serve until retirement in 1879, his entire career spent in mounted units. Francis B. Heitman, *Historical Register and Dictionary of the United States Army, from Its Organization, September 29, 1789, to March 2, 1903* (Washington: Government Printing Office, 1903), 823.

16. Cyrus Gray to Post Adjutant, Fort Concho, May 20, 1880, RHFCT.

17. Haley, *Fort Concho*, 157. Emily Andrews, wife of Colonel George L. Andrews, Twenty-fifth Infantry, gives an interesting description of Johnson's Station and Head of the Concho, as well as Kickapoo Springs and Escondido Springs, all stopping places on her trip from Austin to Fort Davis in 1874, in Emily K. Andrews, "A Woman's View of the Texas Frontier, 1874: The Diary of Emily K. Andrews," ed. and ann. Sandra L. Myres, *Southwestern Historical Quarterly* 86 (July 1982): 49-80.

18. Roscoe P. Conkling and Margaret B. Conkling, *The Butterfield Overland Mail 1857-1869* (Glendale, California: The Arthur H. Clark Company, 1947), vol. 3.

19. Special Orders No. 162, Fort Concho, December 22, 1869; Special Orders No. 164, Fort Concho, December 25, 1869; Special Orders No. 170, Fort Concho, December 30, 1869, RHFCT.

20. Special Orders No. 164, Fort Concho, December 25, 1869; Special Orders No. 170, Fort Concho, December 30, 1869; Special Orders No. 41, Fort Concho, March 27, 1870, RHFCT.

21. Special Orders No. 77, Fort Concho, March 26, 1871; Special Orders No. 227, Fort Concho, October 25, 1874; Special Orders No. 175, Fort Concho, September 3, 1875, RHFCT.

22. Conkling and Conkling, *Butterfield Overland Mail*, vol. 3.

23. Haley, *Fort Concho*, 156-57.

24. Ibid., 157.

25. Special Orders No. 133, Fort Concho, October 19, 1869, RHFCT.

26. Haley, *Fort Concho*, 157.

27. Special Orders No. 227, Fort Concho, October 25, 1874; Special Orders No. 167, Fort Concho, August 23, 1875; R. G. Smither to Henry Williams, March 26, 1879, RHFCT.

28. Eugene Driscoll to Post Adjutant, Fort Concho, August 20, 1875, RHFCT.

29. R. G. Smither to Commanding Officer, D Company, Tenth Cavalry, April 22, 1877, RHFCT.

30. Haley, *Fort Concho*, 156-57.

31. Patrick Dearen, *Castle Gap and the Pecos Frontier* (Fort Worth: Texas Christian University Press, 1988), 50.

32. A. L. Myer to W. C. Hemphill, October 21, 1872, RHFCT.

33. M. F. Eggleston to Commanding Officer, Camp Charlotte, August 2, 1879, RHFCT.

34. Ibid.

35. James H. Lane to John W. French, November 25, 1879, RHFCT.

36. J. Law to Acting Assistant Adjutant General, District of the Pecos, April 25, 1879, RHFCT.

37. "Memoirs of William George Wedemeyer," vol. 2, 113, Fort Davis National Historic Site. See Thomas T. Smith, *The U.S. Army and the Texas Frontier Economy 1845-1900* (College Station: Texas A&M University Press, 1999), 166-69, for a summary of the construction of the military telegraph network across Texas.

38. A. Haugh to Adjutant General, Department of Texas, August 24, 1882, RHFCT.

39. J. Rendelbrock to I. M. Starr, February 20, 1872, RHFCT; Patrick Dearen, *Portraits of the Pecos Frontier* (Lubbock: Texas Tech University Press, 1993), 124. For additional information, see *The New Handbook of Texas*, s.v. "Camp Elizabeth."

40. R. G. Smither to Commanding Officer, E Company, Tenth Cavalry, July 28, 1879, RHFCT.

41. R. G. Smither to Post Quartermaster, Fort Concho, August 22, 1880; B. H. Grierson to Commanding Officer, F Company, Sixteenth Infantry, February 21, 1881, RHFCT.

42. J. O. Shelby to Calvin Esterly, July 30, 1881, RHFCT.

43. "Memoirs of William George Wedemeyer," vol. 2, 121.

44. C. R. Tyler to Post Quartermaster, Fort Concho, July 18, 1882, RHFCT.

45. J. O. Shelby to P. L. Lee, October 30, 1881, RHFCT.

46. A. Haugh to Adjutant General, Department of Texas, August 24, 1882, RHFCT.

47. J. O. Shelby to Commanding Officer, Head of the North Concho, November 30, 1881, RHFCT.

48. B. H. Grierson to Assistant Adjutant General, Department of Texas, April 5, 1882, RHFCT.

49. Lieutenant Allen, Acting Post Adjutant, Fort Concho, to Commanding Officer, C Company, Sixteenth Infantry, November 11, 1882, RHFCT.

50. M. M. Maxon, "Twenty Years in the Saddle: Reminiscences of His Military Experience 1869 to 1889," Maxon Family Papers, Fort Davis National Historic Site.

51. Frank M. Temple, "Grierson's Spring," *Fort Concho Report* 15 (winter 1983): 5. See Leckie and Leckie, *Unlikely Warriors*, 250-75, for an account of Grierson's work in mapping the portion of West Texas under his responsibility and establishing the network of small military posts there.

52. Maxon, "Twenty Years."

53. Temple, "Grierson's Spring," 9.

54. Cyrus Gray to Post Adjutant, Fort Concho, May 20, 1880, RHFCT. An infantry soldier of the time, passing through Grierson's Spring on the march, gives a brief description of it and the nearby country in E.A. Bode, *A Dose of Frontier Soldiering: The Memoirs of Corporal E.A. Bode, Frontier Regular Infantry, 1877-1882*, Thomas T. Smith, ed. (Lincoln: University of Nebraska Press, 1994), 172-73.

55. R. G. Smither to Post Quartermaster, Fort Concho, April 18, 1879, RHFCT.

56. J. Law to Acting Assistant Adjutant General, District of the Pecos, April 25, 1879, RHFCT.

57. William B. Kennedy to Assistant Adjutant General, District of the Pecos, October 15, 1878, RHFCT.

58. Maxon, "Twenty Years."

59. William Black to Assistant Adjutant General, District of the Pecos, October 20, 1880, RHFCT.

60. R. G. Smither to Commanding Officer, E Company, Tenth Cavalry, July 28, 1879, RHFCT.

61. B. H. Grierson to Assistant Adjutant General, Department of Texas, April 5, 1882, RHFCT; A. Haugh to Adjutant General, Department of Texas, August 24, 1882, RHFCT.

62. B. H. Grierson to Assistant Adjutant General, Department of Texas, April 5, 1882, RHFCT; Haley, *Fort Concho*, 338.

CHAPTER 10

1. B. W. Aston, "Federal Military Reoccupation of the Texas Southwestern Frontier, 1865-1871," *Texas Military History* 8 (1970): 128.

2. Francis B. Heitman, *Historical Register and Dictionary of the United States Army, from Its Organization, September 29, 1789, to March 2, 1903* (Washington: Government Printing Office, 1903), 706. See also Dan L. Thrapp, *Encyclopedia of Frontier Biography* (Lincoln: University of Nebraska Press, 1988), vol. 2, 976.

3. Don E. Alberts, *Brandy Station to Manila Bay: A Biography of General Wesley Merritt* (Austin: Presidial Press, 1980), 189-92.

4. Ibid.

5. Charles M. Robinson, III, *Frontier Forts of Texas* (Houston: Lone Star Books, 1986), 56. For more detailed information on Shafter's campaign, see Paul H. Carlson, *Pecos Bill: A Military Biography of William R. Shafter* (College Station: Texas A&M University Press, 1989), 55-61.

6. Joseph A. Stout, Jr., *Apache Lightning: The Last Great Battles of the Ojo Calientes* (New York: Oxford University Press, 1974), 73.

7. Ibid., 74, 88-90. For a narrative of Victorio and his struggles with the United States, see Dan Thrapp, *Victorio and the Mimbres Apaches* (Norman: University of Oklahoma Press, 1974).

8. Bruce J. Dinges, "The Victorio Campaign of 1880: Cooperation and Conflict on the United States-Mexico Border," *New Mexico Historical Review* 62 (January 1987): 83-87.

9. Frank M. Temple, "Colonel B. H. Grierson's Administration of the District of the Pecos," *West Texas Historical Association Year Book* 38 (October 1962): 85-87. Additional information on Grierson's strategy and efforts can be found in William H. Leckie and Shirley A. Leckie, *Unlikely Warriors: General Benjamin H. Grierson and His Family* (Norman: University of Oklahoma Press, 1984), 250-75.

10. William H. Leckie, *The Buffalo Soldiers: A Narrative of the Negro Cavalry in the West* (Norman: University of Oklahoma Press, 1967), 223-24.

11. Thrapp, *Victorio and the Mimbres Apaches*, 286-90. For a detailed account of the fight at Tinaja de las Palmas, see Douglas C. McChristian, "Grierson's Fight at Tinaja de las Palmas: An Episode in the Victorio Campaign," *Red River Valley Historical Review* 7 (winter 1982): 45-63.

12. Dan L. Thrapp, *The Conquest of Apacheria* (Norman: University of Oklahoma Press, 1967), 208.

13. Robinson, *Frontier Forts of Texas*, 57.

14. Arlen L. Fowler, *The Black Infantry in the West 1869-1891* (Westport, Connecticut: Greenwood Publishing Corporation, 1971), 25-27. See Barry Scobee, *Fort Davis, Texas, 1583-1960* (El Paso: by the author, 1963), 71-74, for incidental information on some of these small posts.

15. Roscoe P. Conkling and Margaret B. Conkling *The Butterfield Overland Mail 1857-1869*, (Glendale, California: The Arthur H. Clark Company, 1947), vol. 2, 23.

16. W. J. Sanborn to Post Adjutant, Fort Davis, April 30, 1871, Fort Davis Selected Documents, Record Group 98, National Archives (hereafter cited as FDSD) (Microfilm, Rolls NMRA 66-783 [7675] 8-9 and 65-855 [10427], Fort Davis National Historic Site).

17. Edward Hatch to C. E. Morse, February 5, 1868, Headquarters Records of Fort Stockton, Record Group 393, National Archives (hereafter cited as HRFS) (Microfilm M-1189).

18. D. H. Cortelyon to Ira W. Trask, September 19, 1868, HRFS.

19. W. R. Shafter to James F. Wade, June 18, 1871, HRFS.

20. General Orders No. 17, Department of Texas, November 9, 1871, M. L. Crimmins Collection, Center for American History, University of Texas at Austin.

21. "Incidents Involving Hostile Indians Within the Influence of Fort Davis, Texas 1866-1891," Archives of the Big Bend, Sul Ross State University, Alpine, Texas; J. H. Taylor to Commanding Officer, Fort Stockton, telegram, June 11, 1877, HRFS.

22. J. F. Ukkerd to W. H. W. James, August 9, 1880, FDSD.

23. Conkling and Conkling, *Butterfield Overland Mail*, vol. 2, 30-31.

24. Wesley Merritt to H. Clay Wood, July 5, 1869, "El Muerto and Barrel Springs," Card Files, Fort Davis National Historic Site (hereafter cited as CF). Brief descriptions of Barrel Springs and El Muerto by a soldier of the period can be found in E. A. Bode, *A Dose of Frontier Soldiering: The Memoirs of Corporal E. A. Bode, Frontier Regular Infantry, 1877-1882*, Thomas T. Smith, ed. (Lincoln: University of Nebraska Press, 1994), 177-78.

25. Wayne R. Austerman, *Sharps Rifles and Spanish Mules: The San Antonio-El Paso Mail, 1851-1881* (College Station: Texas A&M University Press, 1985), 218.

26. F. C. Godfrey to M. M. Blunt, September 29, 1877, HRFS.

27. B. Baker to Post Adjutant, Fort Davis, June 22, 1880, FDSD.

28. Conkling and Conkling, *Butterfield Overland Mail*, vol. 2, 31-33.

29. Wesley Merritt to H. Clay Wood, July 5, 1869, "El Muerto and Barrel Springs," CF.

30. William Bayard to Commanding Officer, Fifth Military District, September 28, 1869, "El Muerto," CF.

31. Ibid.

32. George L. Andrews to Commanding Officer, Department of Texas, July 21, 1877, "Station Guards," CF.

33. L. H. Carpenter to Assistant Adjutant General, Department of Texas, July 11, 1879; W. H. W. James to Post Master, Fort Davis, August 7, 1880, "Stagecoaching," CF.

34. Conkling and Conkling, *Butterfield Overland Mail*, vol. 2, 33-34.

35. George L. Andrews to Commanding Officer, Department of Texas, July 21, 1877, "Station Guards," CF.

36. Austerman, *Sharps Rifles and Spanish Mules*, 292.

37. Ibid.

38. Conkling and Conkling, *Butterfield Overland Mail*, vol. 2, 35-38.

39. Ninth Cavalry Regimental Returns, December 1867, Record Group 94, National Archives (Microfilm M744, Roll 87).

40. Edward Hatch to C. E. Morse, January 24 and February 5, 1868, HRFS. Details on army organization at the higher levels in Texas during the Reconstruction period can be found in William Richter, *The Army in Texas During Reconstruction, 1865-1870* (College Station: Texas A&M University Press, 1987). For more extensive organizational information on the army in Texas between 1866 and 1886, see Thomas T. Smith, *The Old Army in Texas: A Research Guide to the U.S. Army in Nineteenth-Century Texas* (Austin: Texas State Historical Association, 2000).

41. Ninth Cavalry Regimental Returns, June 1868 and October 1871. Boice's connection with the military was over long before that time. He had risen from sergeant to lieutenant colonel during the Civil War, but apparently he found no place in the peacetime army, at least not under his real name. He enlisted in the Second Cavalry under the name of Guy Traver in September 1865 and served for over a year as an enlisted man under that assumed identity. He received a commission in his real name in the Ninth Cavalry and even a promotion to captain in 1867. Two years later, however, the army cashiered him. Heitman, *Historical Register and Dictionary of the United States Army*, 228.

42. D. H. Porter to P. A. Ekin, May 20, 1871, FDSD.

43. Robert Smither to L. H. Carpenter, June 4, 1878, FDSD. Carpenter was a soldier with a superb record. He rose from a private in 1861, to colonel of a black cavalry regiment in 1865, winning several brevet promotions for gallantry. He served for the first seventeen years after the war in the Tenth Cavalry. For his actions in Kansas and Colorado against hostile Indians during September and October 1868, he won the Congressional Medal of Honor. After service with several other cavalry regiments, he retired in 1899 at the rank of brigadier general. Heitman, *Historical Register and Dictionary of the United States Army*, 284.

44. Acting Assistant Adjutant General, District of the Pecos, to Commanding Officer, Fort Davis, telegram, October 2, 1878, FDSD.

45. L. Carpenter to Post Adjutant, Fort Davis, June 27, 1880, FDSD.

46. John H. Nankivell, comp. and ed., *History of the Twenty-fifth Regiment United States Infantry 1869-1926* (n.p., 1927), 30.

47. House, *Report of the Secretary of War*, 46th Cong., 3d sess., 1880, H. Exec. Doc. 1, pt. 2, 159-61; McChristian, "Grierson's Fight," 45-63.

48. Post Adjutant, Fort Davis, to Commanding Officer, Fort Quitman, June 20, 1882, FDSD.

49. George S. Andrews to Commanding Officer, Department of Texas, August 13, 1872, "Presidio," CF.

50. Thomas G. Williams to E. O. C. Ord, September 28, 1875, FDSD.

51. George S. Andrews to Adjutant General, United States Army, November 17, 1875, "Presidio Crisis," CF.

52. Leon C. Metz, *Border: The U.S.-Mexico Line* (El Paso: Mangan Books, 1989), 165-67.

53. Ibid.

54. John French to Post Adjutant, Fort Davis, February 11, 1877, FDSD.

55. Fort Davis Post Returns, March 1881-March 1882, Record Group 94, National Archives (Microfilm M617, Roll 298).

56. House, *Report of the Secretary of War*, 48th Cong., 1st sess., 1884, H. Exec. Doc. 1, 145.

57. M. M. Maxon, "Twenty Years in the Saddle: Reminiscences of His Military Experience 1869 to 1889," Maxon Family Papers, Fort Davis National Historic Site.

58. Orders, Camp Peña Blanca, June 4, 1878, Maxon Family Papers, Fort Davis National Historic Site.

59. Temple, "Grierson's Administration," 90.

60. Robert Smither to Commanding Officer, Fort Stockton, October 7, 1878, HRFS.

61. Nankivell, *History of the Twenty-fifth Regiment*, 30.

62. Conkling and Conkling, *Butterfield Overland Mail*, 391-93.

63. General Order No. 2, Headquarters, Subdistrict of the Presidio, March 30, 1870, HRFS.

64. House, *Report of the Secretary of War*, 46th Cong., 2d sess., 1879, H. Exec. Doc. 1, pt. 2, 105.

65. Temple, "Grierson's Administration," 91.

66. House, *Report of the Secretary of War*, 46th Cong., 3d sess., 1880, H. Exec. Doc. 1, pt. 2, 137.

67. Maxon, "Twenty Years," 28-29.

68. J. J. Bowden, *Surveying the Texas and Pacific Land Grant West of the Pecos*, "Southwestern Studies," no. 46 (El Paso: Texas Western Press, 1975), 27.

69. McChristian, "Grierson's Fight," 49.

70. M. L. Courtney to Post Adjutant, Fort Davis, October 7, 1878, FDSD.

71. Acting Assistant Adjutant General, District of the Pecos, to Commanding Officer, Fort Davis, June 14, 1878, FDSD.

72. M. L. Courtney to Post Adjutant, Fort Davis, October 7, 1878, FDSD.

73. House, *Report of the Secretary of War*, 1880, 137-39.

74. George S. Andrews to Adjutant General, United States Army, November 17, 1875, "Presidio Crisis," CF. For background on Milton Faver, the colorful owner of the ranch, see Scobee, *Fort Davis, Texas*, 74-77.

75. "Incidents Involving Hostile Indians," Archives of the Big Bend.

76. George S. Andrews to Adjutant General, United States Army, November 17, 1875, CF.

77. House, *Report of the Secretary of War*, 1880, 120-21, 138.

78. Ibid., 138.

79. James B. Gillett, *Six Years with the Texas Rangers 1875 to 1881* (New Haven: Yale University Press, 1925), 284-85; McChristian, "Grierson's Fight," 50.

80. Gillett, *Six Years*, 285-86; Adjutant General, United States Army to Marfa Chamber of Commerce, February 15, 1938, Clay Miller Collection, Archives of the Big Bend, Sul Ross State University (Copy at Fort Davis National Historic Site).

81. L. H. Carpenter to Assistant Adjutant General, District of the Pecos, June 13, 1880; L. Carpenter to Post Adjutant, Fort Davis, June 27, 1880, FDSD; McChristian, "Grierson's Fight," 50.

82. B. H. Grierson to Adjutant General, Department of Texas, August 5, 1883, Clay Miller Collection, Archives of the Big Bend, Sul Ross State University (Copy at Fort Davis National Historic Site). For more information on how the army leased the land for its Texas posts, see Thomas T. Smith, *The U.S. Army and the Texas Frontier Economy 1845-1900* (College Station: Texas A&M University Press, 1999), 80-81.

83. B. H. Grierson to Assistant Adjutant General, Department of Texas, telegram, October 29, 1880, FDSD.

84. Ibid.; Gillett, *Six Years*, 287.

85. Alberts, *Brandy Station*, 194.

86. Robert D. Read to Post Adjutant, Fort Davis, June 20, 1880, Clay Miller Collection, Archives of the Big Bend, Sul Ross State University (copy at Fort Davis National Historic Site); Nankivell, *History of the Twenty-fifth Regiment*, 16.

87. Daniel Murphy to Commanding Officer, Fort Davis, March 7, 1871, FDSD.

88. Post Adjutant, Fort Davis, to R. G. Armstrong, August 8, 1881; Colonel, First Infantry, to Adjutant General, Department of Texas, September 5, 1881; W. R. Shafter to F. E. Pierce, September 23, 1881, "Pinery Notes," CF.

89. W. Lea to Adjutant, Fort Davis, February 24, 1871, FDSD.

90. Post Adjutant, Fort Davis, to Daniel F. Callinan, December 10, 1881; Post Adjutant, Fort Davis, to C. R. Ward, September 3, 1883, "Pinery Notes," CF.

91. W. R. Shafter to Adjutant General, Department of Texas, July 19, 1881, "Pinery Notes," CF; F. E. Pierce to Post Adjutant, Fort Davis, September 30, 1881, FDSD.

92. Assistant Adjutant General, Department of Texas, to Commanding Officer, Fort Davis, telegram, August 17, 1882, FDSD.

93. Assistant Adjutant General, Department of Texas, to Commanding Officer, Fort Davis, April 23, 1884; W. H. Clapps to Post Adjutant, Fort Davis, June 12 and June 17, 1884, FDSD.

CHAPTER 11

1. James C. Cage and Tommy Powell, *Fort Quitman* (McNary, Texas: n.p., 1972), 3-5.

2. Ibid., 11.

3. Fort Quitman Post Returns, May-June 1868, Record Group 94, National Archives (Microfilm M-617, Roll 985).

4. Ibid., July 1868.

5. George Ruhlen, "Quitman: The Worst Post at Which I Ever Served," in *The Black Military Experience in the American West*, John M. Carroll, ed. (New York: Liveright, 1971), 107.

6. Cage and Powell, *Fort Quitman*, 11-17.

7. Ruhlen, "Quitman," 107-10.

8. Fort Quitman Post Returns, July 1869-January 1877.

9. Ruhlen, "Quitman," 112.

10. Dan L. Thrapp, *The Conquest of Apacheria* (Norman: University of Oklahoma Press, 1967), 204.

11. Ruhlen, "Quitman," 112; Commanding Officer, Fort Quitman, to Commanding Officer, Fort Davis, telegram, August 11, 1880, Fort Davis Selected Documents, Record Group 98, National Archives (hereafter cited as FDSD) (Microfilm, Rolls NMRA 66-783 [7675] 8-9 and 65-855 [10427], Fort Davis National Historic Site).

12. Post Adjutant, Fort Davis, to Lieutenant Whitall, February 8, 1881; Commanding Officer, Fort Davis, to Adjutant General, Department of Texas, April 27, 1881; Post Adjutant, Fort Davis, to S. Finley, July 24, 1881; Assistant Adjutant General, Department of Texas, to Commanding Officer, Fort Davis, July 5, 1882, FDSD. Ruhlen, "Quitman," 113.

13. Eddie J. Guffee, "Camp Peña Colorado, Texas 1879-1893" (master's thesis, West Texas State University, 1976), 13-15. For additional information, see *The New Handbook of Texas*, "Camp Peña Colorado," by Richard A. Thompson.

14. Camp Peña Colorado Post Returns, March 1880 and June 1884, Record Group 94, National Archives (Microfilm M-617, Roll 901).

15. Guffee, "Camp Peña Colorado," 18.

16. Ibid., 22-25.

17. F. L. Carrington to Post Adjutant, Fort Davis, September 19, 1881; W. H. Beck to Post Adjutant, Fort Davis, September 30, November 18, and November 30, 1881, FDSD.

18. AnneJo P. Wedin, *The Magnificent Marathon Basin: A History of Marathon, Texas, Its People and Events* (Austin: Nortex Press, 1989), 20.

19. Travis Roberts, interview by Jim Cullen, July 26, 1986, Archives of the Big Bend, Sul Ross State University, Alpine, Texas.

20. Peña Colorado Post Returns, March 1880-March 1885.

21. Ibid., March-May 1880.

22. Guffee, "Camp Peña Colorado," 73-75.

23. Special Orders No. 1, Department of Texas, January 2, 1885, FDSD.

24. Peña Colorado Post Returns, April 1885.

25. Guffee, "Camp Peña Colorado," 31-32. For additional information, see *The New Handbook of Texas*, s.v. "Camp Neville Springs," by Richard A. Thompson.

26. Wedin, *Magnificent Marathon Basin*, 29.

27. Ruhlen, "Quitman," 113-14.

28. "Fort Hancock (Camp Rice)," Card Files, Fort Davis National Historic Site (hereafter cited as CF).

29. Commanding Officer, Fort Davis, to Vincent, Adjutant General, Department of Texas, telegram, April 28, 1882, FDSD.

30. Assistant Adjutant General, Department of Texas, to Commanding Officer, Fort Davis, July 5, 1882, FDSD.

31. "Fort Hancock (Camp Rice)," CF.

32. T. Lebo to Post Adjutant, Fort Davis, November 3, 1882, FDSD.

33. T. A. Baldwin to Post Adjutant, Fort Davis, September 30, 1883, FDSD.

34. W. H. Smith to T. A. Baldwin, March 26, 1884; J. S. Jouett to T. A. Baldwin, April 26, 1884, FDSD.

35. "Fort Hancock (Camp Rice)," CF.

✳ ✳ ✳ BIBLIOGRAPHY ✳ ✳ ✳

PRIMARY SOURCES

MANUSCRIPT MATERIAL

Card Files. Fort Davis National Historic Site.

M. L. Crimmins Collection, Center for American History, University of Texas at Austin.

"Incidents Involving Hostile Indians Within the Influence of Fort Davis, Texas 1866-1891." Archives of the Big Bend. Sul Ross State University, Alpine, Texas.

Maxon Family Papers. Fort Davis National Historic Site.

Clay Miller Collection. Archives of the Big Bend. Sul Ross State University. Copy held by Fort Davis National Historic Site.

National Archives. Medical Histories of Posts, Fort Richardson. Record group 94. Microfilm in possession of Texas Parks and Wildlife Department.

_____. Fort Brown Post Returns. Record Group 94. Microfilm M-617, Roll 152.

_____. Fort Clark Post Returns. Record Group 94. Microfilm M-617, Rolls 214-15.

_____. Fort Davis Post Returns. Record Group 94. Microfilm M-617, Rolls 297-98.

_____. Fort Duncan Post Returns. Record Group 94. Microfilm M-617, Roll 336.

_____. Fort Elliott Post Returns. Record Group 94. Microfilm M-617, Roll 346.

_____. Fort Griffin Post Returns. Record Group 94. Microfilm M-617, Roll 429.

_____. Fort Hudson Post Returns. Record Group 94. Microfilm M-617, Roll 495.

_____. Fort McKavett Post Returns. Record Group 94. Microfilm M-617, Roll 688.

_____. Camp Peña Colorado Post Returns. Record Group 94. Microfilm M-617, Roll 901.

_____. Fort Quitman Post Returns. Record Group 94. Microfilm M-617, Roll 985.

_____. Ninth Cavalry Regimental Returns. Record Group 94. Microfilm M-744, Roll 87.

_____. Ringgold Barracks Post Returns. Record Group 94. Microfilm M-617, Rolls 1020-1021.

_____. Fort Davis Selected Documents. Record Group 98. Microfilm, Rolls NMRA 66-783 (7675) 8-9 and 65-855 (10427) 1, at Fort Davis National Historic Site.

_____. Headquarters Records of Fort Stockton. Record Group 393. Microfilm M-1189, Rolls 1-8.

_____. Records of Fort Elliott, Texas. Record Group 393. Microfilm in possession of Panhandle-Plains Historical Museum, West Texas A&M University, Canyon, Texas.

_____. Records of Fort Griffin, Texas. Record Group 393. Microfilm in possession of Texas Parks and Wildlife Department.

_____. Records of Fort McKavett, Texas. Record Group 393. Microfilm in possession of Southwest Collection, Texas Tech University, Lubbock.

_____. Records of Fort Richardson, Texas. Record Group 393. Microfilm in possession of Texas Parks and Wildlife Department.

_____. Records of Headquarters, Fort Concho, Texas. Record Group 393. Microfilm in possession of Fort Concho National Historic Landmark.

Texas State Archives. Special Orders of Adjutant General of State of Texas, August 1870-April 2, 1897. Adjutant General's Record Group (RG 401). Archives Division—Texas State Library.

"Memoirs of William George Wedemeyer." Fort Davis National Historic Site.

GOVERNMENT DOCUMENTS

U. S. House. *Report of the Secretary of War.* 40th Cong., 2d sess., 1867. H. Exec. Doc. 1.

_____. *Report of the Secretary of War.* 40th Cong., 3d sess., 1868. H. Exec. Doc. 1.

_____. *Report of the Secretary of War.* 41st Cong., 3d sess., 1870. H. Exec. Doc. 1, pt. 2.

_____. *Report of the Secretary of War.* 42d Cong., 2d sess., 1871. H. Exec. Doc. 1, pt. 2.

_____. *Report of the Secretary of War.* 42d Cong., 3d sess., 1872. H. Exec. Doc. 1, pt. 2.

_____. *Report of the Secretary of War.* 44th Cong., 1st sess., 1875. H. Exec. Doc. 1, pt. 2.

_____. *Report of the Secretary of War.* 44th Cong., 2d sess., 1876. H. Exec. Doc. 1, pt. 2, Map 49. Copy in "United States Military Telegraph Records," box 3H137. Center for American History, University of Texas at Austin.

_____. *Report of the Secretary of War.* 45th Cong., 3d sess., 1878. H. Exec. Doc. 1. pt. 2.

_____. *Report of the Secretary of War.* 46th Cong., 2d sess., 1879. H. Exec. Doc. 1, pt. 2.

_____. *Report of the Secretary of War.* 46th Cong., 3d sess., 1880. H. Exec. Doc. 1, pt. 2.

_____. *Report of the Secretary of War.* 48th Cong., 1st sess., 1884. H. Exec. Doc. 1.

NEWSPAPERS

Denison (Texas) Daily Cresset, 1875.

Panhandle News, 1877.

PUBLISHED PRIMARY SOURCES

Andrews, Emily K. "A Woman's View of the Texas Frontier, 1874: The Diary of Emily K. Andrews." Edited and annotated by Sandra L. Myres. *Southwestern Historical Quarterly* 86 (July 1982): 49-80.

Armes, George A. *Ups and Downs of an Army Officer.* Washington: n.p., 1900.

Bode, E. A. *A Dose of Frontier Soldiering: The Memoirs of Corporal E. A. Bode, Frontier Regular Infantry, 1877-1882.* Edited by Thomas T. Smith. Lincoln: University of Nebraska Press, 1994.

Boyd, Mrs. Orsemus Bronson. *Cavalry Life in Tent and Field.* 1894. Reprint, with an introduction by Darlis A. Miller. Lincoln: University of Nebraska Press, 1982.

Carter, R. G. *On the Border with Mackenzie; or Winning West Texas from the Comanches.* New York: Antiquarian Press, Ltd., 1961.

Charlton, John B. *The Old Sergeant's Story: Winning the West from the Indians and Bad Men in 1870 to 1876.* Edited by Robert G. Carter. New York: Frederick H. Hitchcock, 1926.

Flipper, Henry O. *Black Frontiersman: The Memoirs of Henry O. Flipper.* Compiled and edited with an introduction and notes by Theodore D. Harris. Fort Worth: Texas Christian University Press, 1997.

Gillett, James B. *Six Years with the Texas Rangers 1875 to 1881.* Edited by M. M. Quaife. New Haven: Yale University Press, 1925.

McConnell, H. H. *Five Years a Cavalryman; or, Sketches of Regular Army Life on the Texas Frontier, Twenty Odd Years Ago.* 1888. Reprint, Freeport, New York: Books for Libraries Press, 1970.

Parker, James. *The Old Army: Memories 1872-1918.* Philadelphia: Dorrance & Company, 1929.

INTERVIEWS

Roberts, Travis. Interview by Jim Cullen. Cassette recording. July 26, 1986. Archives of the Big Bend, Sul Ross State University, Alpine, Texas.

SECONDARY SOURCES

BOOKS

Alberts, Don E. *Brandy Station to Manila Bay: A Biography of General Wesley Merritt.* Austin: Presidial Press, 1980.

Altshuler, Constance Wynn. *Cavalry Yellow and Infantry Blue: Army Officers in Arizona Between 1851 and 1886.* Tucson: Arizona Historical Society, 1991.

Austerman, Wayne R. *Sharps Rifles and Spanish Mules: The San Antonio-El Paso Mail, 1851-1881.* College Station: Texas A&M University Press, 1985.

Baker, T. Lindsay, and Billy R. Harrison. *Adobe Walls: The History and Archaeology of the 1874 Trading Post.* College Station: Texas A&M University Press, 1986.

Bowden, J. J. *Surveying the Texas and Pacific Land Grant West of the Pecos.* Southwestern Studies No. 46. El Paso: Texas Western Press, 1975.

Cage, James C., and Tommy Powell. *Fort Quitman.* McNary, Texas: n.p., 1972.

Carlson, Paul H. *Pecos Bill: A Military Biography of William R. Shafter.* College Station: Texas A&M University Press, 1989.

Carroll, John M., ed. *The Black Military Experience in the American West.* New York: Liveright, 1971.

Carter, William H. *From Yorktown to Santiago with the Sixth U.S. Cavalry.* Austin: State House Press, 1989.

Conkling, Roscoe P., and Margaret B. Conkling. *The Butterfield Overland Mail 1857-1869.* 3 vols. Glendale, California: The Arthur H. Clark Company, 1947.

Dearen, Patrick. *Castle Gap and the Pecos Frontier.* Fort Worth: Texas Christian University Press, 1988.

_____. *Portraits of the Pecos Frontier.* Lubbock: Texas Tech University Press, 1993.

Davidson, Homer K. *Black Jack Davidson, A Cavalry Commander on the Western Frontier: The Life of General John W. Davidson.* Glendale, California: The Arthur H. Clark Company, 1974.

Dunlay, Thomas W. *Wolves for the Blue Soldiers: Indian Scouts and Auxiliaries with the United States Army, 1860-90.* Lincoln: University of Nebraska Press, 1982.

Fowler, Arlen L. *The Black Infantry in the West 1869-1891.* Westport, Connecticut: Greenwood Publishing Corporation, 1971.

Haley, J. Evetts. *Fort Concho and the Texas Frontier*. San Angelo, Texas: San Angelo Standard-Times, 1952.

Haley, James L. *The Buffalo War: The History of the Red River Indian Uprising of 1874*. Garden City, New York: Doubleday & Company, 1976. Reprint, Norman: University of Oklahoma Press, 1985.

Hamilton, Allen Lee. *Sentinel of the Southern Plains: Fort Richardson and the Northwest Texas Frontier, 1866-1878*. Fort Worth: Texas Christian University Press, 1988.

Heitman, Francis B. *Historical Register and Dictionary of the United States Army, from Its Organization, September 29, 1789, to March 2, 1903*. Vol. 1. Washington: Government Printing Office, 1903.

Hollon, W. Eugene. *Beyond the Cross Timbers: The Travels of Randolph B. Marcy, 1812, 1887*. Norman: University of Oklahoma Press, 1955.

Jackson, W. Turrentine. *Wagon Roads West: A Study of Federal Road Surveys and Construction in the Trans-Mississippi West 1846-1869*. Berkeley: University of California Press, 1952.

Kenner, Charles L. *Buffalo Soldiers and Officers of the Ninth Cavalry 1867-1898: Black and White Together*. Norman: University of Oklahoma Press, 1999.

_____. *The Comanchero Frontier: A History of New Mexican-Plains Indian Relations*. Norman: University of Oklahoma Press, 1969, 1994.

Kinevan, Marcos E. *Frontier Cavalryman: Lieutenant John Bigelow with the Buffalo Soldiers in Texas*. El Paso: Texas Western Press, 1998.

Leckie, Shirley A., ed. *The Colonel's Lady on the Western Frontier: The Correspondence of Alice Kirk Grierson*. Lincoln: University of Nebraska Press, 1989.

Leckie, William H. *The Buffalo Soldiers: A Narrative of the Negro Cavalry in the West*. Norman: University of Oklahoma Press, 1967.

_____. *The Military Conquest of the Southern Plains*. Norman: University of Oklahoma Press, 1963.

Leckie, William H. and Shirley A. Leckie. *Unlikely Warriors: General Benjamin H. Grierson and His Family*. Norman: University of Oklahoma Press, 1984.

Metz, Leon C. *Border: The U.S.-Mexico Line*. El Paso: Mangan Books, 1989.

Mulroy, Kevin. *Freedom on the Border: The Seminole Maroons in Florida, the Indian Territory, Coahuila, and Texas*. Lubbock: Texas Tech University Press, 1993.

Nankivell, John H., comp. and ed. *History of the Twenty-fifth Regiment United States Infantry 1869-1926*. N.p., 1927.

Pierce, Michael D. *The Most Promising Young Officer: A Life of Ranald Slidell Mackenzie*. Norman: University of Oklahoma Press, 1993.

Pratt, Richard Henry. *Battlefield and Classroom: Four Decades with the American Indian, 1867-1904*. Edited and with an introduction by Robert M. Utley. New Haven: Yale University Press, 1964.

Prucha, Francis Paul. *A Guide to the Military Posts of the United States 1789-1895.* Madison: The State Historical Society of Wisconsin, 1964.

Richardson, Rupert N. *The Frontier of Northwest Texas 1846 to 1876.* Glendale, California: The Arthur H. Clark Company, 1963.

Richter, William. *The Army in Texas During Reconstruction 1865-1870.* College Station: Texas A&M University Press, 1987.

Rickey, Don, Jr. *Forty Miles a Day on Beans and Hay: The Enlisted Soldier Fighting the Indian Wars.* Norman: University of Oklahoma Press, 1963.

Rister, Carl Coke. *Fort Griffin on the Texas Frontier.* Norman: University of Oklahoma Press, 1986.

Robinson, Charles M., III. *Bad Hand: A Biography of General Ranald S. Mackenzie.* Austin: State House Press, 1993.

_____. *Frontier Forts of Texas.* Houston: Lone Star Books, 1986.

_____. *The Frontier World of Fort Griffin: The Life and Death of a Western Town.* Spokane, Washington: The Arthur H. Clark Company, 1992.

Ruhlen, George. "Quitman: The Worst Post at Which I Ever Served." In *The Black Military Experience in the American West,* John M. Carroll, ed. New York: Liveright, 1971. First published in *Password* 11 (Fall 1966).

Sandoz, Mari. *The Buffalo Hunters: The Story of the Hide Men.* New York: Hastings House, 1954.

Schubert, Frank N. *Black Valor: Buffalo Soldiers and the Medal of Honor, 1870-1898.* Wilmington, Delaware: SR Books, 1997.

Scobee, Barry. *Fort Davis, Texas: 1583-1960.* El Paso: by the author, 1963.

Shipman, Mrs. O. L. *Taming the Big Bend: A History of the Extreme Western Portion of Texas from Fort Clark to El Paso.* N.p., 1926.

Smith, David Paul. *Frontier Defense in the Civil War: Texas' Rangers and Rebels.* College Station: Texas A&M University Press, 1992.

Smith, Thomas T. *The Old Army in Texas: A Research Guide to the U.S. Army in Nineteenth Century Texas.* Austin: Texas State Historical Association, 2000.

_____. *The U. S. Army and the Texas Frontier Economy, 1845-1900.* College Station: Texas A&M University Press, 1999.

Steinbach, Robert H. *A Long March: The Lives of Frank and Alice Baldwin.* Austin: University of Texas Press, 1989.

Stout, Joseph A., Jr. *Apache Lightning: The Last Great Battles of the Ojo Calientes.* New York: Oxford University Press, 1974.

Stovall, Allan A. *Nueces Headwater Country: A Regional History.* San Antonio: The Naylor Company, 1959.

Sullivan, Jerry M. *Fort McKavett: A Texas Frontier Post.* Austin: Texas Parks and Wildlife Department, n.d.

Tate, Michael L. *The Frontier Army in the Settlement of the West.* Norman: University of Oklahoma Press, 1999.

Taylor, Joe F., ed. and comp. *The Indian Campaign on the Staked Plains, 1874-1875: Military Correspondence from War Department Adjutant General's Office, File 2815-1874.* Canyon, Texas: Panhandle-Plains Historical Society, 1962.

ter Braake, Alex L. *Texas: The Drama of Its Postal Past.* State College, Pennsylvania: The American Philatelic Society, 1970.

Thrapp, Dan L. *The Conquest of Apacheria.* Norman: University of Oklahoma Press, 1967.

_____. *Encyclopedia of Frontier Biography,* 3 vols. Lincoln: University of Nebraska Press, 1988.

_____. *Victorio and the Mimbres Apaches.* Norman: University of Oklahoma Press, 1974.

Utley, Robert M. *Frontier Regulars: The United States Army and the Indian, 1866-1891.* New York: Macmillan Publishing Company, 1973.

Wallace, Ernest. *Ranald S. Mackenzie on the Texas Frontier.* Lubbock: West Texas Museum Association, 1964.

_____. *Ranald S. Mackenzie's Official Correspondence Relating to Texas, 1871-1873.* Lubbock: West Texas Museum Association, 1967.

Wedin, AnneJo P. *The Magnificent Marathon Basin: A History of Marathon, Texas, Its People and Events.* Austin: Nortex Press, 1989.

Williams, Clayton W. *Texas' Last Frontier: Fort Stockton and the Trans-Pecos, 1861-1895.* Edited by Ernest Wallace. College Station: Texas A&M University Press, 1982.

Wooster, Robert. *The Military and United States Indian Policy 1865-1903.* New Haven: Yale University Press, 1988.

_____. *Soldiers, Suttlers, and Settlers: Garrison Life on the Texas Frontier.* College Station: Texas A&M University Press, 1987.

ARTICLES

Aston, B. W. "Federal Military Reoccupation of the Texas Southwestern Frontier, 1865-1871." *Texas Military History* 8 (1970): 123-34.

Bender, A. B. "Opening Routes across West Texas, 1848-1850." *Southwestern Historical Quarterly* 37 (October 1933): 116-35.

Campbell, T. N., and William T. Field. "Identification of Comanche Raiding Trails in Trans-Pecos Texas." *West Texas Historical Association Year Book* 44 (October 1968): 128-44.

Carlson, Paul H. "William R. Shafter, Black Troops, and the Finale to the Red River War." *Red River Valley Historical Review* 3 (Spring 1978): 247-58.

_____. "William R. Shafter, Black Troops, and the Opening of the Llano Estacado, 1870-1875." *Panhandle-Plains Historical Review* 47 (1974): 1-18.

Carroll, H. Bailey. "Nolan's 'Lost Nigger' Expedition of 1877." *Southwestern Historical Quarterly* 44 (July 1940): 55-75.

Crimmins, M. L. "Fort Elliott, Texas." *The West Texas Historical Association Year Book* 23 (October 1947): 3-12.

_____. "Old Fort Duncan: A Frontier Post." *Frontier Times* 15 (June 1938): 379-85.

Dinges, Bruce J. "The Irrepressible Captain Armes: Politics and Justice in the Indian-Fighting Army." *Journal of the West* 32 (April 1993): 38-53.

_____. "The Victorio Campaign of 1880: Cooperation and Conflict on the United States-Mexico Border." *New Mexico Historical Review* 62 (January 1987): 81-94.

Ellis, L. Tuffly, ed. "Lieutenant A. W. Greely's Report on the Installation of Military Telegraph Lines in Texas, 1875-1876." *Southwestern Historical Quarterly* 69 (July 1965): 66-87.

Essin, Emmett M., III. "Mules, Packs, and Packtrains." *Southwestern Historical Quarterly* 74 (July 1970): 52-63.

Graham, Roy Eugene. "Federal Fort Architecture in Texas during the Nineteenth Century." *Southwestern Historical Quarterly* 74 (October 1970): 165-88.

Holden, W. C. "Frontier Defense, 1865-1889." *Panhandle-Plains Historical Review* 2 (1929): 43-64.

Hutto, John R. "Pioneering of the Texas and Pacific." *West Texas Historical Association Year Book* 12 (July 1936): 124-33.

McChristian, Douglas C. "Grierson's Fight at Tinaja de las Palmas: An Episode in the Victoria [sic] Campaign." *Red River Valley Historical Review* 7 (Winter 1982): 45- 63.

Miles, Susan. "The Soldiers' Riot." *Fort Concho Report* 13 (Spring 1981): 1-20.

Nunn, W. Curtis. "Eighty-six Hours Without Water on the Texas Plains." *Southwestern Historical Quarterly* 43 (January 1940): 356-64.

Porter, Kenneth Wiggins. "The Seminole Negro-Indian Scouts, 1870-1881." *Southwestern Historical Quarterly* 55 (January 1952): 358-77.

Ramsey, Grover C. "Camp Melvin, Crockett County, Texas." *West Texas Historical Association Year Book* 37 (October 1961): 137-46.

[Sheffy, L. F., ed.]. "Letters and Reminiscences of Gen. Theodore A. Baldwin: Scouting after Indians on the Plains of West Texas." *Panhandle-Plains Historical Review* 2 (1938): 7-26.

Smith, Thomas T. "Fort Inge and Texas Frontier Military Operations, 1849-1869." *Southwestern Historical Quarterly* 96 (July 1992): 1-26.

_____. "U. S. Army Combat Operations in the Indian Wars of Texas, 1849-1881." *Southwestern Historical Quarterly* 99 (April 1996): 501-32.

Steinbach, Robert H. "The Red River War of 1874-1875: Selected Correspondence Between Lieutenant Frank Baldwin and His Wife, Alice."

Southwestern Historical Quarterly 93 (April 1990): 497-518.

Storey, Brit Allan, ed. "An Army Officer in Texas, 1866-1867." *Southwestern Historical Quarterly* 72 (October 1968): 242-51.

Tate, Michael L. "Indian Scouting Detachments in the Red River War, 1874-1875." *Red River Valley Historical Review* 3 (1978): 202-25.

Temple, Frank M. "Colonel B. H. Grierson's Administration of the District of the Pecos." *West Texas Historical Association Year Book* 38 (October 1962): 85-96.

_____. "Grierson's Spring." *Fort Concho Report* 15 (Winter 1983): 3-14.

Thompson, Theronne. "Fort Buffalo Springs, Texas Border Post." *West Texas Historical Association Year Book* 36 (1960): 156-75.

Utley, Robert M. "A Chained Dog: The Indian-Fighting Army." *American West* 10 (July 1973): 18-24.

Wallace, Edward S. "General John Lapham Bullis, the Thunderbolt of the Texas Frontier, I." *Southwestern Historical Quarterly* 54 (April 1951): 452-61.

_____. "General John Lapham Bullis, the Thunderbolt of the Texas Frontier, II." *Southwestern Historical Quarterly* 55 (July 1951): 77-85.

Wallace, Ernest, and Adrian Anderson. "R. S. Mackenzie and the Kickapoos: The Raid into Mexico in 1873." *Arizona and the West* 7 (Summer 1965): 105-26.

Whisenhunt, Donald W. "Fort Richardson: Outpost on the Texas Frontier." *Southwestern Studies* 5, no. 4 (1968): 3-11.

White, Lonnie J. "Indian Battles in the Texas Panhandle, 1874." *Journal of the West* 6 (April 1967): 278-309.

Wooster, Robert. "The Army and the Politics of Expansion: Texas and the Southwestern Borderlands, 1870-1886." *Southwestern Historical Quarterly* 93 (October 1989): 151-68.`

UNPUBLISHED THESES, DISSERTATIONS, AND PAPERS

Carlson, Paul H. "William R. Shafter: Military Commander in the American West." Ph.D. diss., Texas Tech University, 1973.

Dinges, Bruce J. "The San Angelo Riot of 1881: A Reassessment," paper read to the Texas State Historical Association, Houston, Texas, March 5, 1993, copy in "Riots—Fort Concho" file, Museum Research Library and Archives, Fort Concho National Historic Landmark, San Angelo, Texas.

Guffee, Eddie J. "Camp Peña Colorado, Texas 1879-1893." Master's thesis, West Texas State University, 1976.

Sellers, Rosella R. "The History of Fort Duncan, Eagle Pass, Texas." Master's thesis, Sul Ross College, 1960.

✗ ✗ ✗ ✗ ✗ INDEX ✗ ✗ ✗ ✗ ✗